WANDA'S WAR

MARSHA FAUBERT

Wanda's War

An Untold Story of Nazi Europe,
Forced Labour, and a
Canadian Immigration Scandal

GOOSE LANE

Edited by Jill Ainsley.
Copy edited by Jess Shulman.
Cover and page design by Julie Scriver.
Cover illustrations: A photograph of Wanda Gizmunt in the late 1940s (collection of George Surdykowski) overlaid on an image of German soldiers combing the rubble after victory in the Battle of Westerplatte against Polish forces on September 7, 1939 (Bundesarchiv | AP).
Map by Marcel Morin, Lost Art Cartography.
Images pages 75 and 79 captured from "Fulda 1945. End of WW2," accessed at https://www.youtube.com/watch?v=qFiPtbvQRPw, July 12, 2022.
Printed in Canada by Friesens.
10 9 8 7 6 5 4 3 2 1

Library and Archives Canada Cataloguing in Publication

Title: Wanda's war : an untold story of Nazi Europe, forced labour, and a Canadian immigration
    scandal / Marsha Faubert.
Names: Faubert, Marsha, author.
Description: Includes bibliographical references.
Identifiers: Canadiana (print) 20220415285 | Canadiana (ebook) 20220415471 |
    ISBN 9781773102757 (softcover) | ISBN 9781773102764 (EPUB)
Subjects: LCSH: Gizmunt, Wanda. | LCSH: Immigrants—Canada—Biography. |
    LCSH: Poland—History—Occupation, 1939-1945. | LCSH: World War, 1939-1945—
    Conscript labor—Germany. | LCGFT: Biographies.
Classification: LCC DK4410 .F38 2023 | DDC 943.805/3092—dc23

Goose Lane Editions acknowledges the generous support of the Government of Canada, the Canada Council for the Arts, and the Government of New Brunswick.

Goose Lane Editions is located on the unceded territory of the Wəlastəkwiyik whose ancestors along with the Mi'kmaq and Peskotomuhkati Nations signed Peace and Friendship Treaties with the British Crown in the 1700s.

Goose Lane Editions
500 Beaverbrook Court, Suite 330
Fredericton, New Brunswick
CANADA E3B 5X4
gooselane.com

For George
And for our children, whose stories also begin here

is it true that their pillows
are stuffed with soil
softer than any feather

—Valzhyna Mort, "Polish Immigrants"

Contents

INTRODUCTION
QUESTIONS

"In the war, my mother was a slave labourer in Nazi Germany."
George casually mentioned this fragment of his mother's history during an otherwise ordinary conversation in the graduate pub, where we had ended up after an evening at the legal clinic where we both volunteered. A couple of law-school misfits, we were getting to know each other and comparing notes about our families' working-class origins. George's Polish surname, Surdykowski, marked him as even more of an outlier than I was, but this piece of information was a discordant note, a fact so far removed from our current lives that I struggled to absorb it.

My knowledge of the war period was limited to what I had learned in high-school history class or what my parents might have mentioned—which was very little. My father spent the war years as an army training officer in western Canada and had little to say about that time. In my high school, a small Catholic school run by a collection of nuns and brothers, the Second World War was supposed to have been on the grade twelve curriculum, but our history teacher, Brother Peter, seemed more interested in the Russian Revolution. Odd, given that his own war experience in Holland likely left him with a bitter hatred of the Nazis. But still, "Better dead than red," he wrote on the blackboard, leaving it there for weeks while we concentrated mostly on Lenin and Stalin.

Like most of the post-war generation, I had some knowledge of concentration camps and the Holocaust, but I knew nothing about slave labourers, the millions of ordinary Europeans whose lives were exploded not just by bombs but also by the deportations, starvation, and cruelty the Nazi invaders imposed on them. My sense of the history of war was limited to the story of armies and battles, of victors and the vanquished.

George didn't linger too long on his mother's past, though. It was his philosophy that "the past is history, the future is perfect." At the time, hearing the second part of the mantra, I admired his sunny optimism and thought I could use some of that in my life. Later I came to understand that the first part was more significant in his family life. Not only was the past history, but it did not seem to exist. Where and when was his mother, Wanda, born? What actually happened to her in the years before and during the war? What about his father, Casey, who had been imprisoned in Siberia and then went on to fight in Italy with the Polish army at Monte Cassino? Who were his father's family, and where were they now? As time went on, I asked George these questions, but he had no answers. His younger brother, Chris, recalled once asking Wanda where she came from, but she waved him off. "Gdzieś na wsi," she said—somewhere out in the country, meaning nowhere he would know. Life before Canada was rarely the topic of conversation in their childhood home; that was certainly true by the time I arrived on the scene. In a family that did not even celebrate birthdays there seemed no point in pursuing my questions. If the past was history, who was I to try to dig it up?

On a warm afternoon in early summer, not long after I first met him, George and I sat with his parents on the back patio of their house, making awkward small talk. They had produced from the garage some aluminum folding chairs, the kind with plastic webbing, for the occasion. As we chatted, I eyed the grapevine climbing up the side of the house and spotted a robin's nest hiding behind the massive leaves.

A low hedge surrounded the patio, but there were no flowers to be seen, only a bed of hen-and-chick plants, low-maintenance succulents that hugged the ground and provided little in the way of visual interest. This was not a space used for the kind of idle afternoons I often enjoyed at my parents' home, reading or basking in the sun.

It was early in my relationship with George, and I was politely getting to know his parents. The first indication that things were not as they seemed was his father's name—Casey. He was actually named Kazimierz, but all the awkward consonants had been stripped away for his life in the world of English speakers. My appearance on the scene may have been a disappointment to Wanda. She had grown attached to one of George's previous girlfriends, who continued to telephone her and share gossip and girl talk. When George decided to quit his job at the liquor store to go to law school, his parents tried to discourage him. "You have a government job with a pension! Why would you give that up?" Even worse, I was a law student too, an unlikely candidate for the kind of domestic life they envisioned for their son: an easy job, a house nearby, some grandchildren, Sunday dinners. What kind of home could I make for him?

We walked to the rear of the yard so I could admire their garden, the real purpose of the space: a ten-by-thirty-foot rectangle filled with potatoes, cabbages, tomatoes, onions, beets, cucumbers, peppers, and dill. Wanda and Casey supplied themselves with produce for the winter, much of it canned or pickled, and whenever we visited they sent us home with baskets of food (frozen pierogi or cabbage rolls in the winter months). The trees in the yard were not for shade or decoration: peaches, apples, pears, and plums, the latter showing up in jams and cakes made by Wanda. It was a miniature farm. Casey supplied the labour, and the garden was, like the house, tidy and meticulously ordered. No dust in the house, no weeds in the garden.

I must have asked about their war years that day. Casey, who rarely spoke, said only that he had been in Siberia and talked about being in a tent so cold that ice formed on the inside. A tent in Siberia? That's what I remember him saying. I also recall that he said his mother was there too, but George doesn't remember the conversation this way. Wanda talked about the Germans in her Polish village rounding up the Jews and shooting them in the forest. She said nothing about her later time in Germany. I absorbed this information, speechless and wondering how to respond. Who asks for details after hearing something like that? In the uncomfortable silence that followed, we returned to the banal talk of daily life that brought us to the safer ground of the present. How was school, or the jobs we had that summer?

Inside the house, there was no helping out with meals and cleanup; all that was required was for me to stay out of the way. "I would rather clean than cook," Wanda said more than once. The lace curtains in all the rooms fell stiffly from the curtain rods. In the kitchen, the aluminum kettle and coffee pot were always shiny, as if never used. Every surface was bare except for a few vases of plastic flowers or vines, free of dust and clutter. At Christmas, an old artificial tree was decorated with delicate folded paper stars and snowflakes, hung in a regular pattern. The interior of the house was as static and undisturbed as a museum exhibit.

On occasions when we arrived for dinner, there would be no signs of cooking. The sink and counter would be empty and clean. Pots containing food already cooked were on the stove, or perhaps hiding in the oven, waiting to be heated. The kitchen table was already set. The business of life was hidden from view.

This is not to say that food was incidental to life in Wanda's house. In spite of her dislike of cooking, she was a master at Polish cuisine. Every meal included at least three dishes more than we could consume. If meat was the main course, there would also be cabbage rolls, pierogi or maybe *bigos* (a stew made of meat, sausage, and sauerkraut), as well as potatoes and vegetables. Canned or frozen, the latter were a grudging concession to healthy eating. Gravy materialized from somewhere, usually unrelated to the meat, always with mushrooms. Wanda hovered, sitting down long after everyone else began eating, and picked at her food without interest. If we had wine, she would drink a couple of sips and claim to be tipsy.

At these meals Casey sat, sphinx-like, at the head of the table. Having lived with a father who loved to talk and had opinions on every subject, even ones he knew nothing about, I had no idea how to interpret this silence. Casey seemed perpetually tired, his movements always slow, his eyes half closed, as if he had used up his life force long before I met him. As usual, I watched George and followed his lead. Since there seemed to be little interaction between father and son, I focused my attention on Wanda, as did George and his brother, Chris. She, in turn, directed her gaze at her boys.

"Mother love is like no other love," she once told me. I was supposed to take this to refer to my love for my children, but I could also see that for Wanda, her children were her world. Both George and his brother had lived at home in their university years, enjoying a level of freedom unheard of in my own home. They seemed to set the rules, came and went as they pleased, with no complaint from their mother, who cooked and cleaned up after them. If anything, she revelled in stories of their exploits. I poked fun at George for his pampered student life, but I realize now that Wanda was prepared to pay this price to have her sons with her for as long as possible. When they finally moved away, a hole opened up in her world, one that she struggled to fill.

"When are you coming?" In George's weekly calls with Wanda, this was her question. Life had overtaken us, and visits to either set of our parents became less frequent. With the oppressive workload typical of young lawyers, we found ourselves with little time to spare. Work, a house, and then two children of our own all took priority. We made our trips up and down the highway from Toronto (120 kilometres to his family, 220 to mine) several times a year for major holidays and birthdays. No one in either of our families seemed that interested in the opposite journey, perhaps overwhelmed by the thought of travel to the big city. Our family relationships took place in these brief visits. There was no time for slow conversations, afternoons cooking or baking or just sitting, the kind of visits where people reveal themselves to each other in insignificant details. If I had had time, I might have felt guilty. As it was, I could barely keep myself afloat.

#

January 1988. I was working at home one afternoon — I had just started a job that allowed me to do that part of the time — when George came home unexpectedly. "I just had a call at work," he said. "My father died." In his shock, he seemed puzzled, as if he were repeating words in an unknown language. A friend of Wanda's had found out where George worked, looked up his office number, and contacted him. Snow had fallen the previous evening. Casey had gone out to clear the driveway with a snow blower when he was felled by a heart attack. Who knew how long he had lain in the driveway before he was discovered? He was sixty-seven, an age George began to dread. Wanda was a widow at the age of sixty.

Casey's funeral on a cold January day had an air of unreality as we all adjusted to the shock of his absence. After the church service, we followed as a hearse took him to the cemetery for burial. At his gravesite, the headstone was there already, with Wanda's name next to Casey's on the stone. We gathered in the bitter cold around the coffin, suspended above a hole in the snowy ground. We were joined by a large crowd of mourners: neighbours from the family's first neighbourhood, union representatives from the rubber workers' union to which Casey belonged, members of the Polish Legion, and a contingent of friends. Wanda's closest friend, Niusia, had come from Connecticut to be with her.

A man in the remnants of his Polish army uniform, a medal on his coat and a beret on his head, gave a eulogy in Polish. George wasn't sure who he was, but he would have marched with Casey and the other men from the Polish Legion in the Remembrance Day observances that George watched as a child with his mother. I tried to follow along and asked George to translate when he mentioned their time in Italy, at Monte Cassino: "dobry chłop, dobry żołnierz" — good man, good soldier. Many of these mourners had followed the same path to Kitchener as Casey and Wanda. Unlike us, they knew the stories behind those few words without being told, and they knew that as with Casey, when their time came, those stories would be buried.

George remembers his mother kneeling in the snow, motionless, for what he thought was too long. When he reached out to help her up, she pushed him away. She didn't want to be consoled. Oblivious to the cold snow, she was deep in the memory of what she had lost.

In the aftermath of Casey's unexpected death, Wanda was stunned and unmoored. Her friends surrounded her, keeping her company and consoling her. Niusia took time off work to stay for several weeks after the funeral and help her through the worst of her grief. This would have been the time for us to stay at Wanda's side too, to reorganize our lives and help her manage all the things that her husband once did, like driving her to church and shopping, because she didn't drive. But I had been sick all that winter, worn down by repeated colds or bouts of the flu. Soon after the funeral, I developed a bizarre autoimmune problem that left me with widespread joint pain and swollen bruises on my legs. I could barely hold a cup, let alone our children, and so they went off to daycare until George could pick them up and care for them at the end of the day. Instead of us dropping off food for Wanda, friends were dropping off food for us. It took a few weeks for a diagnosis to be made and the right drugs prescribed. At the same time, my mother was undergoing the first round of chemotherapy for the cancer that would claim her life a few years later. I felt surrounded by thoughts of illness and death, briefly paralyzed by the enormity of life's burdens. I was no help to anyone.

Spring came, I recovered, and Wanda's life gradually developed a new pattern. She gave up the garden and slowly had the fruit trees removed from the backyard. She kept up her work with the Polish Women's Auxiliary, cooking for weddings and funerals and organizing other events. Card games, visits with friends, and needlework filled her days. Niusia's visits became more frequent and lengthy after she retired, and the two women occasionally travelled to Florida, or to a Polish community in northern Ontario. George's brother, Chris, became a steady support in her life after he moved back to Kitchener, remaining in the area as he opened a new optometric practice, married, and began his own family.

Wanda's end came almost as abruptly as Casey's. In November

2003, she stayed in our home to be with our daughter while we travelled for a week. There was no hint of anything amiss; a neighbour mentioned she had seen Wanda outside, sweeping up the last of the oak leaves on the patio. But a month later, she came to stay again, this time to go to the Princess Margaret Hospital for an MRI exam. She had oral cancer, discovered in a routine dentist appointment. It was more advanced than we would have suspected. Maybe she knew something was wrong for some time and chose to ignore it. She had been a widow for fifteen years, and she was prepared for her own death. She declined treatment. She told George which dress she wanted to be buried in and where to find it. In their last visit, Wanda and George had their final conversation, when, in George's words, they "said everything they had to say to each other." Three months after her diagnosis, George had to go find the dress. Not wanting to make any trouble for him, she had organized everything ahead of time, leaving no loose ends behind her.

One of life's bitter tasks is dismantling the home of our parents after their death. Some may uncover long-held secrets that illuminate the questions of a life, but for most the process is simply the last physical contact with a loved one through their possessions. To dispose of the cherished objects of a parent feels like a final betrayal.

Wanda and Casey's home sold quickly. George and I gathered there with Chris and his wife, Tracey, to remove the items that would not be sold in an estate sale—some furniture for our son's apartment, a few keepsakes. We offered Wanda's friends a chance to take a work of embroidery or some of the table linens she had cross-stitched. Between us, we gave away, sold, or threw out almost everything. In a few ruthless afternoons we wiped out the accumulation of a lifetime, as if it never happened.

In all the rush, we discovered two cookie tins of photos and other keepsakes and a partially filled photo album, never before seen by either George or Chris. Without lingering over them, George took one of the tins and the album to store in a cupboard in our basement, where they were left, unopened, for several years. When I finally looked in the cookie tin for the first time, I found Casey's medals from the war, his military identification papers, and some photos of him as a young soldier. A few were obviously taken after the war, showing Casey wandering like an ordinary tourist through city squares, or on a boat, in what appears to be Italy. At first glance, there seemed to be nothing of his from before the war. What about Casey's father and siblings? If his mother was with him in Siberia, what happened to her? And the nagging question, the one that has never been answered: why did his father never speak of any of his experiences to George? The story of Casey's deportation to Siberia was only one of many mysteries about his past. A copy of his newspaper obituary, which Wanda had tucked into the memorial book from the funeral home, said that he had three brothers and three sisters, unnamed, and that only a brother, Joseph, survived him in Poland. George didn't remember ever hearing about any of Casey's brothers and sisters; he didn't even know where his father was born.

I also found Wanda's identification card from the displaced persons camp where she lived after the war, stamped with the name of the camp, Wildflecken. Many of the pictures were of Wanda just after her arrival in Canada, and others showed her with her friends, including Niusia, during their time in Quebec and after they moved to Ontario. Then the photos shift, as the women find partners and appear as bridesmaids at each other's weddings. Visits to Wanda's family in Boston — her mother; her brother, Joe; and her sister, Kasia — were recorded in some of the photographs.

As with Casey, there were no photos in the tin of Wanda's life before Germany. Then I remembered an album of family photos that Wanda gave to George one Christmas and pulled it off the shelf. It is mainly a record of George's childhood and teenage years, complete with pictures of him in his football uniform or with his girlfriend of the time. But the first page is about Wanda's past, two illustrations of her unspoken history that she wanted George to have. In one photo, a man stands woodenly in front of a painted canvas backdrop, posing for a professional photographer. I can see the family resemblance in George, the same mouth and jaw line, and the perfectly formed

Wanda and Niusia in Kitchener, ca. 1948
(Courtesy George Surdykowski)

straight nose with a narrow bridge, also shared by our son. I wondered how this photo survived the war and what had happened to this man, who was never mentioned in the stories of George's childhood trips to Boston to visit Wanda's mother. The other photo, also obviously of pre-war vintage, appears to be of Wanda's mother. The writing on each photo cryptically contains their last name, Gizmunt, but only the first initial of the subject: *A*, for him, and *H*, for her. I asked George what his grandmother's first name was, but all he could offer was *"babcia."* What reason would he have had to know her first name? Nobody ever used it. About his grandfather, he knew nothing at all.

The photos in the tin took me through Wanda's and Casey's journeys from captivity to freedom, but they left me with more questions than I would have known to ask in their lifetimes. What sort of childhoods did they have in Poland? Where had they been sent to work as forced labourers during the war, and what were their living conditions? What was life like in the displaced persons camp in Germany? What had happened to their families, and why did they make their way alone to Canada? And why couldn't they return to Poland when the war ended?

As I prodded George to remember things he wanted to leave buried, I knew it seemed odd, and maybe even a little unhealthy, that my curiosity about George's family exceeded his own. Like Faulkner, I think the past is never dead, or even past, and I comb my memories for meaning and explanations, and sometimes comfort. George finds little of interest in the past. He prefers to accept people and events at face value and, as lawyers sometimes say, to govern himself accordingly. He doesn't clutter his mind with speculation and ideas that can't help him. It works for him. Why would he need more? We've been having some version of this conversation for about forty years, with no consensus in sight.

Did we learn our attitudes to the past from our mothers, or are they found somewhere in the strands of our DNA? My mother had her own version of exile, a voluntary one, not comparable to Wanda's, coming east to Ontario from Calgary when she married my father. The life she found here couldn't compete with the one she left behind, but she imbued our childhoods with happy stories of her own—her dog, her mother and father, the mountains, her sorority, her job as a telephone operator. Although her family was not well off, the Depression left few marks other than thriftiness, which was cast as a virtue, and her lack of education, which left her with the scar of unrealized ambition. Her war was not a tragic one. But it was clear to her children that life in the south end of the smelly industrial city of Sarnia, among my father's unruly Irish Catholic family, was a disappointment to her. Wanda's life seemed to be the photographic negative of my mother's—memories of a sad and chaotic childhood buried, so they wouldn't get in the way of the new and better life she set out to create in exile.

Hoping to find more details about the Gizmunt family, I persuaded George to reconnect with his uncle Joe to fill in some of the missing pieces of his family's life. After so much time had passed, this was not a simple request. What would he say to an uncle he hadn't seen in a couple of decades? But George got in touch with him, and we visited Joe and his wife, Maria, at their home near Boston. By now over eighty years old, Joe was a diminutive man, even smaller than the last time we had seen him, at Chris's wedding, but he felt well and still kept a small garden in the backyard. He wore a T-shirt, screen-printed with a photo of two of his grandchildren and captioned, "I ♥ my Dziadek." He seemed happy to see his nephew and to share details about the Gizmunt family that were so basic it seemed almost impossible that Wanda had never spoken of them. He also recalled many painful experiences. It wasn't something he discussed with his sons—much as it was with Wanda, the occasion never arose, and he didn't know if they would be interested. I will never forget him shaking with laughter and wiping his eyes, remembering himself in the labour camp, picking lice from the hair of his armpits. "It's funny," he said. "It wasn't funny then, but now it's crazy."

During two visits with Joe, a picture of the life of the Gizmunt family in Poland slowly emerged. The two photographs from George's album, with their cryptic inscriptions, were his grandparents, Antoni and Helena. There were no later photos of Antoni because he died before the war, in 1937. In Helena's photo, dated 1917, she is seated on a chair in front of some curtains, holding a leaflet or a magazine with an illustration on the first page. Beside her is a table with more magazines on top, and a stack of books is on the lower shelf. The setting suggests an attempt to convey the image of gentility. Her long hair is braided, the braid fastened beside her ear with a clip. She wears a long dark skirt; her checked blouse is trimmed with lace, and a necklace of beads is around her neck. It is not the costume of a peasant. In the other photo, Antoni is dressed, incongruously, in a sailor's suit. "He was in the navy," Joe explained.

Joe also finally gave a name to their home in Poland, which we at first understood to be Opole. There is more than one Opole in today's Poland, and it turned out that none of them was Wanda's home. Through his son, Joe later clarified that the town they grew up in was Opol, in a larger region of Polesie, within twenty kilometres of Pinsk, Belarus.[1]

Helena Gizmunt (née Bujko),
ca. 1917, Belarus (Courtesy George Surdykowski)

On today's maps, place names in Belarus are either in the Belarusian alphabet or spelled differently than the Polish version. And there is more than one alphabet in use in the region. My own search revealed no Opol or Opole in Belarus, but after experimenting with alternative spellings, I finally located Opaĺ (also Opoĺ, Опаль, and Ополь) in the Brześć Oblast (province) of Belarus, some sixty kilometres northwest of Pinsk.[2] This placed the Gizmunt family in a part of Poland that is no longer Poland and in the path of both Soviet and Nazi occupations during the war, only adding to the mysteries about Wanda's past.

I knew nothing about the Soviet occupation of Poland or its place in Poland's tortured relationships with its neighbours to the east. I began searching for answers to my questions, reading through historians' accounts of the Soviet and Nazi occupations of Poland, forced labour and displaced persons camps in Germany and the Soviet Union, and post-war immigration to Canada. I travelled with George to Germany and Poland, hoping to see some of the places where Wanda or Casey may have been and to explore whether any traces of the war remained. I followed crumbs of information from obscure websites and social media dedicated to preserving the stories of Poles who had shared Wanda's and Casey's experiences, and I searched through archives where I found fragments of details about Wanda's and Casey's journeys. If I couldn't have their words to tell me what had happened, I thought I could reconstruct their lives from the written record.

I realized that Wanda's and Casey's stories were proxies for millions of European civilians whose lives were disrupted by the war in ways that are little known today. And their arrival, among the first of tens of thousands admitted into Canada after the war, brought to the surface the evolving values and attitudes toward newcomers of my own country at a turning point in its history. The meagre history lessons I had absorbed in school omitted any suggestion of the impact of epic historic events on the lives of ordinary people, but I had only to look at Wanda's and Casey's lives to understand it.

My investigations only touched the surface of the trauma and hardship of Wanda's and Casey's early lives, and I felt the injustice both of what they had endured and of how they had so carefully hidden it from their sons and grandchildren. In a recent essay of introduction to the memoir of a gulag survivor, historian Timothy Snyder writes, "we speak of memory, but memory is empty without witness." As I learned about the world they came from, it became clear that both Wanda and Casey had survived horrific treatment and losses at the hands of Poland's enemies. I began to understand that there was tragedy for them not just in their experiences but also in the fact that such a profound part of their history was invisible to their children. While their silence may have served a purpose for them, the memory of their struggle deserved its own witness.

It was not just curiosity that drove my efforts to find the truth about Wanda's and Casey's pasts. As lawyers, both George and I have spent our careers in the administrative justice system, listening in our roles as arbitrator or adjudicator as people told their stories of unfairness or injustice in their lives. The more I learned about Wanda's and Casey's lives, the more cruelly ironic it seemed that the one story we had never listened to was of the profound injustice at the heart of George's family. What justice had been offered to Wanda and Casey and the millions who had shared their trials? And what meaning would the word *justice* have had for them? The answers to these questions were more complex than I expected. Perhaps, I thought, Wanda and Casey would have felt justice in knowing their children finally heard and understood what they had been through, and what they had lost.

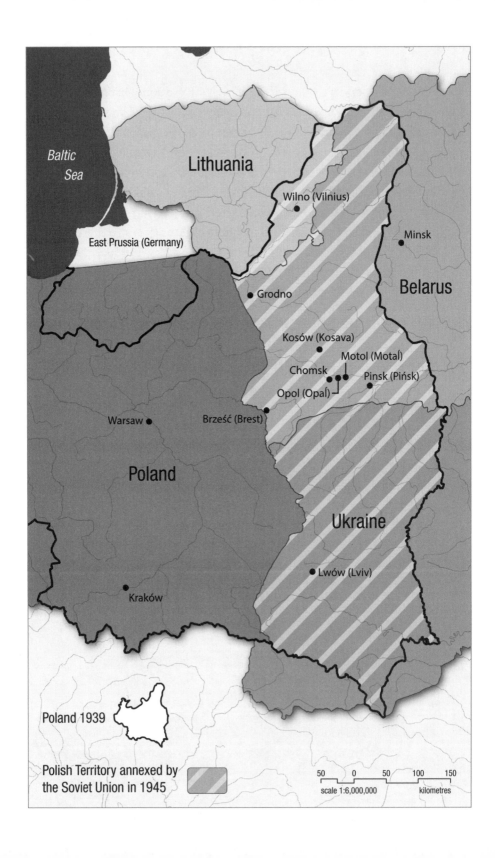

Baltic
Sea

Lithuania

Wilno (Vilnius)

Minsk

East Prussia (Germany)

Grodno

Belarus

Kosów (Kosava)

Motol (Motal)

Chomsk

Pinsk (Pińsk)

Opol (Opal)

Warsaw

Brześć (Brest)

Poland

Ukraine

Lwów (Lviv)

Kraków

Poland 1939

Polish Territory annexed by
the Soviet Union in 1945

50   0   50   100   150

scale 1:6,000,000   kilometres

CHAPTER 1
BORDERLANDS

A Fatherland is soil and graves. By losing memory, nations lose life. Zako-pane remembers. Outside the cemetery in Zakopane, a mountainous resort area in Poland near the border with Slovakia, we paused while our guide, Tomasz, translated the inscription on a plaque at the entrance. Memory, soil, and graves. To the modern visitor, the invocation suggests the spirit of a Poland dominated by the Nazis in the Second World War, but Tomasz wanted us to know that the past that haunts Poland reaches much further back than 1939 and casts taller shadows from the east than from the west.

The name of the town Zakopane means *buried*, symbolizing its location in a valley between the Tatra Mountains and Gubałówka Hill. Memory is long in Poland, and although its history is buried everywhere, it is always close to the surface for the Poles, so that past and present seem to coexist simultaneously. To many Poles, the Soviet liberation of Poland in 1945 was merely another occupation by an opponent in a centuries-old struggle. In the early days of the war, this opponent had already occupied parts of eastern Poland and killed, imprisoned, or deported hundreds of thousands of Poles. If this story is less known to Westerners, it is largely because of the silencing of Poles during forty-five years behind the Iron Curtain and the secrecy of Soviet records of the war.

Over the centuries of its existence, Poland's borders have changed numerous times as armies advanced and retreated across its lands;

for more than one hundred years, it was obliterated from the maps of the world altogether. A series of "partitions" between 1772 and 1795 carved off slices of Poland and divided them among three empires —Prussia, Austria, and Russia—until nothing remained. The question of what exactly was partitioned exposes the roots of persistent conflicting claims to the lost territories. In 1569, the Kingdom of Poland and the Grand Duchy of Lithuania formed the Polish-Lithuanian Commonwealth, reconfiguring the two entities in the process. Lithuania's more southerly East Slavic lands, now associated with modern Ukraine, came under Polish rule; lands that are part of present-day Belarus remained under Lithuanian jurisdiction. The agreement, known as the Union of Lublin, noted that a new state had been "created and joined out of two states and two nations into one people."[1]

Historians caution against making assumptions about the religious, linguistic, or ethnic identities of the citizens of the new republic equating the member nations with their modern counterparts. But this has not stopped modern nationalist movements from relying on medieval constructs of nations to support their territorial disputes. Timothy Snyder has noted that Poles refer to the early modern commonwealth as Polish, Lithuanians can prove that medieval Vilnius was not Polish but Lithuanian, and Russians consider the centuries of east Slavic membership in the commonwealth as a "meaningless prelude to their 'reunification' with Russia."[2] Writing of the centuries-old enmity between Poland and Russia, Czesław Miłosz described its origins as obscure as "the motives for a hereditary vendetta between two families who live on the same street."[3]

Tomasz's lengthy description of Poland's shifting borders didn't seem to have much to do with Wanda and Casey, and it took some time to understand that it held the key to both of their fates during and after the war. The region where Wanda was born, Polesie (or Polesia) originates at the crossing of the Bug and Pripyat river valleys and straddles the border between Belarus and Ukraine, stretching from Poland to Russia. Opal is located just above the east-west corridor that runs from Pinsk to Brześć, at the northwestern edge of the Polesie (or Pripyat) Marshes, a vast area of sandy lowlands once covered by a labyrinth of tributaries, ponds, marshes, and streams on both sides of the Pripyat River. Winston Churchill, in his book *The World Crisis*, described the region as "the cradle of the Slav race," a region of "primeval bog and forest" as large as Scotland, in which the few roads were causeways, creating a massive gulf dividing Europe and Asia. When Wanda's father was in the navy, he may have been in the units that patrolled the Pripyat marshes in a fleet of small gunboats.

A satellite view shows today's Opaĺ as a small rural town or village, with most houses along a single road attached to long, narrow strips of cultivated land. The surrounding countryside consists of larger fields or forested areas. The marshy region is much smaller today than the one described by Churchill, since many of the wetlands have been drained since the war to create arable farmland.[4] A topographical map of the area from 1926 shows a village named Opol, with a scattering of houses bordering the road that went through the village, not so different from today's map. But where the recent map shows farm acreages north of the road, in 1926 that area was mainly wetlands with some small forested areas, stretching out for many miles.

When American explorer Louise Arner Boyd visited the Pripyat marshes in 1934, she found Poland's most sparsely populated and primitive rural area, appearing much as it would have one hundred years earlier. A 1919 demographic map reinforces a sense of Polesia as a predominantly peasant society. It shows almost no signs of a Polish presence; the rural areas north and south of the road between Brześć and Pinsk were mainly inhabited by the *tutejsi*, or the people belonging to here, with a minority of Belarusian (also called White Ruthenians) in places. Not far from Opol, the towns of Chomsk and Drohiczyn were home to a mix of Jewish and *tutejsi* residents, while the larger cities of Brześć and Pinsk were predominantly Jewish.

Isolated from the modern world by its inaccessibility, the area's transportation was mostly on waterways, in flat-bottomed wooden canoes or barges. Boyd found any roads that existed to be in "deplorable condition," usually navigated with one-horse wagons. Many travelled long distances on foot, on paths through the forests or marshes. The area was more easily travelled in winter, when the waterways froze and could be crossed on foot or sleigh.

In a region threaded by rivers, streams, and marshes, fishing was a significant occupation, but the men also harvested willow branches for weaving, and marsh grasses and reeds for animal bedding and roof thatching. One-horse plows were used in the fields, and it was not uncommon to see horses, plows, and other equipment transported by boat from one piece of property to another. Peasants grew hardy vegetables such as cabbage, potatoes, carrots, and beets for their own consumption, and flax for weaving into cloth. Houses were constructed of wood, with roofs of thatched straw, reeds, or grass. It was a life that was largely self-sufficient and unmechanized, almost a relic of a time long past. To Boyd, the area seemed to have been "almost ignored" under the Russian regime, missing out on whatever modernization was taking place elsewhere.[5]

This was the remote and simple place that Wanda was thinking about when she told her son Chris that her home was "gdzieś na wsi," somewhere out in the country; nowhere he would know.

Helena was born in 1897, making her twenty years old in the photograph in George's album. She came from an educated family and had three brothers. One brother was a schoolteacher, another ran a distillery or brewery, and the third brother was the wastrel—a gambler and a drinker. Given her birthdate, Helena would have been thirty when her first child, Wanda, was born, relatively late in life for a woman of her generation. Three more children followed during the next decade: Józef, Kasia, and Ryszard.

The family had a small farm—probably much like those in the satellite image of the town, with a small strip of land adjacent to the house—with a couple of cows and pigs. Helena was sickly—it was something to do with her lungs—and she couldn't help with the farm work. Antoni had to take care of the animals, as well as his job outside the home. The town consisted of about four hundred houses. There were not many Jewish families, maybe two, and there were more Russians (Joe's word, perhaps meaning Belarusians) than Poles. In Joe's eyes, religion determined the difference between them: "If you went to the Catholic Church, you were Polish. If you were Orthodox, you were Russian."

Antoni died in 1937, when Wanda would have been ten years old. He was a blacksmith and was killed while handling a horse. Joe believed that the accident with the horse had caused some kind of heart injury or attack, although it sounded more like a punctured lung or massive internal bleeding caused by a crush injury.

After Antoni's death, most of the family went to live with one of Helena's brothers—the teacher. The youngest child, Ryszard, was sent to live with another uncle in northwest Belarus, near the present-day borders of Lithuania and Poland, and never again lived with his mother and siblings. Perhaps he was sent to stay with Helena's other brother temporarily, for the summer of 1939, and was stranded when the war broke out. But, given her circumstances, it's equally plausible that Helena sent her youngest son to live with her brother indefinitely and couldn't bring herself to tell her young children the truth. Either way, the outbreak of the war made Ryszard's return to his family impossible.

If the rudimentary life in the rural village of Opaĺ marked Wanda's early life, Polesie's place in the larger geography of Poland played an even larger role in determining her future. Polesie was part of Poland's eastern borderlands, or *kresy* as they are known in the region—once an ethnically and linguistically diverse region that stretched from Lithuania in the north, passed through Belarus, and ended in Ukraine. Usually defined as the six provinces along the Polish-Soviet border, Poland's claims to the region rested on its historical presence before the partition years, dating at least as far back as the sixteenth-century formation of the Polish-Lithuanian Commonwealth. But, as Czesław Miłosz points out in his memoir, *Native Realm*, the commonwealth was not a national state, and loyalties were based on regional attachments.

During the first half of the twentieth century, the *kresy* would experience the worst of two world wars, losing millions of its people in massacres, deportations, and starvation while opposing armies occupied and claimed the space for their own. Its location, wedged between Russia and Poland and at the heart of the geopolitical struggle between Tsarist Russia and Imperial Germany (and later, the Soviet Union and Nazi Germany), defined its fate. In somewhat neutral terms, historian Franziska Exeler described the region as "a place where imperial and national rivalries met, overlapped and played out; a political laboratory where various actors could test out their national and social engineering projects; and a space where contested boundaries between different political domains became visible."[6] More explicitly, historian Kate Brown described it as "the epicenter of destruction, the bastard child of progress," "a theater for war and destruction," and "an arena in which warring parties have time and again fallen into the exhausted embrace of worn-out prizefighters." The people of the borderlands, of all Europeans, felt the cumulative effect of these conflicts most acutely.

The short version of history dates the birth of Poland's Second Republic to the end of the First World War and the collapse of the partitioning empires that surrounded it. The Poles were successful in gaining recognition of an independent Polish state, but the Treaty of Versailles established only the border between Germany and Poland; in a region that had been unsettled for centuries, the outcome was not hard to predict. As historian Norman Davies observed, "the collapse of all established order in Central and Eastern Europe condemned the infant republic to a series of nursery brawls."[7]

It took six different armed conflicts between 1918 and 1921 to finally settle the outlines of Poland's border. Uprisings and outright wars were fought in Ukraine, Silesia, Poznan, Lithuania, and on the southern border with Czechoslovakia. The eastern border of Poland was settled—but not permanently, as it would turn out—in the Polish-Soviet War fought over the borderlands of Belarus and Ukraine.[8] Perhaps not fully appreciating the risk posed by a Soviet possession of Poland, or maybe just depleted by their own losses in the war, western governments offered no help in the conflict. British Prime Minister Lloyd George complained that "the Poles have quarrelled with all their neighbours and they are a menace to the peace of Europe."[9]

The Polish-Soviet War would be the last time Poland successfully defended its borders against the Soviets. The country's soldiers rallied to defend Warsaw, where they kept the Russians from crossing the Vistula and forced their retreat. Before the war finally ended, the last great cavalry battle in European history took place near Zamość, where the Poles were victorious once again.[10] In the negotiated peace, formalized by the Treaty of Riga in 1921, the western part of Belarus, including Brześć Oblast, fell within the newly created eastern border of Poland. For the first time, Wanda's mother, Helena, was a Pole living in Poland, not Russia. But for Belarusian nationalists, the treaty was a setback in a quest for autonomy and independence. The short-lived Belarusian Democratic Republic ended, with the eastern territory ceded to the Soviet Union in a newly created Belarusian SSR.[11]

Wanda was born six years after the Treaty of Riga in a place that held only a fragile connection to the Poland of her ancestors. The first years of the new Polish Republic were chaotic. Self-governance did not come easily for the Poles, who had adopted the habit of opposition after over a century of living within three different cultures. Like other European nations, the new country was in ruins after six years of war and destruction. Millions of acres of agricultural land had been devastated, and the retreating Germans had carried out a "de-industrialization" of the country, destroying factories, bridges, and transportation services. In this atmosphere, the Polish government had to create an entire state apparatus from scratch. It set about launching health and social insurance schemes and establishing an education system that halved illiteracy by 1939.[12]

During this time, the Polish government adopted a policy of "Polonisation" of the *kresy*. Thousands of soldiers were granted land

there, and other Poles migrated to the region to take advantage
of government assistance and cheap land. These military settlers,
osadnicy wojskowi, were required to remain in the reserve army,
providing an ongoing military presence in the area.[13] Poland had
aspirations to introduce civilization into a region it considered
historically Polish but largely undeveloped and primitive as a result of
over a century under Russian domination.

It is hard to say whether this experiment would have succeeded
had it not been for the intervention of another war, but the demographics of the *kresy* suggest that it would have met with conflict
and failure in many parts of the region. Poles, Russians, Belarusians,
Ukrainians, Jews, and even Germans, each speaking their own language and practising their own religion, had followed the armies to
the borderlands over the centuries, colonizing the region with each
new occupation. The *kresy* contained the Pale of Settlement, the
area of Imperial Russia in which Jews were permitted to reside. In
the northeast part of the *kresy*, in and around Wilno, Poles represented a majority of the population, but elsewhere, the demographic
mixes varied. In a 1931 Polish census, native Polish speakers were in
the majority in the three northern provinces of Białystok, Wilno, and
Nowogródek, but in Volhynia, to the south of Polesie, Poles consti-
tuted only 16.6 percent of the population.

This diverse mix of intermingling cultures is at odds with the
national mythologies of the countries that exist in today's *kresy*,
which present as homogeneous ethnic territories. Writing of the
town of Buczacz (located in today's Ukraine), historian Omer Bartov
described life in the region as "premised on constant interaction
between different ethnic communities." Jews did not live segregated
from the Christian population in isolated shtetls but integrated into
the larger community. A market day in predominantly Jewish Pinsk
brought together peasants—the men in birchbark sandals over legs
wrapped in cloth, the women sometimes barefooted and in babush-
kas—with townspeople in suits, dresses, and leather footwear.
Everything from lumber and hay, livestock and game, to cloth and
sheepskin, produce and wild mushrooms—all transported by horse

and cart or wooden boat—were sold in markets across the *kresy* that resembled the monthly gathering by the River Pina.

Not all who lived in the *kresy* shared the romantic Polish view of it as an outpost of Polish civilization in opposition to Russian despotism. Many in the *kresy* chafed at the reforms the new Polish government imposed on them and resented the landowning *osadnicy* and Polish elites who governed over non-Polish minorities (or even, sometimes, majorities). Peasants, who were largely illiterate, objected to the introduction of compulsory education and refused to cooperate in sending their children miles away to attend school. Czesław Miłosz observed that "Warsaw conducted an absurd policy," forbidding the Belarusians from having their own schools and discouraging them from any attempts to organize themselves.[14] Historian Kathryn Ciancia writes that Poland's modernizing agenda in the *kresy* soon collided with the reality of the emergence of nation-states in eastern Europe, describing the region as an "economic, political, and security nightmare for the fledgling state."[15]

The map of Poland, with its changing borders, gives a sense of the frailty of existence for those in the land where Wanda and her family were born, where fortunes shifted frequently with the arrival and departure of yet another army. Those fortunes would shift again, disastrously, with the beginning of yet another war on the lands where they lived.

In today's Russia, the Second World War is known as the Great Patriotic War, which began only when the Nazis invaded the Soviet Union in June 1941. According to Russian mythology, the war ended with victory over the Nazis, brought about by Stalin's leadership and the sacrifice and heroism of the Soviet people, a vindication of Communism and the Russian spirit.

For the Polish inhabitants of the *kresy*, though, the war began on September 1, 1939, the day the Nazis launched their offensive in Poland. By the end of September, Poland's losses were devastating. In Warsaw alone, one of the worst-hit cities, about 40,000 civilians were killed during the artillery and air bombardment of the city. Over 66,000 soldiers and airmen died, another 133,000 were wounded, and almost 700,000 were captured.[16] Not long after the Nazis advanced across Poland from three directions simultaneously, flattening towns and cities with tonnes of bombs and artillery, those in the *kresy* understood that a different kind of war had come to them.

The Soviet Union had signed a treaty of non-aggression with Nazi Germany, the Molotov-Ribbentrop Pact, on August 23 that year. The agreement did more than just protect the Soviet Union from invasion. In secret protocols, the two powers agreed to divide Poland between them, leaving the Soviets to take control of the Baltic states and parts of Finland and Romania. The *kresy*, which was to be annexed by the Soviet Union, was largely spared in the western Nazi offensive, for the simple reason that the Nazis never intended to occupy it. All that remained was for the Red Army to take possession of the eastern territories, which it considered to be part of the Soviet Union all along.

By the time the Soviets entered eastern Poland on September 17, 1939, what remained of the Polish army was incapable of mounting any meaningful resistance, and the Soviet occupation was accomplished without significant combat. More than twelve million people living across 190,000 square kilometres of territory became subjects of the Soviet Union. Five days later, the residents of Brześć witnessed a joint German-Soviet victory parade to mark the handover of the city from German to Soviet control. The eastern parts of the Polish Republic were renamed Western Belarus and Western Ukraine, territories that stretched from Hungary and Romania in the south to Lithuania in the north and were bordered on the west by the Nazi-run general government that controlled the rest of Poland. The Brześć region, where Wanda and her family lived, fell in the territory of Western Belarus. With this occupation, the country of Poland, once described by Vyacheslav Molotov as "the monstrous bastard of the Peace of Versailles," once again ceased to exist.[17] Wanda's twelve years of living as a Pole within Poland were over, although she never left home.

To Belarusian nationalists, the Soviet occupation of Poland in 1939 resulted in a "reunification" of the country, restoring the land that Poland had taken in the Polish-Soviet War.[18] When the Soviets entered the eastern territories in September, it was under an order declaring that they came "not as conquerors but as liberators of our brother Belorusians [*sic*] and Ukrainians and the workers of Poland."[19]

For Wanda and her family, as for the other Poles in the region, the Soviet occupation was no liberation. It was not safe to be a Pole in the eastern provinces as the Soviets embarked on their occupation. It was especially unsafe to be a landowning or educated Pole or anyone considered a member of the "elite" or ruling class. Even before the Red Army arrived, Soviet agents were dispatched to organize friendly receptions for the incoming army, ushering in a period of anarchy before the army established its authority. Longstanding ethnic tensions in the region spilled over, and incidents of brutality and destruction of property went on for days.

The first months of the war were devastating for the Gizmunts. When the Soviet army occupied eastern Poland, their uncle disappeared one day, presumed to have been murdered. But it wasn't the Soviets who killed him; the peasants did it. He was most likely a victim of the violent chaos that preceded the Soviet occupation, in which the entering Soviets encouraged locals to exact their revenge for the years of Polish rule. Leaflets circulated calling for assaults on Polish landlords with whatever tools were at hand. "*Poliakam, panam, sobakam — sobachaia smert,*" (for Poles, Pans [gentry], and dogs — a dog's death) one proclaimed. For several days, a general dispensation was given for the populace to do as it pleased. In parts of the *kresy*, a "peasant jacquerie" emerged, embarking on a campaign of terror, pillage, and violence.[20] Some Poles hid in the forest, but most watched nervously. Thousands were killed throughout eastern Poland, "often with primitive and premeditated brutality."[21] Teachers like Wanda's uncle were not just members of the hated elites but symbols of the oppressive policy of compulsory education in Polish.

Once again left to fend for herself, and probably fearing for her family's safety, Helena joined households with Antoni's sister — a single woman, older than Helena, with no children of her own. Together, this little group of two women and three young children clung together to face the occupation of their home by two different enemies.

Following this initial period of lawlessness, the Sovietization of eastern Poland began; the objective was the destruction of Polish culture in the region. Libraries, newspapers, and bookstores were closed. Worship was forbidden. Wanda, Joe, and Kasia were sent to school to learn the Russian language and become communists. The old elites were arrested, and some were killed. Polish currency was abolished, savings were confiscated, and landowners were stripped of their property. A plebiscite was held, with the results determined in advance, annexing Western Ukraine and Western Belarus to the Soviet Union. All inhabitants were required to register and accept Soviet citizenship; resisters were arrested and imprisoned.

The one-party dictatorship took control of the territories and set up an informant network. Neighbours were encouraged to betray neighbours. The Soviets captured approximately 150,000 Polish soldiers in the fall of 1939. Some were handed over to the Germans, some were released, and some deported to Siberia, but many were murdered. The most notorious was the massacre of as many as 22,000 Polish prisoners of war, including 14,500 army officers executed at Katyń, Mednoye, and Kharkov, locations in the Soviet Union.[22]

The Soviets also carried out waves of deportations of targeted groups: professionals, local government officials, settlers, small farmers, foresters, and those deemed "anti-Soviet" or "nationalist." With no visas or passports, Jewish refugees from western Poland were arrested, exchanging certain death in Nazi concentration camps for deportation and imprisonment in Soviet camps. Estimates of the number deported vary widely, from as few as 320,000 to over one million; they were sent to gulags or to "special settlements" in Siberia and Kazakhstan in four different actions. About 125,000 of them came from western Belorussia.[23]

The Polish journalist and writer Ryszard Kapuściński was a seven-year-old boy in nearby Pinsk when the Soviets entered eastern Poland in September 1939. His book *Imperium* offers a view of the Soviet occupation through a child's eyes, much as Wanda and her siblings would have experienced it a mere sixty kilometres away. Immediately, signs of war were everywhere. Crowds of refugees carrying bundles and suitcases filled the streets. Red Army soldiers, pathetically dressed in rags and old boots, carrying empty linen bags instead of knapsacks, along with their guns and bayonets, patrolled the town. The children returned to school, where they didn't need to be told not to ask questions about their lessons on Stalin and Lenin, learning a new alphabet, as well as a new way of living in an atmosphere so tense and heavy that it felt like a minefield: "We were afraid even to take a deep breath," Kapuściński remembered, "lest we set off an explosion."[24]

At school, the NKVD (state police) arrived with white shirts and red scarves for the children, who were now members of the patriotic Soviet youth group Pioneers. As children do, they made games out of trading the stamps of Soviet leaders, no different than North American children trading hockey and baseball cards. These light-hearted games didn't last. Before long, Kapuściński noticed dozens of freight cars gathering on the tracks near the train stations, along with swarms of Red Army and NKVD men. Later, he watched as wagons filled with people and bundles pulled up to be loaded into the cars. The deportations had begun, and a new fear infected the homes of Poles in the borderlands.

The deportations happened at night. A peasant wagon, pulled by a horse, stopped outside a house. The commanding officer shouted at the residents, giving them fifteen minutes to pack. The residents frantically gathered their possessions and some food and climbed on the wagon, which pulled away in the darkness. After a trip through the muddy streets, the deported were loaded onto freight cars. "What did it mean—to fill a car?" Kapuściński asked. "It meant to stuff these people into it using knees and rifle butts so that there would be no room left even for a pin."

At school, all the talk was of deportations; at home, mothers and fathers didn't sleep, listening for footsteps in the silence of the night.

No one knew when they would come, or for whom. The children could see no rules or logic to those who were taken from their homes. Classmates, even the teacher, disappeared from school, but no one asked where they were. Eventually, Kapuściński's class dwindled to half its size. Then, the hunger began. The shops had no food to sell. Children raided gardens, especially the unguarded ones of those who had already been deported, and parents would drive to nearby villages to trade jewellery or clothing for flour or poultry.

Winter in the Polesie region in 1939-40 came early, a "frosty, icy hell." One day, Kapuściński and his sister watched from behind some bushes as a transport filled with people sat on the siding, waiting to depart. Grownups told him they were going to Siberia. He didn't know where that was, but it was clear from the way they said the word that "even thinking about this Siberia was enough to make one shudder." He listened as moans and cries came from the direction of the siding; wagons went from one car to the next, collecting those who had died of hunger or exposure in the night. After the soldiers closed the doors, they tied them shut with wire, tightening it with pliers.

In a smaller town, away from the railway hub, Wanda might have been spared the sight of the cattle cars filled with Poles awaiting transportation to Siberia. But she and her family must have felt vulnerable to the same fate as the other Poles being deported. Her father had been in the Polish navy, her uncle a teacher. Her uncle's violent death could only have instilled terror in the family. For the next two years, they lived in fear of their own deportation as they adjusted to the new reality of life in a Soviet town.

CHAPTER 2
THE GULAG

The German philosopher and essayist Walter Benjamin once famously said, "to live means to leave traces." Any traces of his past that lived on in Casey's memory, unspoken in life, vanished with his death. The physical traces of his early life were almost as obscure. Unlike Wanda, he left behind no family to consult and few records that could bring to life the world he inhabited before he arrived in Canada. His obituary said that he had three brothers and three sisters, unnamed, and that only a brother, Joseph, survived him in Poland. The few objects of Casey's found in Wanda's cookie tin would be my only tools to reconstruct his origins and life before arriving in Canada.

One of the two photos Casey left behind is a group photo, a formal portrait, of a father and mother with five children—three boys and two girls—posed in front of some trees. It has no inscription to identify the subjects, but it is likely a photo of his family, missing two of the siblings. The youngest child, a boy, appears to be no more than five or six, and he resembles Casey more than the other two boys. The expression of reticence on his face, his inner stillness, and the smile he was not fully committed to convince me he is Casey. The young boys have jackets over their shirts, the girls wear dresses, and the older son and his father are dressed in suits and ties. The father sports a bushy moustache, a full head of hair, and a serious look. His wife, who appears older and more worn than her husband, sits beside

The Surdykowski family with young Casey on the left, ca. 1925
(Courtesy George Surdykowski)

him, staring glumly at the camera. The photo is heavily creased, and its edges are ragged, as if Casey had carried it around with him since he left home. A large part of the bottom is missing, enough space for there to have been two smaller children seated in front. But given the age of the parents, it seems more likely the two missing siblings were older and had already left home or simply did not survive childhood. In another photo, a man, dressed in a double-breasted suit and tie, stands in a busy square with a young boy and a pre-teen girl. The stamp on the back of the photo is from the Tabac of Mme. Marchand, in Rue de la Barre, Lyon. The photo is inscribed, in Polish, "a souvenir for brother Kasika [Casey]—photo [from] last Easter 1947."

An inspection of Casey's military documents only led to more questions. His military record says he was born on March 20, 1920, to father, Feliks, and mother, Józefa. It gives his birthplace as Marianowo —the name for at least seventeen villages, towns, or cities in today's Poland. The area and province given, Złotówo-Pomorskie, only adds to the confusion. Two Marianowos are in Pomorskie, but neither of them appears close to any of the four Złotówos in the region. Łukasz, our guide from Poland, explained that a realignment of boundaries after the war meant that the Marianowo in question was probably located in a different province. Shifting my search produced another four towns or villages named Marianowo. The most I can say is that Casey came from west-central Poland and not from the area in eastern Poland the Soviets occupied in the early days of the war.

How, then, did he end up in a camp in Siberia? Had it not been for the opening of Soviet archives in Russia after the fall of the Soviet Union, the answer to that question would have been forever buried. In the days of glasnost, when it was finally possible to speak openly about the abuses of Stalinism, Memorial, a non-governmental organization dedicated to supporting democracy and human rights in Russia and documenting the victims of Stalin-era repressions, emerged. With virtually no film footage or photography and few surviving artifacts of gulags and prisons, Memorial has relied mainly on archives opened up by the KGB to assemble information about the estimated one million dead and over eleven million persecuted in Soviet state repression. One of Memorial's stated objects is to "call everyone by name."[1] Since 2009, it has held an event each October 29 in several cities in Russia and around the world, in which people read out the names of those executed during Stalin's terror. Another project, The Last Address, attaches metal plaques to the walls of buildings where victims lived before their arrests. For many victims of Stalinism, the record of their names or a simple address in an archive is all that exists as proof of lives interrupted or ended by a hostile state.[2]

Memorial has also compiled a database of the names of people unjustly persecuted in the Soviet Union. Today, it contains three million names, or about one quarter of the estimated total of the victims of Soviet repression. Memorial joined with the KARTA Center Foundation, a social archive of twentieth-century Poland, to create databases of groups of Polish citizens who suffered repression in the former Soviet Union. They scoured Soviet and Polish archival sources to generate an Index of the Repressed—the Poles deported to Siberia, prisoners of war, and murdered prisoners. The digital database is accessible through Poland's Institute of National Remembrance, created to preserve the memory and record of the victims, losses, and damage Poland suffered during and after the Second World War.

Memorial's work makes it possible to learn more about Casey's past than was known in his lifetime. I found Casey, his parents, and his two older sisters in the Index of the Repressed (although finding the female members of his family required searching not for Surdykowski but for Surdykowska) and on a spreadsheet naming all the Poles deported to the Arkhangelsk Oblast. The index also helpfully contained links to a compilation of archival documents. Together, these records furnished me with names, years of birth, the place they were living when they were arrested, and their dates of release.

Casey's father, Feliks, was born in 1877; his father was named Jan. Casey's mother, Józefa, was born in 1879. His sisters, Zofia and Zuzanna, were born in 1909 and 1911 respectively, and Casey, or Kazimierz to use his Polish name, was born in 1920. The Polish Institute and Sikorski Museum in London maintains a registry of the names of military settlers deported to the Soviet Union, and this confirms that the Surdykowski family moved from central Poland to the Brześć region, not far from where Wanda grew up, as *osadnicy wojskowi*, part of the movement of Poles into the eastern borderlands of the reconstituted Poland of the 1920s, where they established farms on acreages created from state land. They were grouped in colonies, known as *osady*, and eked out a living on about twenty hectares of land per family.

Life in the *osada* was hardscrabble. The farms may have been vacant land, forested, or damaged by the war. With few tools or farm animals, the Poles set about clearing land and building houses to live in. Some locals, who may have been tenants of the farms before the Soviets lost control of the area, resented the Poles' presence. Even if their position seemed enviable to the locals, Poles who took up the offer of property in the *kresy* likely left behind an even more difficult life in partitioned Poland and were looking for their own chance at a fresh start. But their status as settlers or colonists in the *kresy* formerly associated with the Polish military made them an obvious first target for exclusion when the Soviets began their occupation of the region in 1939.

Military settlers in the *kresy*, those Poles who had taken up land in the region after serving in the Polish army during the First World War or the Polish-Soviet War, were the first to be deported; a decree in December 1939 placed all Polish settlers, whether military or civilian, on the list of undesirables to be removed from their homes and deported east to forced labour, mainly in forestry. In another decree, the Politburo approved the disposition of their property. State and collective farms would acquire their land, tools, large animals, and machinery; teachers and doctors took possession of their homes; and their furniture and other domestic supplies were distributed as needed by state institutions like schools and hospitals.[3]

In the stories of the *sybiracy*, the name given to Poles who were deported from the eastern borderlands by the Soviets, Siberia is more than simply a geographic location, the vast territory covering thirteen million square miles from the Ural Mountains to the Arctic and Pacific watersheds. It represents a state of being: exiled, disappeared, and forgotten, sentenced to endless work in conditions as hostile and unforgiving as their Soviet masters. In fact, not all the *sybiracy* ended up in Siberia. Some were sent to work on farms in Kazakhstan, and others were sent to the Arkhangelsk region in northeastern European Russia, just below the Arctic Circle on the White Sea. No matter where they ended up, though, their exile was known as Siberia, and their memories of their journey consistently begin with the shock of roundups at gunpoint in the night.

Exile to the regions beyond the Ural mountains had long been a form of punishment in Russia, dating back to the seventeenth century. Violent criminals, degenerates, and other outsiders were removed from society and used to settle the vast interior of the country, replacing its native people with a Russian society.[4] More recently, internal exile in the Soviet Union came to be associated with the gulag, a system of prison camps scattered across the vast, unpopulated northern and eastern regions of the USSR, used in mass repression carried out against real or imagined opponents of the Soviet system. Not all who were exiled were imprisoned as criminals. Many were sent to work on collective farms, in special settlements, or in corrective labour camps. Collectively, these camps provided the free labour that fuelled the Soviet Union's economic expansion, allowing it to develop its vast natural resources in wood and minerals in the north and east. During the war, forced labour produced munitions and military equipment.

Throughout the mid-1930s, the special settlements (*spetsposelka* in Russian; *specjalny posiołek* or *specposiołek* in Polish) housed the largest contingent of prisoners in the Soviet Union. The first inhabitants were the kulaks, prosperous peasant families or "rural capitalists" who had to be removed to support collectivization and the transformation of the agrarian nation into a modern industrialized country. Later, the settlements were replenished with "socially dangerous elements." At their peak in 1931, 1.8 million people lived in special settlements scattered across the northern territories of subarctic Russia, Siberia, the Urals, Kazakhstan, and the far east.

The conditions in the special settlements were harsh and brutal, particularly for the original inhabitants, who had to clear the land and build their own housing. Typically, they constructed log houses of about one thousand square metres to house eight families. They were given insufficient rations, and many died of starvation; others survived by eating birchbark, silage, leaves, and grass.[5]

It was no great leap for the Soviets to use these same camps to dispose of potential enemies from the newly occupied Polish territories. Casey's journey to a *specposiołek* began, as it did for thousands of other Poles, in the depths of a bitterly cold winter night on February 10, 1940. Soldiers arrived at their home, ordering the family to gather their possessions and searching for weapons to seize. The Surdykowskis boarded a wagon waiting to take them to the train station at Kosów, where they were ordered into a dirty red boxcar known as the Red Cow, overcrowding spaces meant for no more than forty people — or eight horses. Escort troops surrounded the stations to prevent escape.

In a journey that may have taken weeks, Casey lived in the crowded and forced intimacy of the cattle car with dozens of people he may not have known. The passengers would have mourned their passage from Poland into Russia, peering from the tiny opening in the wall of the train at the snow-covered expanse outside the train. From time to time, the train stopped for the guards to dispense the meagre daily food ration; food consisted of bread and water offered once a day, and occasionally soup, or whatever food could be scrounged from villagers during train stops along the way. Local Soviet citizens along the rail line, familiar with the convoys of people being taken from their homes for a life sentence in the gulag, sometimes took pity on the prisoners, offering bits of food, or *kipyatok*, the boiled water that passed for tea everywhere Casey went. The sight of boxcars filled with deportees was nothing new for the villagers, who commiserated with the Poles about their fate.

In the cattle car, men, women and children clamoured for a spot near the stove (when there was one), which may not have provided much heat in any case. The toilet was no more than a hole in the floor, which may have been surrounded by a blanket in a feeble attempt to preserve privacy. In the winter cold, many died on the journey east, only to be buried beneath the snow when the train made an occasional stop at a village along the way. They lived this way for anywhere from three to six weeks, the uncertainty of their future multiplying the misery and humiliation of the trip.

It is hard to know exactly where the train stopped before the passengers had to get off. Casey's final destination, the *specposiołek* at Pachikha, is 280 kilometres southeast of Arkhangelsk, and about the same distance from Kholmogorski, but any road to the settlement is circuitous. Even today, there is no train that goes there from any direction. In 1940 it would have been reachable only by ice road in the winter or horse cart in the summer. After a long journey cramped in a frigid cattle car, the final leg of the family's journey would have been the most arduous. In early March, moving through the forest or along the river in the snow and ice, with little food or comfort, the trip must have felt unendurable.

When they finally arrived, they discovered a settlement buried in the taiga bordering the Yula River. The area is home to one of the last large stands of intact forest in the world, estimated to be roughly four thousand years old. The forest is predominantly spruce, and it teems with wildlife—elk, bear, wolves, lynxes, and even reindeer. Salmon spawn in the taiga rivers. Hunting, fishing, and gathering mushrooms and berries provide food for local inhabitants who have the time to do so.

A Polish journalist for the *Kurier Galicyjski*, Adam Kaczyński, travelled to the area in 2012 to visit the settlement at Pachikha. He found remnants of the lives of the former Polish exiles, who eked out a living at logging and farming potatoes in their short time there. Kaczyński reported that at the end of March 1940, 259 people made their way to Pachikha, 106 of whom were deemed qualified to work. After they arrived, the commandant, Nikiforov, gave them three days to rest. He informed them that they were there for good, and that they were there to work.[6] The Poles heard the same Russian phrase on their arrival at the camps or settlements across the Soviet Union: *zdes zhit budete*, here you shall live; meaning, you will never leave this place. Those already living in the settlement encouraged the newcomers to accept their fate with the sanguine advice, *privýknete, a kak ne privýknete to podókhnete*—you will get used to it, or if you don't, you'll croak.[7]

At Pachikha, the Poles joined a collection of Soviet citizens—kulaks, enemies of the people, and other undesirables—who had arrived there to construct the settlement in 1935. They lived in log buildings, including uninsulated barracks furnished with plank beds. The Poles were allotted garden plots, which meant that the family had to clear trees and remove the rocks before planting when the spring finally arrived. With the rocks they built boundary walls, creating a "Polish field," a term still used by local hunters. Today only traces of barracks, a mill located on a stream flowing out of a nearby lake, a row of poplars, and a cemetery remain to mark the presence of the Polish deportees.

One vivid account of the logger's life in the Arkhangelsk Oblast appears in *A World Apart*, the 1951 memoir of the Polish writer Gustaw Herling. Herling was arrested when he attempted to enter Soviet-occupied Poland to join the Polish Army in September 1939. Initially held in prison, he was transferred to a labour camp at Yercevo, near Arkhangelsk, where he remained until his release. His journey out of the gulag, at least until the end of the war, was the same that Casey followed.

In Herling's account, prisoners walked miles each way to work in the forest, in clothing made from rags and boots made from torn felt or even scraps of car tires. Many did not undress at night for fear their clothing—dirty, fragile, and threadbare—might disintegrate at their touch. Every season had its hazards: the misery of bitter cold and snow in the winter, rain and mud in the spring and fall, and heat, humidity, and ravenous bugs in the summer. Lice and hunger were constant in all seasons.

There is no memoir of Poles in the gulags or special settlements that does not describe at length the daily hopeless battle to defeat lice. Julius Margolin, a Jewish Pole from Pinsk who was deported to the Russian far north, had a daily ritual of eating his bread each morning and then "reading the latest news"—killing the lice he could find on his clothes and body. "We picked them off the bread and our faces, off the collar and the pillow of our neighbour, and we crushed them with gloomy satisfaction, as if they were our jailers."[8]

Food servings were based on productivity, guaranteeing that those who could not contribute would eventually starve. Bread was the basic unit of food, supplemented by weak soup and a spoon of boiled barley. Death was an ever-present companion, and every prisoner knew, as Herling wrote, "that his death was approaching with a speed which excluded the consciousness of dying."[9]

In another logging camp at Kvasha, about two hundred kilometres south of Pachikha, Stefan Waydenfeld had an existence that must have been very close to Casey's. There were no guards or barbed wires to keep the Poles there, but they were unnecessary. The remoteness of their exile meant that nobody could leave on their own and survive. The settlement staff assigned work, and everyone lived by the same principle: "he who does not work does not eat." The able-bodied were assigned to the forest brigade and spent their days felling trees, removing branches, and, with the help of horses, hauling the logs to the river, where they would float downriver to Arkhangelsk. The work did not stop in the winter, when logs were carried across an ice road to the river bank. To keep warm, the workers improvised, adding layers and lining their clothing and boots with newspaper to cope with the cold. The lucky ones were granted a pair of *valenki*, the coveted felted wool boots that were the best insulation available for the frigid winter. Days off were rare, although crews were not sent to work when the temperature dipped below −40° Celsius.[10]

For Gustav Herling, the spiritual perils of the gulag were as hazardous as the physical. He believed that "a mental condition of full consciousness is more dangerous in slavery than hunger and physical death."[11] The reality of exile and the indignity of forced labour could be more crushing to the spirit than the daily physical discomforts, especially if one dwelled on thoughts of what might have been. Margolin traced the stages of dehumanization and shame that came with life in the gulag, beginning with the journey to the camp. "Everything is suppressed in an ordinary camp inmate: his logic and feeling of justice and his personal right to attention to his most elementary bodily and spiritual needs. The only thing left is resignation and the recognition of his absolute worthlessness and lack of rights."[12]

Another *sybirak*, Edward Herzbaum, observed in his diary that he feared death less than his life of continuous hunger, growing weakness, and inescapable coldness. Everything around him translated to pain of some kind: feet, riddled with sores, rubbed against frozen shoes useless in the snowy forest; snow seemed to "bite off pieces of the body"; wind pierced the face and neck; and hunger taunted with its memories of the feeling of chewing food with a full mouth. He was gripped by despair, "not the feverish sudden kind, but the terribly cold, helpless, motionless despair which suffocates you very slowly and hurts with every thought, like a hidden wound which hurts you when you move some part of your body."[13] Life must have been particularly hard for Casey's aging parents. His mother and father were sent to live in the Pineski Dom Inwalidow, an invalids' home, in March 1941.

How did Casey survive? Instead of embarking on his life with the usual dreams and energy of young men, he was thrust into a wretched world with no end in sight. He was a quiet and stoic man, but it is hard to know how much of this was his personality before he arrived at Pachikha. Was his spirit crushed, never to recover? The gulag had no room for the soul. Better to live the days in mechanical oblivion, avoiding disappointment by refusing hope.

Reading Herling and the memoirs of other *sybiracy*, it is not surprising that Casey never spoke of this time to his children. Not just because he was a quiet introvert; how could he have explained such a world? It seems almost too incredible to be true. And if, as Herling says, a denial of full consciousness was essential to survive the experience, then it is easy to understand why someone would refuse to awaken the memory of that time, only to share it with children living the relatively soft life of boys in mid-century Canada, who would never be able to comprehend what had happened to their father.

CHAPTER 3
WAR AND AMNESTY

The first full day of summer, June 22, 1941, probably began for Wanda much like any other day in Opaĺ. As the eldest daughter of a sickly mother, her days would have consisted of chores, helping her mother look after her younger brother and sister, or, now fourteen, she might have worked outside the home to help support her family. Rumours of an impending German attack circulated in the countryside, but the family may not have been aware that for some time the Germans had been amassing troops at the Russian border a little over one hundred kilometres to the west, or that just that morning, they had launched a massive assault across the 2,900-kilometre front from the Finnish border in the north down to the Black Sea. The sound of Nazi fighter planes buzzing overhead that day, on their way to bombing raids on major cities and strategic centres, would have been enough to signal the invasion, even before the Soviet foreign minister Vyacheslav Molotov went on air at noon to broadcast the news.

Operation Barbarossa, the largest invading force assembled in the history of war, saw over three million German soldiers and more than three thousand tanks cross into the Soviet Union. Taken by surprise, the Soviets were at first disorganized in their response, allowing the Nazis to make swift progress across the western provinces, marching at the rate of fifty kilometres each day. Roads that often saw little traffic were choked with dust from armoured vehicles. Within days, the Nazis occupied the towns and villages around Opaĺ, and by the end of August, they controlled a large swath of territory from Tallinn in the north to Odessa in the south and as far east as Smolensk in Belarus.

Some of the citizens who had suffered or chafed under Soviet rule at first saw the Nazis as liberators, going so far as to welcome the soldiers with bread and salt. Soon it became obvious that the Nazi objective was not the liberation of those oppressed by the Soviets. Looting was widespread, with soldiers stealing food, livestock, and equipment from farmers and stores. Some local citizens joined in, plundering Jewish homes and carrying out hastily organized pogroms of their own.

More systematic violence followed this early chaos. Franziska Exeler, a scholar of Belarus during and after the Nazi occupation, identifies four elements in the Nazi plan: the mass murder of the Jews, the enslavement of the Slavic population, the economic exploitation of the occupied territories, and the eradication of communism.[1] The Nazis planned to transform the Soviet Union into an agrarian colony and turn most of the Baltic states and Ukraine over to German farmers. They considered most Soviet citizens "useless eaters" who would only divert food and resources from the Germans, and they envisioned their death through starvation; in the case of the population of Belarus, they planned to eliminate about six million people.

While their grandiose plans for *lebensraum* for the German people would have to await the end of their conquest of the Soviet Union, the Nazis immediately embarked on their campaign to eliminate the Jews. The western Soviet Union was the site of thousands of *aktions* carried out by Nazi troops, mainly by the Einsatzgruppen (death squads) who followed the Wehrmacht (Nazi forces) into the country. Unlike the death camps the Nazis established in occupied Poland for killing with industrial efficiency, the murder of the Jews in the Soviet Union was individual, personal, and in some ways disturbingly intimate. Joe and Wanda never forgot the Jews whom the Nazis shot in the forest. "And then, that was it," Joe said, his shock at this event apparent more than seventy years later.

The town of Opal̃ does not appear in any searches of Holocaust remembrance sites, suggesting few Jewish residents, but many towns and villages nearby do appear in those records. At first, German detachments avoided the isolated villages along the road where Opal̃ is situated. But by early August, a unit of the SS (*Schutzstaffel* or Protective Echelon) cavalry brigade arrived in Chomsk, about fifteen kilometres west of Opal̃, with instructions from Heinrich Himmler, the Reichsführer of the SS, to murder every Jew in the villages north of the main railway line from Brześć to Pinsk. They rounded up about two thousand Jewish men, women, and children, marched them out of town to a field where the men were forced to dig large ditches for their graves, and shot them with machine guns.[2]

In Motal̃, some twelve kilometres east of Opal̃, most of the town's three thousand Jews were executed in the first week of August and left in a mass grave. "We had not yet been able to absorb the events of the war from a short time ago and the change of Polish to Soviet authority which turned upside down all the accepted ways of life and traditions that stood for generations and which brought down the mighty while it raised the lowly," A.L. Polick, a survivor, later wrote, "before we managed to recover from the legal collapse brought on by the entrance of the Russians who confiscated the best parts of the town and stole with their laws the fruits of years of labor by different hands, once again war." Polick described the complete collapse of society in rural Polesie with the arrival of the Nazis. "All our friends, with whom we maintained personal and business connections, became our enemies."[3]

The Nazis declared that anyone associating with a Jew would be killed. Many villagers simply avoided or distanced themselves from them, rather than risk their own deaths. Anyone helping a Jew could be betrayed by a neighbour, so it was no longer safe to trust anyone. When Jews were forbidden to go out in public, their stores were looted. Nazis also looted the homes of the Jews they murdered. Townspeople took for their own use any possessions the Nazis left behind. Villagers betrayed their Jewish neighbours to the Nazis, with some even descending to the same bestial depths and carrying out random killings. But Polick also witnessed the other extreme, as some neighbours shared information, hid him in their attics or barns, showed him routes to hiding places in the marshes or the forest, and left food and water for him by the roadside. Without them, he would not have survived. But for the vast majority of Jews, there was no help.

No one living in the region during the Nazi occupation could have been unaware of the violence and racial hatred. As a fourteen-year-old girl, Wanda might not have known the full extent of what happened, but the cruelty and destruction that surrounded her in those days of the war could not have left her untouched.

By the time the Nazis invaded the Soviet Union in June 1941, Casey must have grown accustomed to sudden changes in fortune. The truce that led to his release determined the course of Casey's life, sending him on a journey so strange that he could never have imagined it. Under the terms of the Sikorski-Maisky Agreement there would be an amnesty for "all Polish citizens who are at present deprived of their freedom on the territory of the USSR either as prisoners of war or *on other adequate grounds.*"[4] The amnesty granted to the Polish exiles was unprecedented in the history of Soviet gulags. It would lead to the release of as many as 340,000 people: 265,000 from special settlements and exile, and the remainder from prisons or camps and prisoners of war. But in its wording, the pact clung to the legitimacy of the Soviet claim to the eastern borderlands and the program of ethnic cleansing that led to the deportation of those thousands in the first place.[5]

The pact re-established the Polish state, but worryingly, the Polish government-in-exile of Prime Minister Władysław Sikorski agreed to determine Poland's borders at a later date. Although many in Sikorski's cabinet advised him to insist on the return of the seized lands, he relied instead on the hope that they could be regained at the end of the war. With no bargaining power, it was undoubtedly the best deal the Poles could make. The pact forced Poles into an uneasy alliance with the Russians against a shared enemy, each of them barely containing their mutual suspicion and mistrust. For the Poles who were released, it left their return to their homeland in grave doubt.

The pact permitted the Poles to create a new division of the Polish army on Soviet soil, the Polish Second Corps. Command of the army was given to General Władysław Anders, who was at the time an inmate of the Lubyanka prison at the NKVD headquarters in Moscow. Anders was a charismatic figure whose leadership and determination were so profound and far-reaching that the troops he led would come to be known by his name, the Anders Army. A fierce advocate for the welfare of the Poles coming out of Soviet exile, he was a thorn in the side of the other Allied leadership, a quality that endeared him even more to his soldiers.

As a Pole who had grown up in Russian-controlled Poland and served in the Russian army during the First World War, Anders had the confidence of both the Poles and the Soviets. In the new war, he had commanded the Nowogródzka cavalry brigade for the Polish army and was wounded in clashes with both the German and Soviet armies. He and his troops had been captured by the Soviets and imprisoned in Lwów, and then Lubyanka. After learning of his new command, Anders left the prison in a chauffeured NKVD car, dressed in a shirt and trousers but with no shoes on his feet.[6]

For the thousands released from the gulags, the beginnings of the army were even more humble. The Soviets offered limited food or supplies, and often withheld money or information from the prisoners. The local NKVD was responsible for issuing travel documents. Some prisoners' freedom of movement was restricted, and others were released only after significant delay. With no organized evacuation or information about where to go, the deportees walked, hitchhiked, rafted down rivers, or climbed on the backs of passing vehicles to make their way to the nearest train station, searching for the rumoured army. For some, the journey took months. After his release from the gulag, Gustaw Herling travelled for weeks, sleeping on station floors, begging for food, and picking up odd jobs. When he finally arrived in Sverdlovsk, he and some other Poles met, "with almost religious awe," the first Polish officer they had seen in Russia. He told them the nearest office of the army was in Chelyabinsk, in west-central Russia, and that a division of the army was forming in Kazakhstan. After Chelyabinsk, Herling spent another month travelling in a "goods truck" to Lugovoye, Kazakhstan, where he was accepted into a regiment on March 12, 1942.

Thieves, illness, officials to be bribed, hunger, endless waiting in train stations and unsanitary refugee camps, crowded trains, and continuous uncertainty about the future: these were the conditions faced by thousands of Poles making their way across the Soviet Union in search of a way out of the country.

The Poles left Pachikha by raft, first going into the woods to fell trees, cut them into logs, and tie them together with rope or tree branches. Others made bread and gathered mushrooms, berries, and edible plants from the forest to add to whatever food they had been able to produce in their gardens. The Polish journalist Kaczyński found one witness to the exodus, Mrs. Eudokia, "the oldest babushka" in Pachikha. "To this day I remember when the amnesty was proclaimed and the Poles, with their whole families, floated on rafts down along the Yula, then the Pinega, to Karpogory," she recalled of the day the Poles left the settlement. "What stuck in my memory the most is the rafts and bonfires burning on them. Later in Karpogory they boarded a ship. I remember saying goodbye to one of the departing groups. They waved and shouted: 'Duśka, come with us to Poland!'" The jubilance of the Poles probably did not last long; if any of them returned to Poland, it would not be for some years.

Casey's travel across Russia must have taken him many months. He and the other members of his family were released from Pachikha on September 7, 1941, and his army records show that he arrived at an unnamed location on April 18, 1942, and was sworn in on May 3, assigned to the Twelfth Podolski Lancers (12 Pułk, Ułanow Podolskich), an infantry corps attached to the Third Carpathian Rifle Division. There is no record of what happened to Casey's parents after their release, apart from the fact that by 1947 his father, Feliks, was living in Wrocław, the city known as Breslau, Germany, before the border was moved in 1945. It appears Casey's sisters, Zofia and Zuzanna, didn't leave the Soviet Union. They were last reported as arriving in the Poltava region (now in Ukraine) in June 1944 with an "SK-695 eszelon" (part of the women's auxiliary), according to the Russian State Military Archive. What is clear is that after their official release date in September 1941, the family dispersed. What happened next to Casey's sisters, whether his mother Józefa survived the journey that followed her release from exile, or how any of them spent the remainder of the war—or their lives—remains a mystery.

The Polish army established a command post at Buzuluk, southeast of Moscow, with other camps at Totskoye and Tatischevo. The army assembled in the first winter after the amnesty, and conditions were primitive and harsh, reaching the level of a humanitarian crisis. The Polish writer and artist Józef Czapski, who would become a pivotal aide to Anders in the search for thousands of missing Polish army officers, was one of those on hand to greet the men and women who made their way to the assembly camps. A member of the waning European aristocracy, educated and multilingual, he was an officer in the Polish army in the Polish-Soviet War of 1919. After the war, he studied art and painted in Kraków and Paris; in the early days of the Second World War the Soviets captured and imprisoned him with other Polish army officers in Gryazovets. During his time in prison, he occupied himself and the other prisoners by delivering lectures on Proust, composed entirely from memory. At Totskoye on the southern Russian steppe, he became aware of the massive scope of the Polish deportations as waves of deportees—as many as two thousand in one day—arrived in search of the army's support and shelter. Czapski spent months in a "gradual, daily immersion in a vast ocean of human misery, hearing how families had been torn apart, children had gone missing or had died of hunger, and how thousands of our comrades had disappeared in the tundra and the mines."[7]

After his time in the taiga, Casey must have been overjoyed to be free and among other Poles, and he may even have been eager to join the battle against the Nazis. But after all he had been through, he could be forgiven for being confused about who was his ally and who was his enemy. Like the other deportees, Casey likely arrived in no shape to go into battle.

The Polish deportees were tired, hungry, and often sick or injured. In clothing worn and ragged from their labour of the last two years, they looked like beggars. They wrapped rags around their legs in place of boots and tied their coats closed with string. They lived in tents, twelve men in each, where they slept on ground they covered with straw and branches scrounged from the surrounding area. To try to minimize the cold, they piled snow on the tents and constructed primitive stoves and slept with head coverings to make sure their hair did not freeze to the side of the tent.[8] When Casey described sleeping in a tent with ice on the inside, he may have been talking about the army camp.

In the early days, General Anders's first task was to restore his recruits to health. Already weak, they were susceptible to diseases such as dysentery, which the lack of sanitation made rampant. Medical supplies were scarce, and death was common. In the winter of 1941-42, as many as three hundred people died each day in the Polish camps.[9] Józef Czapski estimated that more Polish soldiers died of typhus and dysentery in Turkestan alone than were later killed in combat at Monte Cassino. The complexities of the alliance with the Soviets made it increasingly difficult for Anders to deal with the challenges of feeding, clothing, and equipping his troops. There were disputes about the number of men to be recruited, food rations were cut, promised supplies were not delivered, and loans were delayed.

The growing realization of an earlier betrayal by Poland's new ally aggravated underlying tensions. Anders expected that as many as 180,000 Polish soldiers were in the Soviet Union, plus 5,000 regular officers and 4,000 reserve officers. But as the men arrived at the assembly camps, the number of officers was alarmingly low. In a first meeting between Sikorski, Anders, and Stalin in December 1941, the Poles gave Stalin a list of 4,000 missing officers, incomplete because it was created from memory. Stalin suggested they "may have escaped

The Anders Army camp in Kołtubanka, Chkalovsk Oblast, USSR,
December 1941 (Czesław Zembal, Courtesy Archiwum Fotografii Ośrodka KARTA)

to Manchuria," knowing that he had in fact ordered their murders the
year before.[10] Anders dispatched Czapski to Moscow with letters of
introduction to meet with whatever Soviet officials he could engage
who might have information to share about what had happened to the
officers. The trip was fruitless; Czapski went from office to office, each
meeting ending with the suggestion that he try talking to someone
else who would be sure to know the officers' whereabouts.

Convinced of the impossibility of working directly with the Soviets,
Anders orchestrated the removal of his troops from the Soviet Union,
ensuring they would not be engaged in the fighting on the Eastern
Front. The army moved farther south, spread out across Kazakhstan,
Uzbekistan, and Kirghizstan, and finally left the Soviet Union in the
spring and summer of 1942. Altogether, 115,000 Poles — the majority
of them soldiers — left the Soviet Union that year. Any deportees
who did not manage to get to the assembly centres by then were left
behind, as were the thousands of others who were not released in the
amnesty. Some of their descendants can still be found in ethnic Polish
communities in Kazakhstan and northern Russia.[11]

Casey's war records include an identity card from 1946, commemorating his odyssey from the Soviet Union with the Polish Second
Corps. On the front of the card is a map, showing Warsaw in the
centre of Europe and a line drawing the route from "Z.S.S.R. – Iran –
Irak – Palestyna – Egipt – Italia." By August 1942, the army had moved
to Iran, travelling either across the Caspian Sea to the Iranian port of
Pahlevi or overland from Tashkent to Mashhad in the northeast corner of Iran. Anders is often described as a Moses figure, leading his
men into the promised land, and their first experiences in Iran must
have led many of them to believe they had arrived. They encountered
friendly people, the heat of summer, and an undreamt abundance of
food, including the first fresh fruit they had seen in years. For the mal-
nourished, the sudden improvement in diet carried hidden risks. Many
suffered (and some perished) from consuming food they could not
digest.

On arrival, the soldiers were separated from the civilians and
taken to a camp where they stripped and showered. Then they were
powdered with insecticide, had their heads shaven to rid them of
lice, and issued new uniforms. Now looking more like soldiers, they
continued their trek across Asia. They travelled to Tehran on the
narrow winding roads over the Elburz mountains and then to Iraq,
where they joined British training camps near Mosul and Kirkuk. The
soldiers went through combat training in the desert, learning to use
unfamiliar equipment in the heat of an Iraqi summer.

Józef Czapski described the first summer after leaving Russia as a
period of almost joyful hope. The beauty of the Iraqi desert captivated
him, and he described it in painterly terms: "the pure peacock blue
of the sky, the subtle geometry of the white tents," a landscape fully
saturated with light "the way Corot painted it." At night, "the cupola
of the sky without a single tiny cloud or a single tree to obscure it,
all but shining with myriad stars."[12] The army set about restoring the
spirits of the men, with courses for the youngest soldiers, who had not
finished school, and an imprint that published books, pamphlets, and
essays, some written by the soldiers, for them to read. Finally healthy
and fit, the men began to see themselves for the first time as part

of the Allied forces and to dream of the possibility of returning to a liberated Poland after defeating Hitler. Reports from Poland about the waves of deportations of Poles for forced labour in Germany and mass executions in Warsaw only strengthened their resolve.

Later in 1943, convoys of trucks transported the men of the Second Corps and their weapons and supplies five hundred miles across the Syrian desert to Palestine. In Palestine, Casey must have joined his fellow soldiers in visiting some of the prominent religious sites, an occasion he could never have imagined as a boy growing up on a farm in Poland. For the rest of his life he kept four souvenir photographs purchased from the Garden of Gethsemane in Jerusalem. Three of them show the exterior and altar of the Church of All Nations, built between 1919 and 1924 with donations from over a dozen countries. The fourth is of a monk strolling the paths in the garden, amidst the ancient olive trees. The story of the "agony in the garden" is well known to every Catholic schoolchild. After sharing his last meal with his apostles, Jesus went to the garden at Gethsemane to pray. In his agony, he first asked God to spare him from his death, and then, accepting his fate, to give him the strength he needed to face his trials. His persecutors found him when one of his disciples, Judas Iscariot, betrayed him with a kiss.

Later in his life, Casey never seemed a particularly religious man. But it is hard to imagine he would have been unmoved walking the paths of the garden and entering the church, in a place of such profound history and deep religious meaning. The photographs are the only reminder of Casey's journey out of Siberia as he moved into his role as a soldier. Perhaps he preserved these images because the symbolism of struggle and sacrifice captured his attention; maybe it was the betrayal at the root of it.

After Palestine, the men moved on to Egypt, the last stop for the Anders Army before they arrived in Italy to join the other Allied troops in the Italian campaign, the beginning of the liberation of Europe.

As the Wehrmacht moved east into the Soviet Union, living conditions for those in the occupied territories steadily deteriorated. For Wanda and her family, the fear and suffering imposed by a new occupier, one who intended not to transform them but to destroy them, replaced the misery of the two years of Soviet occupation. Hitler established a government for the occupied eastern territories. The part of Polesie where Wanda lived was placed under the Reichskommissariat of Ukraine. Non-Jewish locals formed a significant part of the labour used by the Germans, and residents were appointed to serve as mayors or village elders. In each district, a police force under the command of a German police officer was staffed with locals, turning the people against each other and creating opportunities for corruption and exploitation.[13]

Nazi troops were forcibly billeted on townspeople, who were also conscripted into forced labour as the Germans established local administrations. People lived under rigid control. Curfews were established, and the Germans requisitioned for their own use the bulk of the food supply, already significantly depleted by the departing Red Army. Looting by soldiers was widespread, and hundreds of citizens were executed in reprisal for acts of sabotage, real or imagined.[14] Wanda's family of women and three children, two of them girls, must have felt especially vulnerable. Many women were exposed to sexual assault and exploitation. Some were forced into military brothels, others recruited to work in bars set up for German soldiers were sometimes coerced into prostitution. Rape was not uncommon but rarely prosecuted by court martial.

In this atmosphere, a partisan movement sprang up in Belarus, with Stalin's encouragement. Hiding in the forests and marshes by day, the partisans emerged at night for raids on German installations and to collect supplies from often unwilling locals, who had little enough to eat. A cycle of violence ensued, with the Germans exacting reprisals against villagers suspected of harbouring the partisans. Entire villages were destroyed, the residents killed, their livestock seized, and their homes burned down. Franziska Exeler estimates that by the end of the war, the Germans had set over 9,000 Belarusian villages on fire, entirely razing over 5,000 of them and killing some or all of their inhabitants. As many as 345,000 civilians were killed in anti-partisan operations.[15]

As fall turned to winter in 1941, it became clear that the Nazi fantasy of a swift victory over the Soviet Union would not happen. Instead, the Germans faced a long war on the Eastern Front, and when the United States entered the war in December, it increased pressure in the west. There were not enough Germans to provide labour for the war economy. Men were needed to replace the soldiers killed or lost to capture, disease, or injury, and Hitler expressly forbade the general employment of German women.

As the demand for workers increased, Hitler ordered that Russian prisoners of war should be put to work. But of the more than three million captured Soviet soldiers, only a small percentage survived or were in good enough condition to be used as workers.[16] The only option was to recruit workers from the eastern occupied territories. Rather than starving the Slavic people of the Soviet Union to death, the Nazis realized they would need to keep them alive long enough to provide their labour to fuel the war effort.

Forced labour had been part of the Nazi war-production strategy from the beginning of the war. After invading Poland in 1939, the Nazi authorities introduced compulsory labour for all Poles aged between sixteen and sixty. The first deportations from Poland began only a few weeks after the Nazi invasion and continued until after the Warsaw Uprising in 1944, when the Soviet army pushed the Nazis out of Poland.[17] By early 1942, there were already over a million foreign workers in Germany and many others providing labour in the occupied territories. But millions more would be needed, leading Hitler to adopt a new strategy to prop up the Nazi war effort.

In March 1942, Hitler appointed Fritz Sauckel to a newly created role that would be central to the war administration. As "plenipotentiary general for the utilization of labour," Sauckel organized the labour supply for the German economy and the Nazi war machine. For the next three years, he would report directly to Hitler, on paper, at least. Sauckel had complete authority to issue orders to commissioners of occupied lands, the heads of civil agencies, and even to generals and admirals to gather the needed manpower. It was Sauckel who would direct the arrest and deportation of millions to Nazi Germany, including Wanda, irrevocably changing her life.

For Sauckel, the new role was the culmination of his two decades of toil as a loyal Nazi party official. Born in 1894 to a mailman and a seamstress in the northern Bavarian town of Hassfurt, Sauckel's humble origins offered no hint of his eventual rise in the Nazi party leadership. With no money for an education, he left home to become a merchant seaman at the age of fifteen and was taken prisoner when his ship was captured by the French at the outbreak of the First World War. He spent the war years in a French internment camp, frustrated by his inability to take part in the German war effort. On his return to Germany, he settled into the life of a factory worker in a ball-bearing factory in Schweinfurt. But, as with many young Germans of his generation, Germany's defeat and diminished status under the Treaty of Versailles stung, and he quickly became involved in politics.

He later began his slow and steady climb up the Nazi hierarchy as one of the first to join the party in 1923. He remained loyal to Hitler after the failed coup d'état known as the Beer Hall Putsch in November 1923, establishing a cover party for the Nazis while the party was banned in Germany. For his devotion, Hitler appointed him gauleiter (regional leader of the Nazi party) of Thuringia. As one of the party leaders who played a key role in the Nazi takeover of the regions in the Reich, he was a useful and loyal foot soldier to Hitler, and he received a succession of elected and appointed offices in return for his hard work.

And yet Sauckel seemed an unlikely choice for senior Nazi official and mastermind of the German labour-mobilization plan. To those who encountered him, he appeared less a villain than an obsequious and fanatical servant of Hitler, universally disliked and often ridiculed. A short, pudgy man with a balding head and a Hitler-style moustache, he walked "on the balls of his feet like a referee at a wrestling match."[18] Goebbels described him as the "dullest of the dull."[19] But he was respected as an *alter kämpfer*—veteran of

the struggle — and known to be a gifted propagandist. These quali-
ties, together with his unquestioning devotion to Hitler, made him
the ideal bureaucrat to carry out Hitler's orders in one of the most
bureaucratic tasks of the war.

For Sauckel's first assignment, Hitler directed him to raise 1.6 million foreign workers in the three months after his appointment. That
number would multiply several times as the war continued for another
three years, the failure of the Nazi offensive compounded by the devastation of Allied bombing campaigns inside Germany. Soon enough,
trains containing thousands of eastern workers crammed into boxcars
began departing from stations throughout the Baltic states and occupied Soviet Union. Perhaps Wanda and her family thought they might
escape that fate; surely two older women and three children would be
of little use to the Nazis. The next years of the war would require a
delicate balancing act, as Wanda's mother tried to keep her children
fed and healthy while avoiding the attention of partisans, Nazis seeking reprisals, and labour recruiters.

Fritz Sauckel and foreign workers during an inspection tour in Kyiv, June 1942 (Yad Vashem Photo Archive, Jerusalem, 132E08)

CHAPTER 4
OSTARBEITER IN GERMANY

In Reichskommissariat Ukraine, the one thousandth transport of forced labourers was dispatched to Germany in April 1943. Fritz Sauckel was in the eastern territories at the time, meeting with local police and SS officials, on a mission to secure another million workers from the region for deportation to Germany. During his tour, his aides seized the opportunity to celebrate this milestone with an extravagant ceremony held on Hitler's birthday, April 20.[1] The symbolism would have delighted Sauckel.

In truth, though, the faithful had little to celebrate. The tide of the war was turning against Germany. During the winter of 1942-43, the weather and frequent conflicts between Sauckel's office and the Wehrmacht and other German institutions involved in the recruitment of workers disrupted the procurement of new *ostarbeiter* (eastern workers).[2] Sauckel was under pressure to dramatically increase the number of workers sent to Germany. By the beginning of April, he increased the target to ten thousand workers per day. Over the next four months, one million more eastern workers were deported to Germany, most of them Ukrainians.

Not all of the Nazi leadership was in favour of importing workers from the Soviet Union. Nazi ideology considered Slavs to be *untermenschen* (subhuman) and ultimately expendable. The foreign workers would be placed in factories alongside Germans, and many feared either that this would allow racially inferior and communist-indoc-trinated people to contaminate the Germans, or that fraternization of enemy civilians with Germans would humanize them and create doubt about the war effort.[3] To assuage these concerns, a number of regulations governing the treatment of eastern workers were put in place. They were held in closed residential camps, with no freedom of movement. At work, they could be supervised by plant security guards, but they should be segregated from German workers. To clearly identify them as non-western workers, they were required to wear badges with the *Ost* designation. Ruthless suppression of disobedience was permitted, with punishments ranging from the withholding of hot meals to flogging. Anyone attempting escape would be sent to a labour-education or concentration camp, and any-one having sexual intercourse with a German could be executed.[4]

Sauckel also resorted to propaganda to quell any misgivings the Germans might have had about the growing numbers of Russians and other easterners in their midst. In the spring of 1943, he commissioned an illustrated book, *Europe Works in Germany: Sauckel Mobilizes the Labour Reserves*, with chapters on the need for foreign workers, the industries where they worked, their housing and living conditions, and countering the "false enemy propaganda" about their mistreatment; four hundred thousand copies were printed.

Sauckel's propaganda walked a fine line between insisting on the right to exploit foreign workers and claiming they would be treated humanely. In his Labour Mobilization Program, released only a month after his appointment, he wrote that the purpose of the program was to provide resources for Germany and its allies. If the number of vol-unteers was insufficient, "we must immediately institute conscription or forced labor." All of the foreign labourers were to be "fed, sheltered and treated in such a way as to exploit them to the highest possible [degree] at the lowest conceivable degree of expenditure."[5] Sauckel reassured the Germans that the foreign workers would be paid, pro-vided with clean and orderly shelter, and fed according to the same provisions made for German civilians, with "consideration...given to the native customs of the foreign workers."[6]

At the same time, he reinforced Nazi claims about the pervasive evil of capitalist exploitation, Bolshevist terror, and the "Jews and their lackeys" who "force a second world war on Germany." He suggested that through their labour in Germany, the foreigners were saved from a far worse fate. They worked in conditions that, he claimed, "have never before in history been matched in their cleanliness, correctness, care and justice." In their home countries, the workers had been "victims of the lies of the worst, base, and corrupt criminals of Jewish plutocracy and Bolshevist hangmen," but now that they were in Germany, they were "astonished" at its advanced culture and were experiencing "social and medical services that no one ever dreams of in Soviet Russia."[7]

These claims had little relationship to the reality of daily life for the millions of foreign workers. Like the arrests of the Poles by the Soviets in 1940, the deportations followed a familiar pattern. The campaign began with the "recruitment" of eighteen- to twenty-one-year-olds; gradually, the target ages were lowered, and by the end, entire families — including Wanda's — were deported to Germany. Attempts to promote voluntary service met with little success, and the local authorities quickly resorted to "coercive relocation and hostage taking." Armed recruitment commissions roamed the countryside in the eastern territories, arresting young men and women or abusing the families of those in hiding until they surrendered. Letters sent from the eastern territories described how "men and women, including teenagers aged fifteen and above, are reportedly being picked up on the street, at markets and during village celebrations, and then speeded away...the inhabitants are frightened, hide, and avoid going out in public." The commissioners flogged local officials who failed to meet their targets and burned down farmsteads and even entire villages.[8] In the villages and towns of the occupied territories, many fled to the forests to join the partisans and evade the recruitment commissions.

Alfred Rosenberg, the reichminister for the occupied eastern territories, expressed concern that the increase in guerilla bands in the region was largely the result of the "forced measures of mass deportation" executed by Sauckel's "agencies and collaborators," as well as the news circulating throughout the region about the treatment of foreign workers in the Reich.[9] But local authorities sanctioned these methods. In November 1943, Nazi authorities declined to discipline a district commissioner, Fritz Mueller, for his role in burning houses during labour roundups. Even if he were guilty, a September 1942 directive from his superior, the commissioner general in Lutsk, permitted the use of extreme measures: "Estates of those who refuse to work are to be burned, their relatives are to be arrested as hostages and to be brought to forced labor camps."[10]

When the Nazis came for the Gizmunts, they gave the family only a few minutes to gather the possessions they would take with them to Germany. Joe compared their haste to that of a family trying to save things in the face of a coming wildfire. They were among the last to be arrested and had witnessed several rounds of deportation—enough to know it would be pointless to resist. After their arrest, they would have assembled at a transit centre where they were documented, examined, and left to wait for transport. Their transit was no different than that used by the Soviets deporting Poles to Siberia: they would have been loaded into cattle cars with inadequate or no food or toilet facilities. Once they arrived in Germany, they would have been taken to another assembly centre, where they were selected to work in Fulda. At least they had each other for comfort.

Today Fulda is mainly known as a focal point in the development of Christianity in Germany; a disciple of St. Boniface established a monastery there in the eighth century as a base for Charlemagne's political and military conversion of Saxony to the Christian faith. Over the centuries, other significant Christian sites were added: a medieval church, a Benedictine abbey, a Franciscan monastery, and a cathedral, the burial place of St. Boniface and a destination for pilgrims.

On June 5 every year the feast of St. Boniface draws religious pilgrims from across Europe. The churches of Fulda participate enthusiastically in the event, their bells driving people out of bed first thing in the morning and interrupting evening meals with seemingly interminable ringing that echoes across the cobbled squares of the city. Churches dominate the city. The Frauenberg monastery, perched atop a long hill, offers a view of the trees and rooftops of the city outside the village, and the Rhön and Vogelsberg mountains in the distance. The centrepiece of the old city is the early eighteenth-century cathedral, its interior crammed with ornate mouldings, gilded columns and statues, and carved wooden pews, a model of the baroque style.

In a city of churches, the most ancient was also the most obviously spiritual. Looking down from some ramparts onto the street below, St. Michael's Church was built in the early ninth century in the pre-Romanesque style with an austere interior where simple wooden benches provide a place for contemplation. St. Michael's also carries the only hint of war in any of Fulda's religious sites, in the form of a hauntingly beautiful relief sculpture made of four slate panels on the exterior wall of the church. The top left and bottom right panels are flat and unmarked. The bottom left panel depicts rows of skulls of varying sizes, from infant to elderly; and the upper right panel shows the left arm, shoulder, and head of an angel, pointing to the heavens. The skulls are entirely anonymous, but they clearly suggest the remains of Jews buried in mass graves after their slaughter. The sculptor was the German artist Ewald Mataré, whom the Nazis denounced and persecuted as a creator of "degenerate art" in the 1930s but who was rehabilitated in the post-war years.[11]

Wartime Fulda seemed an unlikely place for labourers in the Nazi war industry. Located in the state of Hesse in the centre of Germany, between the Rhön and Vogelsberg mountains, not quite midway between Frankfurt and Sauckel's home in Weimar and situated on a river of the same name, it was a small city of about thirty thousand people when Wanda arrived in 1943.

The Nazis had brought their campaign of propaganda and intimidation to the city, holding parades and mass rallies, just as they did everywhere in Germany. They renamed streets and squares; Friedrichsmarkt became Adolf-Hitler-Platz. Shortly after the *machtergreifung*, the Fulda town council voted unanimously to make Adolf Hitler an honorary citizen. Fulda's newspaper, the *Fuldaer Zeitung*, initially took an aggressive stand against national socialism, but this ended in December 1933, when the SA (*Sturmabteilung* or Storm Troopers, also known as Brownshirts) raided its offices and banned its editor. Afterward, the paper was subject to the same editorial control as all other press in Germany.[12] The overpowering Nazi presence, combined with the shrinking moral authority of the clergy, no doubt contributed to or aggravated anti-Semitic sentiment that already existed in the small city. The fate of Fulda's Jews was the fate of Jews throughout Europe. In this cradle of Christianity, anti-Semitism had thrived over the last millennium. Fulda's small Jewish community had survived serial violence, expulsions, and persecution, but it took the war to almost completely eliminate it. On Kristallnacht, November 9, 1938, the SA burned Fulda's synagogue. By 1939, most of Fulda's Jews had fled or been arrested, and half of those remaining were sent to the death camps.

Naftali Herbert Sonn, a Fulda-born historian who wrote two books about the city, recalled a priest who sheltered two Jewish children and helped them to immigrate to America after the war. Although he described Fulda as a "religious town," for the most part its people were silent as the Nazis persecuted the Jews.[13] Some were openly anti-Semitic. Arnold Goldschmidt was sixteen years old when the Nazis came to arrest him on November 9. He could smell the synagogue burning. Some of Fulda's Jews, including the rabbi, had been told that "there was going to be trouble," so they'd run into the woods. But Goldschmidt's family were taken by surprise when the brownshirts arrived. When they entered his home, the SA threw their possessions, including their silver and gold, out the window. Below, women, neighbours his family had considered friends, "were standing there with aprons, catching the silver and gold." When he and his family went to the home of a previously friendly Catholic family who lived across the street from their business, they refused to open the door. About seventy people were arrested in Fulda, including Goldschmidt.

An image from a reconnaissance plane of the rail-marshalling yards at
Fulda after a bombing (US Army Air Force, photographer/unit unknown)

He remembered that when he was marched to the assembly area for
transport in a cattle car, people spat on him and called him names.[14]

In popular histories of the war, Fulda is not mentioned as a site of
any significant event or strategic importance. In the history books, it is
as invisible as Wanda's home in Opaí. Most information is buried deep
in the blogs and websites of a vast network of amateur historians and
archivists who post photos and videos of soldiers on the march or in
combat, of bombing sites and destroyed cities, of war survivors picking
through the rubble strewn beside the hollowed-out shells of buildings,
and of the dead—soldiers and civilians of all nationalities, in shallow
graves, or in the streets, forests, or rivers where they fell.

One of the most compelling sets of images of wartime Fulda is in a
video of the marshalling yards. Compiled from still photographs taken
on a US air force reconnaissance mission, it shows the destruction
of Fulda from multiple perspectives.[15] In one photo, railway cars
are scattered across the tracks, some upended, others derailed or
destroyed. The seventeenth-century Franciscan monastery looms in
the distance on one of Fulda's seven hills.

If the word *luck* has any meaning in the context of Wanda's life during the war, it could be said that she was fortunate that the transport that brought her to Germany stopped at Fulda. In the engine of the Nazi war machine, the city played only a minor role. With no great military or industrial significance apart from the railyards, a tire plant, and some minor armaments factories, it was initially spared the bombs the Allied forces had dropped on the larger or more strategically important cities that surrounded it. A series of bombing raids devastated Darmstadt, a city about 130 kilometres southwest of Fulda, including an attack on the medieval city centre that created a firestorm and claimed the lives of more than twelve thousand inhabitants. Kassel, about one hundred kilometres north, suffered similar attacks. On one night in October 1943, the RAF deployed 569 bombers over Kassel's city centre, killing at least ten thousand and wounding thousands more.

Fulda did not completely evade the Allied bombs. The meticulously detailed records of bombing missions over Fulda offer an accounting of the number of planes in a mission and the tonnes of bombs dropped, targets hit or missed, and planes and crew members lost or missing in action. Typically, the missions targeted armaments plants, oil refineries, shipyards, airfields, and train marshalling yards—many of the locations where forced labourers would be at work when the bombs hit. Fulda was a target in July and again in September 1944. On the latter occasions, the same days as the attacks on Darmstadt, two hundred B-17s bombed the marshalling yards, the tire plant and other "targets of opportunity." More daylight raids on Fulda were carried out in November and December; one of the targets was the small-arms plant.[16]

The worst bombings occurred at noon on December 27, when 117 B-17s hit the marshalling yards. The attack led to the city's greatest loss of life in the entire war. When the air raid sirens went off around noon that day, those holding a permission card filed into a four-hundred-metre-long concrete tunnel beneath the railyards, the Krätzbach, that had been converted into a bomb shelter. The bombs caused the collapse of one of the entrances, as well as the ceiling in the middle of the bunker. About one thousand people were trapped, and before rescuers could dig them out, more than seven hundred of them died, mainly of asphyxiation. The dead included 262 forced labourers. On January 3, 1945, another 141 B-17s bombed the same target.[17]

An American airman who was part of the December 27 mission saw the results of his own work and witnessed the second strike from the ground as a prisoner of war. George Klare was a twenty-two-year-old navigator when his aircraft was shot down during a mission near Hamburg on December 31, 1944. He parachuted to safety but, along with the other eight members of his crew, was captured by the Germans. He was being transported to an interrogation centre when his train stopped at Fulda; Klare noted with some satisfaction that his recent mission had heavily damaged the tracks, and the train could not proceed.

The prisoners and their escorts had just left the train when they heard bombs in the distance. They sheltered beneath an underpass in the centre of the railyard. Klare dropped to the ground, protecting his head with his arms.

After the raid, Klare and the other prisoners were ordered to unload freight from the burning station. Moments before it collapsed they were permitted to leave the building, escaping without injury. In the meantime, a crowd of angry Germans gathered nearby, glaring sullenly at the Americans. Armed only with a pistol, the German captain in charge of the prisoners would not have been able to control a mob. In an act that mystified Klare, the German quickly ushered the Americans to safety in a nearby building, where they were kept until it was safe to remove them.

Today, beside the Fulda river, a system of paths for hiking and biking stretches for miles through the nearby low-lying mountains. Hidden beside one of the paths is a monument to the war dead, as subtle and understated as the sculpture at St. Michael's Church. A stone obelisk, about ten feet tall and capped with a stone globe, stands next to a low hedge, taller trees in the background. The simple inscription commemorates Fulda's fallen in the First and Second World Wars. Other memorials to the war dead in Fulda are equally hidden or obscure. A small plaque on the embankment next to Mehlerstrasse reads: "On 27 December 1944 700 people who had sought protection in the tunnel of the Krätzbach were killed as victims of the bombing. The city of Fulda commemorates these dead."

The citizens of Fulda who died in the bombing would have been buried by their families in the Fulda cemetery. The more than 270 forced labourers who died that day lie in anonymous graves. A stone in the cemetery acknowledges the "foreign war dead," but does not mention why the foreigners were in Fulda, or how they died.

Life in the labour camps was unmitigated misery. Wanda's housing was likely no better than that inhabited by other forced labourers — "flimsy wooden barracks, open to ice, fleas, lice, snow, and Allied bombs."[18] It shared many of the indignities, pain, and discomfort that Casey experienced in the Russian settlement. Camp rooms were overcrowded and unsanitary, often lacking facilities for even basic hygiene, and diseases such as tuberculosis spread easily. Workers had no access to clothing beyond what they had managed to bring with them. Many suffered from spotted fever or skin disease caused by lice, fleas, bugs, and other vermin endemic to the camps. Wanda's mother's hair fell out. Workers were often forced to work despite illness. Conditions worsened with the onset of bombing in 1943, as many workers lived in the wreckage of their former barracks, where water supplies might be cut off for days at a time.

In theory, the foreign workers were to be paid by their employers. Regulations set out foreign workers' wages (lower than for Germans), but the higher taxes and social insurance payments deducted from their pay and the room and board subtracted by their employers meant they received little or no compensation (Joe only laughed when asked whether he had actually been paid). In return, employers were entitled to "get the maximum amount of work" out of them; the prevailing attitude was that "the exploitation of the workman must be as rational and economical as if he were coal and power."[19] Women, who were a significant part of the foreign workforce, were treated with

A reconnaissance plane image of a labour camp in Fulda

(US Army Air Force, photographer/unit unknown)

equal contempt. Heinrich Himmler reportedly said that "whether ten thousand Russian women collapse with exhaustion in the construction of an anti-tank ditch for Germany only interests me insofar as the ditch gets dug for Germany."[20]

Disputes within the Nazi regime about the diet of the foreign workers centred not on humanitarian concerns but practical ones: how little food was needed to keep them alive so they could perform their duties?[21] It was a zero-sum game; food given to foreign workers would have to be taken from German soldiers and civilians, and the foreign workers could always be replaced. Employers were responsible for providing food, and meals were eaten in the plant or the camp. The eastern workers were not permitted to travel outside the camps, and they could not supplement the meagre offerings provided. Their diet consisted of 3.5 kilograms of bread per week, with thin soup at lunch. Very young children sent to the camps with their families were unattended during the day; those as young as eight were put to work.[22] The poor quality and meagre servings of food left workers in a constant state of hunger and malnourishment.

The International Labour Organization, one of the few external organizations to inquire into the lives of the foreign workers during the war, offered an especially poignant description of the wretched hunger of workers in the Junker airplane factory at Dessau. In July 1942, Nazi authorities arranged a tour of the facility for foreign broadcasters and journalists, presumably because they considered it one of the best facilities available. One of the Swedish journalists, Gösta F. Block, noticed that many of the Russian workers, clad in blue overalls bearing the *Ost* badge, were barefoot; they had no replacements for their worn-out shoes. In the canteen, some of them went around with spoons, scraping out whatever soup other workers had left behind in the tin bowls. The journalists were offered some food, which would have been better than usual that day, given the presence of outsiders, but many could not eat it. They dumped the remains into a barrel on which the workers quickly descended like scavenger birds, anxious to consume the rejected food.[23]

None of this mattered to Sauckel. He was not responsible for either the actions of the recruiting officers or the conditions in which the foreign workers were forced to live. His only interest was in the performance of his mission and his service to Hitler. Despite reports of abuse in the roundups and the camps, Sauckel assured Hitler that "never before in the world were foreign workers treated as correctly as is now happening in the hardest of all wars by the German people." Later, he reported to Hitler that their treatment had been regulated in a way that was a "shining example compared with the methods of the capitalist and Bolshevik world." Most importantly, though, he boasted that in the first year of his post, "3,638,056 new foreign workers were given to the German war economy."[24] He had proven his worth to his leader.

For the remainder of the war, the Nazis conscripted labour throughout Europe and Russia, but the majority of the foreign civilian workers were Poles, Ukrainians, and Russians from the occupied eastern territories. In all, about 13.5 million people were employed in forced labour in Germany or in the occupied territories: 8.4 million civilian workers who worked in industry and agriculture; 4.6 million prisoners of war who performed labour, often in contravention of the Geneva Convention; and 1.7 million concentration camp prisoners.[25]

According to Joe, all of the family, except for Kasia, who was too young, worked in a shop, making parts for train repairs. At first, they lived in a camp. They slept in barracks with rows of bunkbeds in columns of three and thin mattresses to lie on. All of them were in the same bunkhouse, boys, girls, and women. When they heard planes approaching, they ran out into the fields, thinking that it would be safer than staying in the building that was the target of the bombs. If a bomb struck them, they would be killed; but they judged this risk to be less than the risk of being hit by flying debris inside a building struck by a bomb.

By the time they were liberated, bombs had destroyed the barracks they lived in, and the Germans had taken them to live in the barn of a farmer. This seems to have happened some time before the December 27 attack that claimed so many lives. Thanks to the cows, Joe recalled, the barn was warmer than the barracks in the camp.

Why didn't they just leave once they were taken to live, unguarded, in the barn? But where would they go? How does a family of two women and three adolescents make their way through a country under siege? Even the minimal amount of food they received as foreign workers would have been more than they could expect as fugitives with no place to hide and nobody to trust. They could have been arrested, ending up worse off than when they started.

The German writer and scholar Victor Klemperer pondered the passivity of the foreign workers. In an entry in his wartime diary, later published in a volume titled *I Will Bear Witness*, he wondered why, if their numbers were so great, they had not revolted against their jailors or engaged in acts of sabotage. "Their huge number, in some factories only a tenth of the workforce German," he noted. "Why does the uprising, the sabotage, on which Eisenhower counted, not take place? Some may think of it — but they also think of the annihilation of insurgent Warsaw!" Then, he recounts a conversation his Aryan wife had with a watchman from a private company, who did twelve-hour shifts in a Polish camp where only a few hundred police officers guarded ten thousand prisoners. The prisoners had, in fact, "mutinied," using "every stick, every piece of iron as a weapon,"

the watchman said, and the guards "nearly got our heads done in."
But then what? Klemperer doesn't say, but even if a number of the
prisoners had managed to escape, how would they have made their way
across Germany to safety? As the war went on, German companies
eventually stopped guarding the bunkhouses, because it would have
been impossible for the foreign workers to move through the German
towns and countryside without being detected and, presumably,
imprisoned or shot.

Klemperer's final comment, that "it is certainly also right that only
a small proportion of these foreigners of very mixed origin are really
hostile to Germany and have a real will to fight it," rings hollow. Could
someone of Klemperer's avowed mistrust and hatred of the Nazis have
believed that the vast majority of foreign workers were willingly in
Germany, working to support the enemy in their own persecution?
As a writer who made a study of the Nazi perversion of the German
language for propaganda purposes, he should have been critical of the
official Nazi line about foreign workers. But propaganda is powerful,
even among those who are inclined to doubt.

Klemperer's passage poses a question that has often been asked:
how could so many, in so many different places, have been cowed
into submission by the Nazis? The same question applies to the
Germans who readily took on the job of dehumanizing the enemy
and subjecting millions to unimaginable atrocities. Those who have
not lived through such times have difficulty imagining the power of
fear. Timothy Snyder, in his recent manifesto *On Tyranny*, reminds
the world of the lessons of the twentieth century as democracy faces
renewed threats. He points out that most of the power of authori-
tarianism is freely given and that there is a human tendency to act
with unthinking conformity in response to threats. How much more
powerful are these tendencies once one has witnessed the punishment given out for resistance? By the time Wanda arrived in Fulda,
she had had ample opportunity to observe how the Nazis dealt with
their enemies. She may have considered acts of defiance, but given her
youth and vulnerability, it's more likely she would have taken a pragmatic view: do what is needed to survive, and let the Allied soldiers

do their jobs. But the lack of control, or inability to strike back at an oppressor, surely deepens the scars caused by abuse.

Acts of sabotage were far fewer than the German security agencies had feared; the number suggested was an average of 6,800 acts each year.[26] With as many as eight million foreign workers labouring almost every day of the year, this would have been a minuscule risk for the Nazi war machine. It is heartening to finally come across an anecdote of one incident as reported by historian Richard J. Evans, an impeccable source. "A German bomb fell through the roof of my wife's grandmother's house in the East End of London in 1943 and lodged, unexploded, in her bedroom wardrobe," Evans wrote. "When the bomb disposal unit opened it up, they found a note inside. 'Don't worry, English,' it said, 'we're with you. Polish workers.'"[27]

Wanda in January 1946 at a displaced persons camp in Fulda

(Courtesy George Surdykowski)

CHAPTER 5
DISPLACED

The final months of the war were perilous for the foreign workers in Germany. In the last eight months of the war, the American and British air forces dropped 729,000 tonnes of bombs over Germany, more than in all the previous months of the war combined. The campaign demoralized the German public, brought the economy to a standstill, and crippled military supply lines, laying the groundwork for the Allied troops' invasion of Germany. The effects of the bombing on the German people were devastating: at least 305,000 civilians dead, more than twice that many wounded, and 7.5 million left homeless.[1] Many German cities were no more than piles of rubble. Although Fulda was not as hard hit as many other cities, almost 1,500 of its 30,000 inhabitants died as a result of the various bombings.

The force of the aerial bombardment may have given the foreign workers hope, when they weren't terrified instead. Some reported that the frequency of the bombs overhead and the disappearance of many of their bosses to join the military told them of the approaching front. Their food supplies dwindled, and they were constantly hungry. It's impossible to imagine the desperation of Wanda's family in the winter of 1945. Living in a barn, cold, hunger, and parasites plaguing them, their clothing and bedding no better than rags, Wanda's family could think only of survival.

As the end of the war neared, Fulda once again came under fire in Operation Clarion, an Allied offensive specifically targeting German

lines of communication and transportation. On February 23, over
1,200 bombers spread out over rail centres in central Germany,
dropping more than 3,000 tonnes on targets that included the
marshalling yards at Fulda.[2] In final airstrikes on March 17 and 19,
eighty-three B-17s dropped their bombs over Fulda, aiming once
again for the marshalling yards. By then, it was obvious to all that
the Nazis were in defeat. The Soviet army had occupied most of pre-
war Poland by the end of January; at the same time, after successfully
pushing back the Nazi forces at the Battle of the Bulge, the western
Allied forces assembled for an attack on the Rhine. In his last speech,
delivered on January 30, 1945, Hitler spoke of victory through
resistance, inspiring no one to believe in the overpowering dominance
of the German forces that once aimed to take over Europe and the
Soviet Union.[3]

On Easter Sunday, April 1, 1945, soldiers of the 101st Infantry of the
US Army reached Fulda, a week after crossing the Rhine in the Allied
campaign to liberate Europe and occupy Germany. As American tanks
and jeeps rolled through the streets, soldiers quickly moved through
the city in house-to-house combat, searching for snipers; others
cleared out the nearby woods.

In the knowledge of certain defeat, Fulda's mayor tried to spare his
city from further losses. He approached the local combat commander
and asked him to refrain from a pointless defence of the city,
preferring surrender to more bloodshed and destruction. In the end,
any resistance was merely symbolic.[4] By April 3, the Americans had
taken control of Fulda, and the war, for Wanda, was over.

What did liberation look like when it finally arrived? Decades later,
celebrations in city squares, soldiers embracing civilians in a spirit of
jubilation, are the first images that come to mind. But for those who
were hundreds of miles from a home that no longer existed, worn and
hurting and facing an uncertain future, the end of hostilities was not
simply the arrival of peace or a moment of elation, but the beginning
of a new kind of upheaval. One Polish worker, Gabriela Knapska,
kept a diary of the last days of the war, and she recorded the day the
Americans arrived at her camp in the midst of gunfire. The end came

as a relief, her happiness somehow numbed by all that had happened. "We always said that we would probably go crazy with joy. But the joy was covered with shadows," she wrote.[5]

For many, in fact, the period surrounding the surrender and Allied occupation of Germany was more dangerous than any other time in the war. As the Red Army drove into Poland, the Nazis began to destroy evidence of their activities in the concentration camps. Many of the prisoners who had survived were forced into death marches, crossing Poland on foot toward Germany. As many as 750,000 prisoners were herded from the camps; one-third of them died along the way, perishing from starvation or disease or shot because they could not keep up.[6] On a much smaller scale, forced labourers in Germany were also at risk as the Germans evaded Allied troops. In the village of Hirzenhain, only fifty kilometres from Fulda, an SS unit shot and killed eighty-seven Polish and Russian labourers to make way for a detachment that wanted to take up quarters in the camp as it fled from the Allies. Several weeks later, liberated forced labourers discovered the mass grave of the victims.[7] In another incident, members of the SS, Wehrmacht soldiers, and civilians murdered fifty-seven people in a forest near Warstein. The dead were among nearly two thousand eastern workers whom the Nazis were driving east in an attempt to evade the advancing Allied armies. On discovering this massacre, the US Army ordered locals to exhume and view the corpses to ensure no one could deny the crime.[8]

Those foreign workers who managed to escape before liberation survived by their wits, looting abandoned homes and stores and hiding in bombed-out buildings. Those whom the Germans caught were imprisoned, beaten, and sometimes executed. Foreign workers still in any of the Nazi-operated camps in the final months of the war would have experienced months of reductions in their already meagre rations, as food was diverted to the military.

The savagery of the end of the war was not confined to acts of the German army. As the Soviet army proceeded west into the country, many soldiers engaged in appalling acts of rape and cruelty against German civilians, seeking vengeance for the murder, starvation, and humiliation the Soviets had suffered at the hands of the Nazis. The Soviets seized more than half a million Germans for forced labour. Timothy Snyder estimates that about six hundred thousand Germans would die at the end of the war, including both those taken as prisoners of war and labourers.[9]

The statistics of death and abuse overwhelm, but they are as depersonalized as the violence they portray. Words are equally inadequate to convey the emotions of the liberated, who confronted freedom, uncertainty, and fear in the same moment. Their first priorities would have been food, shelter, decent clothing, and hygiene. Wanda and her family may have been free, but they would have been unwelcome among the Germans and a burden to their liberators.

Across Germany, as they entered towns and villages, Allied soldiers encountered millions of civilians like Wanda, prisoners or forced labourers held in concentration camps and labour camps. While they anticipated dealing with a hostile civilian population and the release of captured soldiers in prisoner-of-war camps, the massive numbers of refugees seeping out of the camps overwhelmed them. Estimates vary, but the Nazi defeat set free as many as eleven million people in Germany alone.[10] Added to the rivers of homeless people flowing through Germany were ethnic Germans from east-central Europe who were fleeing advancing Soviet troops or were expelled by Czechoslovakia and Poland at the end of the war.

Some of the newly liberated simply started walking, not waiting for help, beginning their long trek homeward as soon as the doors of their camp barracks were opened. One foreign worker, Waleria P., travelled by train for "weeks at a time, wandering." Passing through Czechoslovakia, she slept outside and dug potatoes to eat. Some local people were kind enough to give her hay to sleep on, and some offered her kerosene to get rid of the lice on her head. Later, she rode on a coal train, sitting on top of the coal. Another worker, Kazimiera K., reported that the freed labourers walked with their "beat up suitcases, held together with string…and that wretched blanket from the camp." It was fortunate that it was a warm spring, because they slept on the ground. "But the world was wounded," Kazimiera remembered. "There were bodies of German soldiers, swollen. Here a tree, an apple tree half destroyed, a branch blossoming. Everything seemed unreal." Some people wore rags; others were "dressed up." The trains were packed. "People sat on the roofs of the box cars, the couplings…by some miracle I found myself inside, in the wagon."[11]

In the early days of the war, the Allies had begun planning for the reconstruction of Europe, aware that large numbers of displaced persons would need repatriation to their homelands once the war ended. The 1941 Atlantic Charter set out Churchill and Roosevelt's vision for the post-war world. The charter's principles included a nation's right to choose its own government, the restoration of sovereign rights and self-government to those who were forcibly deprived of them, and a desire for no territorial changes against the freely expressed wishes of the people concerned. The Inter-Allied Committee on Post-War Requirements was created the following month to prepare for likely post-war scenarios and plan for the immediate emergency phase after the end of the war. The first steps toward a platform for international collaboration came in January 1942, when twenty-six countries gathered in Washington and signed the Declaration by the United Nations, affirming the Atlantic Charter's ideals and rejecting the possibility of a separate peace with the Axis powers. The term United Nations was used after that to refer to joint efforts to defeat Nazism and fascism and became the official name of the organization created in April 1945 to maintain international peace and security and ensure cooperation in solving international economic, social, cultural, and humanitarian problems.

In the meantime, the United Nations Relief and Rehabilitation Administration (UNRRA) was founded in November 1943, when forty-four nations formally agreed on the structure of the post-war relief organization. The Soviet Union was among the founders, but given its own devastation, it would be a recipient of aid rather than a contributor of funds. UNRRA would plan, coordinate, and administer measures for the relief of victims of war through the provision of "food, fuel, clothing, shelter and other basic necessities, medical and other essential services." It would help countries resume industrial and agricultural production, and it would make arrangements for the return of prisoners and exiles to their homes.[12] To fuel this level of activity, UNRRA established purchasing offices around the globe, funded by contributions from the member states; the United States was the major contributor, donating two-thirds of the $3.6 billion global cost of the program, with the United Kingdom and Canada adding $600 million and $137 million respectively. UNRRA also took in contributions from NGOs, some of whom donated food or clothing instead of money. By 1947, Americans had donated over seventy thousand tonnes of clothing to the relief effort.[13]

Far removed from the camps and cities of Germany, some UNRRA planners understood that not all of the displaced would want to return to their countries of origin and flagged the impending challenges for UNRRA administrators: "Even though nationality may be restored to the stateless, memories of the horrors and privations of expulsion from their home countries will remain. It is to be hoped that those who find their families scattered in many countries and who desire to rejoin them to start life anew in some other country will not be forced against their will by the operation of rigid procedures to resume residence in a country which offers no attractions or opportunities for them. The opportunities of immigration in the post-war world may admittedly be limited, but it will be a sorry world indeed if places cannot be found for those so situated."[14] It took some time for this view to be accepted by the liberating forces of the Allies.

Once the war ended, the first challenge was immediate relief. The Allied forces designated the French, British, and American armies as the immediate providers of relief, and divided Germany into zones of responsibility for each of them. They then set out to administer to the displaced, fully expecting them all to leave Germany as soon as transport could be arranged. Civilian UNRRA rescue teams moved in to help with the process. They first requisitioned barracks and temporary housing facilities and set up assembly centres where they could tend to the refugees who reached their doors. Here UNRRA registered the displaced, gave them identification papers, fed them, and sprayed them with lice-killing DDT powder. Even this task stretched the resources of the relief workers, who could barely keep up with the speed of the Allied advance into Germany. Journalist Marguerite Higgins described the scene in large cities such as Frankfurt as a state of "near-chaos," with "facilities...so inadequate as to produce extremely grave and often tragic results." Adding to the turmoil, the relief workers had no accommodations ready for the refugees. With no alternatives available, some of them had to be housed in prisoner-of-war and concentration camps. Higgins observed that "it is sometimes quite a job to persuade the laborers who check in at the main receiving center in the town to return to their former quarters."[15] Even the infamous Buchenwald concentration camp served as a displaced persons camp, dubbed Kibbutz Buchenwald and used as a Zionist training farm, until the Soviet army took it over in July 1945.[16] Three months after VE Day, another observer found the displaced persons throughout Germany still living "under guard behind barbed-wire fences" in "crowded, frequently unsanitary and generally grim conditions...hoping for some word of encouragement and action on their behalf."[17]

Despite an atmosphere of near anarchy, by the end of 1945, almost six million people displaced by the war had returned to their homes. But for Wanda and hundreds of thousands of other Poles, as well as many others from the Baltic states and Ukraine, that was not an option. The newly drawn eastern borders of Poland meant that Wanda's home in Opaí was now part of Soviet Belarus. What was her homeland? When the Soviets occupied Poland's eastern borderlands in 1939, their campaign of Sovietization included conferring citizenship on the inhabitants, whether they agreed or not. The Soviets did not accept the notion that an individual could renounce his or her citizenship and considered that all those who came from the areas within the new borders of the Soviet Union as Soviet citizens, subject to forcible repatriation.[18]

After the First World War, the stateless were those whose countries of origin, like Russians fleeing from the revolution or Armenians fleeing the Turks, did not want them back and had revoked their citizenship. Since it was only nations who could confer rights on citizens, these stateless people had no rights and were without the protection of any state. The Second World War produced a different kind of stateless person: those who rejected the protection of the country that claimed them following the arbitrary change in their citizenship. The executions and widescale arrests, suicides, and protests in the immediate post-war period gave weight to the displaced persons' fears of the Soviet Union and forced the Allies to reconsider their expectation of repatriation in all cases.

In February 1946, the General Assembly of the United Nations adopted a resolution that prohibited the forcible repatriation of refugees or displaced persons who expressed "valid" objections to returning to their country of origin (except for "war criminals, quislings or traitors"). Those who remained in Germany were questioned regularly in identity screenings to determine whether they had a "valid" objection to repatriation or were traitors or war criminals. Still, the resolution was a novel human rights protection conferred by an international body and not a state, and it presaged the fuller statement of inalienable human rights enshrined in the 1948 Universal Declaration of Human Rights, which included the right of anyone "to leave any country, including his own" and "seek and enjoy in other countries asylum from persecution." Generally, Latvians, Estonians, Lithuanians, and Poles who originated from the borderland territories east of the new Soviet border would only be repatriated to the Soviet Union if they affirmed their Soviet citizenship.[19]

Relocating to a different area in Poland might have been an option for Wanda's family, but where in Poland would they have gone? What remained of the Polish Republic had never been their home, and after their experience during the Soviet occupation, it is hardly surprising that they were unwilling to live in a state dominated by the Soviets.

In truth, they belonged nowhere.

Wanda's cookie tin of papers and photographs contained only one item of her personal identification. A displaced person's identification card names the holder as Wanda Gizmunt, born April 4, 1927. It lists her nationality as Polish and bears her signature. The card was issued at Fulda, at Camp No. 565, on September 5, 1946, and was stamped in several places by various UNRRA officials at the Wildflecken Assembly Centre.

The UNRRA archives contained many records about Wildflecken, but the identity of Camp 565 remained a mystery. Was the date of issue of the identification card related to Wanda's transfer to Wildflecken? If so, where had she lived before then? A photograph, probably one of the first taken of Wanda after the war, held the answer. In the picture, Wanda posed on a hillside of scrubby grass with a dozen or so girls, all dressed in Scouting uniforms. The back of the photo is inscribed with these words, handwritten in Polish: "Second trip to Asha-fenburger Scouting in Fulda." This might refer to Aschaffenburg, a town on the Main River not far from Frankfurt. Below the writing, the photo is stamped, also in Polish: "Cultural-Holiday Association, Polish Colony Fulda, Polish Camp No. 2, Konstantin Kaserne." At first, I wondered if Konstantin Kaserne was the name of the photographer. German speakers would have known immediately that *kaserne* means barracks in English, but I realized this only when I asked Google to translate the words from German. At the top of the photograph is a long narrow strip, which I first read as a defect in the negative. But when I enlarged the photo, I saw it was actually the top of a building lurking behind the hill, a row of small windows barely visible beneath a low, nearly flat roof. The girls were standing in front of their housing, the Konstantin Kaserne, which had once been home to a German infantry regiment in Fulda.

Wanda's memorabilia included other photos of her from 1946, dressed in her Scouting uniform and posed with other young women, or striding up a dirt path. Although it seems odd to think of Scouts in the displaced persons camps of Germany so soon after the war, it

Polish Girl Scouts in front of the barracks in Fulda, ca. 1945.
Wanda is second from the right in the third row. (Courtesy George Surdykowski)

was a common activity for young men and women recently released
from the labour camps. Scouting had been popular in wartime Poland,
where Scouts took an active role in the underground as messengers
and couriers. In the post-war period, Scouts participated in the relief
effort, establishing Boy Scout and Girl Guide troops in the camps and
providing uniforms, classes, and outings to unoccupied children and
teenagers.[20]

Some suggested that, among Poles in the displaced persons camps,
the association with Scouts was more political or paramilitary than
social. Rumours circulated among the camps that Polish Boy Scouts
were being sent for training with the army of General Anders in
Italy, in the hope of forming opposition to the advance of the Soviets
in Poland.[21] But nothing about the scenes in Wanda's photos is
militaristic; they appear to be no more than groups of young people
taking advantage of the chance to get out of the camp and into the
hills and woods with their peers, enjoying their first experience of an
adolescence they had missed during their years of war and captivity.

For his part, Joe saw more of Germany after the war during his time with the Scouts than he ever saw of Poland.

The movements of hundreds of thousands of survivors and displaced persons can be traced in page after page of names and numbers in one database on the website of the International Tracing Service (ITS), created during the war to trace missing persons, but first one must know the name of the camp they were in and be prepared to scroll through pages of lists. Searching these online archives produced no information about the name of the labour camp where Wanda stayed in Fulda or about her deportation or release at the end of the war. But, buried in the registration lists of displaced persons camps in the American zone, the Gizmunt family finally appeared: Helena, Wanda, Józef, Kazimiera, and the aunt, who was finally identified as Maria—leaving Camp No. 565 for Wildflecken on October 10, 1946.

The photograph of the young girls in front of the barracks is touching, a ragtag bunch of teenage girls in an unaccustomed social gathering, some of them smiling slightly, but most of them with sombre faces. The bleakness of their surroundings makes the scene even more poignant. The bureaucratic list of names in the ITS file is equally moving. For anyone forced to deal with the world of bureaucracy, lists like this can feel like a denial of the humanity of the people who appear on them. And it's easy to see this list in the same light, since it was created only for the convenience of the authorities in order to keep track of people shifted around. But a name on a list is a step up from where Wanda had been for the preceding six years. The page of names, carefully typed by an UNRRA secretary decades ago, finally recorded Wanda's presence and gave a name to her and her family after years of anonymous persecution and deprivation. It says: *I saw you, I noticed you. I know you are here, and I am responsible for what happens to you.*

Casey and a friend in an unknown Italian town

CHAPTER 6
ENEMIES AND ALLIES

On the morning of May 18, 1944, while Wanda was labouring in a repair shop in Fulda, a small patrol from Casey's regiment, the Twelfth Podolski Lancers, entered the ruins of the Benedictine monastery at Monte Cassino after an intense week of combat and raised the red and white Polish flag. The hill at Cassino was a crucial defensive position in the Nazis' Gustav Line running across south-central Italy and the focus of four Allied assaults since the beginning of 1944. The joint forces finally succeeded in breaking through in May that year, and the Polish contribution to the Allied success at Monte Cassino stands as one of the proudest moments of the Polish Second Corps in Italy.

After the ordeal of their captivity and journey across the Soviet Union and the Middle East, the Polish soldiers finally had their opportunity to avenge the loss of their country and restore their honour, and they did not waste their chance. Sadly, in the course of battle, the Poles suffered roughly four thousand casualties; one thousand soldiers lost their lives. Overall, the Allies suffered around fifty-five thousand casualties over the course of the four-month campaign.

The Allied armies' focus shifted to France several weeks later. The invasion of Normandy began with the June 6 beach landings. American and French troops were moved to France, while the Polish Second Corps remained behind in Italy, to help secure a base on the Adriatic coast. After a month of heavy fighting, they secured the port city of Ancona. Casey was present for both battles and suffered a left-leg injury at Corinaldo, near Ancona, but he never spoke about it.

Soldiers have many reasons for not talking about their war experiences. The most obvious are the terror and barbarity of armed conflict, which can haunt them for the rest of their lives. They are exposed to mortal danger from bombs, grenades, bullets, and flying debris, and they witness the violent deaths of their fellow soldiers and enemies. Casey survived, but at what cost to his spirit? He acknowledged his past as a soldier by marching with the Polish Legion in annual Remembrance Day ceremonies, but he made no effort to talk about the war with his sons or otherwise commemorate it. He left his medals to tarnish among Wanda's things. His usually flattened mood and removal from the banter of everyday conversation at the table might have been no more than his personality, already evident in the photo of the little boy in the *kresy*. But to a sensitive person, the trauma of war, preceded by the harsh Siberian captivity, could only magnify an already troubled relationship with the world.

For the Polish soldiers, their satisfaction in their success in battle was mixed with a growing anxiety about the tenuousness of the Polish state and Stalin's intentions for post-war Poland. In January 1943, Stalin withdrew Polish citizenship from Poles remaining in the Soviet Union.[1] When Russia claimed all those born in eastern Poland to be its nationals, some born in that area erased their birthplaces from their military documents.[2] Soldiers with relatives still in the Soviet Union understood that they might never see them again. Matters worsened when, in April 1943, the Germans announced the discovery of the corpses of 3,500 murdered Polish officers buried in mass graves in the Katyń Forest near Smolensk in western Russia. Nearly all the dead were found in their uniforms, identity papers still intact, a bullet hole in the back of each skull. These were some of the officers who, according to Stalin, "may have escaped to Manchuria."

The Soviets denied any involvement in the deaths, denouncing Goebbels as a slanderer and blaming the Nazis for the crime. Certainly, the Nazis were prepared to exploit the situation to drive a wedge between the Allies. When the Polish government-in-exile referred the question to the International Red Cross for investigation, Goebbels arranged for Hitler to make the identical request, allowing the implication that the Poles were collaborating with the Nazis.[3] Stalin broke off diplomatic relations with the Polish government-in-exile and launched a propaganda campaign against the Poles, accusing the Polish government of colluding with the Germans. He endorsed a new political entity, the Union of Polish Patriots, laying the groundwork for a future Poland under Soviet control.[4]

The reaction of the Americans and British to the news was a clear signal of what the future held for Poland. Józef Czapski, who had earlier spent months in Russia making lists and searching for the missing soldiers at General Anders's request, recalled his optimism as he left the Soviet Union, believing that Poland's destiny was in the hands of Great Britain and the United States. In 1941, at the first of their wartime conferences, Roosevelt and Churchill declared their "wish to see sovereign rights and self-government restored to those who have been forcibly deprived of them," and Czapski regarded these words as a commitment that at the end of the war Poland would no longer be Russia's pawn. This declaration could not survive the political realities of such an uneasy alliance as existed with the Soviets. Aware that they appeared to condone the massacre, the British and Americans remained publicly neutral on the issue; they could win the war without the Poles, but not without the Soviets.[5]

The Poles were in an unenviable position; criticism of another ally was discouraged, especially one more powerful than the tiny Polish contingent. The Soviets, on the other hand, had no constraints on voicing their opinions of the Poles. Soviet commissar Andrei Vyshinsky denounced Anders as a "renegade" and "deserter" who had shied away from action on the Eastern Front. Rumours about Anders's character and poor discipline of his troops circulated in the press and in official reports. The consensus at the British Foreign Office was that Anders was a "gallant but truculent soldier" with "little respect for some of the realities of modern world politics."[6]

To Józef Czapski, the news was confirmation of what he had long suspected to be the truth. "The news about Katyń," he wrote, "made every Pole even more deeply aware that we were under lethal threat *from both sides.*"[7]

As the Polish troops battled in Italy in the summer and fall of 1944, it became increasingly apparent that their war would not end in a triumphant return to an independent Poland. Paris was liberated on August 25, 1944, after the Third US Army came to the aid of the French forces in an uprising against the German garrison, but there would be no help for the Armia Krajowa (AK, the Polish Home Army) in the Warsaw Uprising that same month.

By the summer of 1944, the Red Army had pushed the Nazis out of the Soviet Union and had advanced to the Warsaw suburb of Praga, several miles away on the other side of the Vistula River, by July 25. Expecting the imminent arrival of the Red Army, the AK began its attacks on the Germans on August 1, using weapons secretly amassed over the last five years. The fighting was vicious and relentless and, in the end, doomed to failure. Learning of the Polish resistance, Hitler ordered Himmler to annihilate Warsaw and kill all its inhabitants. The Germans unleashed bombs, set fires, and brought in reinforcements. Eventually, the Allies flew supply drops over the city, but they were too little, too late. The Soviets, for their part, remained on the other side of the Vistula, ignoring requests for help and refusing permission for other Allies to refuel at Soviet airfields within range. By the time the uprising ended, sixty-three days after it began, almost 200,000 Poles had died: 18,000 AK soldiers and 180,000 civilians. Another half-million Poles were expelled from the city, many of whom were sent to forced-labour camps. The city was almost entirely reduced to rubble. With the AK in disarray, Warsaw on its knees, and nearly 20,000 German soldiers dead, the Red Army resumed its campaign to liberate Poland.

Martha Gellhorn, then a writer for *Collier's* magazine, followed the Polish soldiers as they fought near Ancona in July 1944. They gathered to listen with "agonized interest" to the news of the Soviet advance across Poland every day. It seemed to her that they could tell her what was happening ten kilometres away or in Poland, but nowhere else. And she could see what had happened in Poland "in every man's face, in every man's eyes."[8] (Her article about her encounter with the Polish soldiers, which *Collier's* never published, later appeared in her book *The Face of War*. Gellhorn noted that "at the time, it must have seemed too critical of our popular allies, the Russians" for *Collier's* to print.) The men made their views about their Russian allies clear: "with their whole hearts they fear an ally, who is already in their homeland," Gellhorn observed. "For they do not believe Russia will relinquish their country after the war; they fear they are to be sacrificed in this peace, as Czechoslovakia was in 1938." She tried to persuade them otherwise; her words, in hindsight, appear foolishly idealistic. She wrote that she told them "that Russia must be as great in peace as she has been in war, and that the world must honor the valor and suffering of the Poles by giving them freedom to rebuild and better their homeland. I tried to say I could not believe that this war which is fought to maintain the rights of man will end by ignoring the rights of Poles."

The soldiers knew that they had already lost the support of their allies. The Soviet propaganda war was successful; it seemed to Czapski that the Red Army offensive impressed the foreign reporters, who bathed Stalin in a "halo of glory." Anyone criticizing Stalin or expressing reservations about the Soviets was suspected of being a Nazi sympathizer. The military press was no better. A caricature of a Polish officer appeared in the US Army's *Stars and Stripes* captioned "one of the fifteen thousand *supposedly* murdered by the Soviet government."[9]

The Nazis had their own campaign to attack the morale of the soldiers. They interrupted broadcasts over Radio Kosciuszko, the radio station of the Polish Second Corps, with their own Radio Wanda, sending out a stream of propaganda inviting the men to abandon the Allies and join with the Nazis. "The Bolsheviks are entering your homeland and burning your houses and raping your women," they taunted. "What are you poor boys doing fighting in Italy?" They also dropped leaflets over the Polish positions, informing them that "the Soviet flag is going to fly over your Fatherland," and "when the Red Army floods Poland, you will never see your family again."

The final blow to Polish morale came with the agreement at Yalta in February 1945. By then, the interests of the main Allies had diverged significantly. Britain, the weakest of the three, was financially straitened and needed the war to end. The attention of the Americans had turned to the Pacific, and they needed Stalin's support in that theatre. There would be no more fighting to restore Poland's pre-war borders. The agreement determined that Poland would be assigned to the Soviet sphere of influence, and the border with the Soviet Union would be located along the Curzon Line, removing sixty-nine thousand square kilometres along Poland's former eastern border—home to both Casey and Wanda—from the Polish Republic. Two great cities, Lwów and Wilno, no longer belonged to Poland. As compensation, Poland would gain East Prussia and some unspecified territory in the west. A tripartite commission would form the government of Poland, which would in the end prove unable to prevent Soviet domination.

Realizing the likely reaction of the Poles, Churchill proposed reminding them that "but for the Red Army they would have been utterly destroyed." He was not going to break his heart about Lwów, he said. He knew the Poles would never say they were satisfied, because "nothing would satisfy the Poles."

The result was crushing to the men who had fought with Anders only to lose their own homeland in negotiations to which they were not a party. Józef Czapski later declared, "I've never met a single Pole capable of analyzing this national tragedy dispassionately."[10] Outraged, Anders at first tendered his resignation and applied to withdraw his men from battle sectors, refusing to demand any further sacrifice of soldiers' blood. Under heavy criticism in the British House of Commons, Churchill defended the Yalta agreement, gratuitously adding his hope that "it may be possible to offer the citizenship and freedom of the British Empire" to those members of the Polish forces who did not want to return to a post-war Poland.[11]

Anders was later persuaded not to resign. In spite of all that had occurred, he asked his soldiers to maintain their "dignity and discipline," and the corps continued to fight in the Allied Spring Offensive

Casey's army ID photo
(Courtesy George Surdykowski)

that liberated Bologna. Later, Harold Macmillan, then the British government's representative at Allied headquarters, was forced to concede that although the Poles had lost their country, they "kept their honour."

In the aftermath of the war, Casey remained in Italy with the other men of the Polish Second Corps, waiting to see how the Yalta agreement would play out in Poland. Several photographs of him during this period show him taking in the sights in city squares or at the seashore, with a friend or as part of a larger groups of soldiers. In all these images, he shows only his familiar half smile. Still, in spite of whatever gnawing disappointment he felt at the loss of his home, this must have been a comparatively pleasant time for him, living as a hero among the grateful Italians, with no more battles to fight or hardships to endure.

His future, though, was much in doubt. In spite of Churchill's vague offer of a new home for the soldiers, the British government, fearing the loss of jobs for its own returning soldiers, had no desire to absorb over one hundred thousand Polish men into its workforce. The new foreign secretary, Ernest Bevin, wanted the soldiers to be repatriated without delay. Anders refused to agree unless the Allies could guarantee free elections in Poland. No one was prepared to make that promise. In Poland, the Soviet occupiers were rounding up Home Army soldiers, accusing them of collaborating with the Nazis. Some were deported, others tortured and even executed. By July 1945, the Americans and the British officially recognized the Stalin-backed Provisional Government of National Unity as Poland's legitimate government. That same government stripped General Anders and seventy-five other officers of their rank and nationality, alleging they had committed crimes against the Polish nation. The Soviets demanded the repatriation of Polish soldiers born east of the Curzon Line. The British refused, insisting that all soldiers in the Polish armed forces who were Polish citizens at the outbreak of the war were entitled to be considered as Poles who could not be forced to return to the Soviet Union.

Józef Czapski reported that of the 112,600 soldiers and officers in the Polish Second Army in 1945, only slightly more than 10 percent opted to return to Poland. Of the tens of thousands of soldiers who had experienced Soviet Russia, only 310 returned. According to Czapski, those who did faced accusations of espionage, interrogations by the Polish security police, imprisonment, and sometimes torture. The men may have been aware that in March 1945, the NKVD had arrested sixteen leading figures of the Polish underground (after inviting them to a meeting and assuring their safety) and flew them to Moscow, where they were interrogated at Lubyanka. They were later imprisoned for anti-Soviet activity after a show trial in July.[12] For the majority, a return to their former homes in what was now a Soviet republic was a risk they were unwilling to bear. The prospect of persecution, the fear of Siberian exile, was real. In any case, to what homes would they have returned? After more than five years and three different occupying powers, the homes they once lived in would have been ruined or possessed by others, lost to them forever.

Casey was among the majority of soldiers who decided not to return to Poland. New owners no doubt occupied the family's farm near Kosów, their tools used by other farmers, a new cook in their kitchen. He may not have known where the rest of his family was, or if they planned to return to what remained of Poland. It may not have mattered to him anyway. After years of forced labour, displacement and combat, it was probably an easy decision to remain in what he assumed was a less hostile part of the world.

Kasia, Joe, Maria, Wanda, and Helena in Germany, ca. 1947

CHAPTER 7

THE WILD PLACE

The photos in Wanda's collection are witness to an evolution that took place in her life during her time in Germany after the war. Who took them, and where, in the upheaval of the displaced persons camp, were they developed? Many are inscribed on the back in Wanda's spidery script, the Polish words too illegible to be translated. The earliest photo portrays Wanda as a serious girl standing in front of a wintry scene, gazing warily at the camera, her eyes shadowed and dull with weariness. Others show her easing into her newly unencumbered life, increasingly with a smile on her face: in her Scouting uniform, striding confidently up a dirt path; posing with friends, male and female, in front of a school building or relaxing on the grass; or in charge of groups of small children on outings in the forest.

Unlike Camp 565, a temporary, makeshift home set up in a small barracks during the chaotic first days after the war ended, Wanda's new home in Wildflecken was a bustling village of Poles, larger than any place she had ever lived. In 1937, the Nazis had chosen a site just north of the village of Wildflecken in the Rhön Mountains of Bavaria for the largest SS training centre in Germany, planting a dense forest of pines to camouflage it from aerial surveillance and removing the name of the village from maps. After the Nazi defeat, the Americans moved in and converted it to a camp for the displaced.

The American writer Kathryn Hulme arrived in Wildflecken in July 1945 to discover a camp buried deep in the woods, covering fifteen square miles, with sixty-five blockhouses containing a total of twenty-eight hundred rooms. Hulme was one of a team of UNRRA field workers dispatched from Frankfurt to run the camp and one of only two on the team who had not spent the war years in Europe. Not much in her history suggested an interest in social work or administration. A graduate of Berkeley and the Columbia School of Journalism, Hulme pursued a writing career by supporting herself as a jack of all trades. She spent some time in Paris as an acolyte of the Russian-born mystic and philosopher George Ivanovich Gurdjieff; in her last job before returning to Europe with the UNRRA, she worked as a welder in the Kaiser Shipyards in San Francisco. Her memoir of her time at Wildflecken, *The Wild Place*, offers a rare insider's view of the people and operations of one of the largest displaced persons camps in Germany.

At the time of Hulme's arrival, the camp held more than fifteen thousand inhabitants, mostly Polish. Before that, about twenty thousand Russians were held there. When the American army arrived to convert the camp to an assembly centre for the displaced, either the departing Russians or the local populace had stripped the camp of much of its fittings and provisions. For their part, the Nazis had left behind the largest munitions dump in Germany—poison gases, land mines, machine guns, and ammunition strewn over acres of the land adjacent to the camp—which took over a year to deactivate.

The UNRRA team set about mastering the logistics of supporting a small town: water, sanitation, heat, and food were the immediate needs. DDT squads met the truckloads of the displaced on their arrival, spraying them once again for lice. Six hospital units provided the residents with a full array of medical treatment and public-health services, including immunizations, venereal-disease screening, isolation for tuberculosis cases, maternal care, and DDT dusting once a month. With only four nurses and a chronic shortage of supplies, the workload must have been oppressive. Wanda received medical attention, probably for the first time in years. Records from the International Tracing Service show she received a full set of immunizations in her time at Wildflecken.

Twenty thousand cubic metres of wood had to be taken from the surrounding forest to fuel the wood stoves of the bunkhouses over the winter. The displaced were put to work in the camp's twelve kitchens, which processed six hundred tonnes of rations each month, and in the sewing workshop, which made clothing for the camp residents. Schools for all ages were set up, the teachers drawn from the Polish inhabitants. By the end of September 1945, as many as three thousand Poles were working in various parts of the camp.

Although the UNRRA ran the camp, it was a ripe environment for enterprising Poles and black marketeers, who found a way to monetize the supplies the army and the Red Cross brought to the camp. In an attempt to keep out black marketeers, camp residents required a pass to come and go, but the security for such a large camp was unsurprisingly porous. Cartons of cigarettes and cans of Spam were currency that had to be heavily guarded and eventually handled only by the youngest workers, who could be trusted not to remove some of the goods for trading.

On her arrival, Hulme was provided with an interpreter, the Countess, a "tall, handsome woman in her early sixties...with the lean *racé* face of the Polish nobility but with all the native hauteur beaten out of it." The Countess introduced her to Ignatz, a truck driver who had resolved to become Hulme's chauffeur. Hulme pointed out that she had no car, but that was no problem for Ignatz. He had already located a car for her, which he had towed from a German garage and worked on in the camp's garage. Between them, the Countess and Ignatz filtered requests, translated, ran interference, and offered inside information and insight to help Hulme navigate the sometimes tricky predicaments of the Polish residents.

Hulme settled into a routine of departures and arrivals, with one hundred thousand people passing through the camp in the first year. The first sight of humans crowded into cattle cars arriving at the Wildflecken train station brought her up short. "A sense of shame invades you. A feeling of objective guilt crystallizes and you stare at the humiliation as if you were responsible for it in some intangible fashion," she wrote, noting that the feeling later repeated "with growing familiarity so that finally you accept it matter-of-factly as just one more debasement that has happened to mankind."[1]

After the challenges of organizing transit for thousands, the camp administrators moved on to winter preparations. This was no easy task, as they needed to bring in a thirty-day winter reserve of food and chop enough wood from the nearby forests to heat the camp. Huge convoys of winter clothing arrived and needed to be sorted and inventoried. On November 11, 1945, heavy snow fell on Wildflecken, the first of many storms in what would become one of the most severe winters on record for the area. The camp was effectively blocked from the outside world in the months of snow and ice, interrupting the cycle of incoming and outgoing displaced persons. For Hulme, life was "reduced to the stark simplicity of the supply line." The only trains that arrived in Wildflecken that winter carried food and coal. The 2,800 rooms in the camp became like cocoons, their windows nailed shut. Lines of blankets erected in the crowded rooms to create privacy produced the "proper incubating steam for swift transmission of respiratory diseases."[2]

The incoming and outgoing cycle began again with the first rail transport on March 27, 1946, when another one thousand people arrived in the camp. Hulme went along with the first transport to leave, a little over two hundred Poles travelling in boxcars bound for Poland in a journey that lasted ten days. There was a palpable sense of relief as the train passed from Germany into Czechoslovakia. When the train arrived at the station in Poland, posters in the pavilion of the Polish Committee of Repatriation announced, "Welcome to Poland—We Will All Work Together." Dance music played over a loudspeaker, and Poles greeted the travellers with food and drink. After the travellers were registered, they would again be Polish citizens and no longer homeless casualties of the war. Hulme returned to Wildflecken with a sense of satisfaction and accomplishment, hopeful that a successful series of repatriation trains would dissipate the fear that pervaded the other residents of the camp.

Her optimism lasted only ten days, until one of the camp administrators returned from a repatriation transport with a report of how Czechoslovakia looked after May Day celebrations, with the hammer-and-sickle flag of the Soviet Union hanging from public buildings alongside the Czech flag. Clearly, the Czechoslovakia that people were returning to was not the liberal democracy they'd known before the war. Worse, though, were the photographs of Poland the camp administrator mounted for public viewing. The Poles noticed that in one photo the crown had been removed from Poland's national symbol, the white eagle, on a corner postbox. They were outraged. This provoked a spate of crowned eagles emanating from the camp's handicraft shops in a variety of materials — and a sudden decline in the number of Poles willing to return to Poland.[3]

This refusal was frustrating, even infuriating, to army and UNRRA repatriation officials, who still aimed to return all displaced persons to their places of origin. Although the American leadership would not force repatriation on those remaining in the camps, this did not stop officials from resorting to tactics of extreme persuasion. The army shifted the displaced from camp to camp, giving them no chance of creating a temporary home. This only meant that by August, Wildflecken's number of inhabitants had swelled to twenty thousand.

Many thought that the Wildflecken leadership was thwarting repatriation efforts. In August 1946, an UNRRA repatriation officer complained that Wildflecken's director, George Masset, "does not show any interest in the development of repatriation movements, neither does he provide any active help to officers coming to this camp [for] repatriation matters," and asked that he be replaced.[4]

Masset stood his ground. In his opinion, the randomness of the visits of repatriation officers did nothing to encourage the Poles to return to Poland. He also pointed out that the UNRRA knew very well that few of the remaining Poles would return home. "If despite our efforts we have been able to repatriate since April only 13% of our population, it must not be forgotten that this population has been entirely composed of Poles gathered up from all the camps in the Zone and having been declared non-repatriable," he argued. "The result of 13% is therefore an appreciable quantity."

One September night, while the residents were sleeping, UNRRA officials moved through Wildflecken, posting a proclamation from officials in Warsaw that promised the Poles a friendly reception, jobs, free transportation in Poland, and a two-month supply of food to be distributed to them on their arrival. Next to the proclamation was a letter to the displaced Poles from General Joseph McNarney, commander of the American zone, urging them to return home as there was little chance for their resettlement outside Poland.

The next day, the camp residents got a preview of the sixty-day food supply in the camp canteen, a total of ninety-four pounds of food per person: a mountain of flour, lard, salt, evaporated milk, tins of fish, rolled oats, and dried peas. To add to the sense of abundance, another table held a display of food for a family of four—376 pounds—enough, Hulme's driver, Ignatz, thought, to trade for a horse or even an acreage in Poland. The Poles filed past the display in awe, dreaming of what they could do with such riches if they returned home. Some did, and the transports started up again, moving as many as eight hundred people out of the camp every four days. But more trains of Poles from other camps were arriving just as fast.[5]

In October 1946, just as Wanda was being transferred to Wild-flecken, an UNRRA area employment meeting was held, and the area employment officer spoke to repatriation and employment officers in no uncertain terms. Camp officials were told to get employable persons to work, but not the Poles. "Do not employ Poles—*repatriate them as they must go home*," the officer instructed. "Take all Poles out of work projects and repatriate unless he or she has a repatriation date then they can work until [the date they] go to Poland." The employment officer insisted that there was "no such thing as an unrepatriable Pole. If they refuse repatriation, they can be used to rebuild Germany; after that they will have a change of heart for dear old Poland."[6]

The Americans and the British had none of the sympathy for the displaced Poles that they showed those from the Baltic states. Part of this stemmed from overt racism, which was evident even at the top of the UNRRA hierarchy. Lieutenant-General Sir Frederick Morgan, known for his role in D-Day planning, was given the task of running the organization created for the purpose of returning the displaced in Germany to their homes. He found the educated, well-dressed Balts "simply charming people," but he loathed the Poles, judging them "hopeless," unkempt, and lazy.[7] Similar attitudes pervaded the UNRRA camp administrators and the military.[8] The citizens of Poland might have won the war, but they had lost the peace. They would simply have to adapt to their new reality and return to their homeland.

By the time Wanda and her family arrived in Wildflecken, they must have already resolved not to return to Poland; otherwise, more than a year after the end of the war, they would have gone. This couldn't have been a comfortable decision. The camp in Fulda was rudimentary, and their lives must still have been difficult. With no alternative in sight, it would have taken great resolve to remain in the camp, particularly since the pressure to return never ended.

The situation came to a head in January 1947, coincidentally around the time of elections in Poland that installed the Soviet-backed government, a result widely considered fraudulent. In November 1946, a Polish liaison officer proposed to screen the inhabitants of the displaced persons camps in the American zone to weed out any ineligible people. The Soviets had insisted on forced repatriation of Soviet citizens, including Ukrainians who tried to avoid returning to the Soviet Union by claiming Polish nationality. The liaison officer singled out Wildflecken as the only camp under UNRRA management that had never carried out a classification of nationality, as had been done in other camps.

In the same month, UNRRA officials met at Wildflecken to discuss the need to weed out the camp's anti-repatriation factions. They speculated that as many as 40 percent of the residents could be considered "from the Ukrainian territory." As for the rest, the officials felt that most had strong anti-repatriation feelings. A policy of segregation had to be adopted in the camp to remove anti-repatriation Poles and those considered to be Ukrainian and ineligible for return to Poland. The Wildflecken director agreed to facilitate the screening and posted a notice that starting January 22, the screening would begin. Disingenuously, the notice claimed that the screening had "no connection with repatriation or politics. It is merely a verification of the claims to Polish nationality and citizenship."

Even the least political resident of Wildflecken would have been suspicious of this order. Who among them had any citizenship papers to prove where they were from? How many were not screened before being transported to Wildflecken from another camp? The anti-repatriation faction in the camp circulated posters calling for a demonstration and boycott of the screening, proclaiming, "Every one of us knows well about conditions in the Country, everyone knows the methods of bolsheviks' knaves!"

On January 22, Polish liaison officers, resplendent in long great-coats and leather boots, their caps trimmed with gold braid, presented themselves to carry out the screening in the mess hall. After a period of calm in the streets, a demonstration of about one thousand Poles gathered in the central square. Inside the building, a small group of protesters surrounded the officers. After some pushing and shoving, the Polish officers escaped the building, reaching their car just as protesters smashed its windows. Watching from inside the building, Hulme saw one of the officers get out to remove some protesters who were rocking the car, only to have his hat knocked from his head and the insignia on his coat torn off. Somehow, the Polish officers managed to escape and drive the car out of the camp. The officers, reporting their version of events, claimed that the attackers shouted "Death to Poles!" in the Ukrainian language.

Two weeks later, a headline in the *New York Times* announced:

DP'S IN CAMP RIOT MOB "SOVIET" AIDES
Poles Beat Repatriation Group
Incident Brings Agreement on Segregation Policy

The zonal UNRRA chief and the US military governor for the zone reached an agreement about future screening of displaced persons: The US army and UNRRA would continue checking their eligibility for

UNRRA care, but "for the time being will dispense with the assistance of Polish officers in determining nationality."[9]

The *Times* also reported that the Polish officers returned the next day to try again, but "were beaten more severely." None of the notes of the UNRRA director, or the chief Polish liaison officer, mention a second incident. Instead, there was a day of feverish consultation about threats that had been made in the night about what would happen if the Polish officers returned, resulting in the cancellation of the screening, at least for the time being. Director Masset, sounding a lot like *Casablanca*'s Inspector Renault, commented, "And the combat ended for lack of combatants. It was a beautiful victory (not for us, most certainly)."

Later, Kathryn Hulme wondered at the Americans' intransigence about repatriation. They could have saved significant time, money, and the distress of hundreds of thousands of people if they had simply begun resettlement efforts as soon as it became obvious that those remaining in Germany would not return home. After the passage of legislation in 1948, the Americans welcomed more than three hundred thousand displaced persons over the next three years, with the entire program costing a mere $1.93 per taxpayer.[10]

Even without the undercurrent of political conflict, Helena must have quickly realized that Wildflecken was a hazardous place to raise her three children. In the space of eighteen months, the family had moved from a barn to a small barracks and finally to a dangerously overcrowded camp where all of the problems of displacement and isolation were concentrated in one place: black marketeering, petty theft and criminality, illegal stills and alcohol abuse, and promiscuity. A high percentage of new mothers were unmarried, and some pregnant women underwent amateur abortions. In other cases, newborns were neglected, resulting in infant deaths. Her family crammed yet again into barrack rooms in close proximity to strangers, the risks of this aimless life demanded that Helena find something productive for her children to do.

Polish students on the steps of a *gimnazjum* (high school)
at Wildflecken, ca. 1947. Wanda is on the left of the
second-to-bottom row. (Courtesy George Surdykowski)

Fortunately, twenty-year-old Wanda found an outlet for her
energies in school. A *gimnazjum*, or high school, had been established
in the camp, and Wanda happily joined in, trying to make up for
her lost years of education. Several photographs show her standing
in front of the school in a group of men and women, apparently a
mix of students and teachers, or beside the school with her friends.
Smiling broadly, she looks delighted to be among them. Everyone is
presentably, even professionally, dressed. What effort, or miracle of
bartering, must have gone into maintaining a veneer of respectability?
Even so, Wanda's coat, which must have been a hand-me-down, fits
her a little too loosely. Another photo shows her mother, Helena,
dressed in a plain dark suit, standing with a group of women on the
steps in front of a *szkoła*, or elementary school. They appear to be a

group of teachers for the younger students. Like Wanda's group, they are clothed in dresses and suits and present an image of seriousness, authority, and decorum, in stark contrast with the unrulier elements of Wildflecken's population. The camp offered a safe place for those who would take advantage of it.

Intelligent, strong-willed, and hard-working, Wanda would have been a good student. By the time I met her, she was an avid reader in both Polish and English and had mastered English without any formal instruction; I sometimes wondered if, like my mother, she regretted not having had the chance to continue her education. For a brief time, she had the ordinary pleasures of youth: the peace of the classroom, the company of her fellow students, and the challenge of learning. In the disordered world of Wildflecken, she found a purpose and a way to move toward adulthood. When the future arrived, Wanda would be ready.

CHAPTER 8
THE RECKONING, PART I

"For two days now, I have been kept here, and again and again I have asked myself, Why? Why? I swear by God that I am an innocent man who wronged no one! My only crime is that I loved Germany." In a jail cell in Salzburg, Austria, Fritz Sauckel tearfully pleaded his case before Edgar Snow of the *Saturday Evening Post*, a first draft of the defence he would eventually put before a panel of judges in Nuremberg.

In April 1945, as the Soviets were approaching Berlin and the western Allied forces were making their way through Germany from the west, Sauckel was one of many of the Nazi elite who fled south to the Alps, hiding out in caves or remote villages, hoping to evade the punishment at the hands of the Allies that was surely bearing down on them.

Some, like Adolf Eichmann and Josef Mengele, managed to make their way out of Europe, using escape routes that came to be known as ratlines, and found safe haven in Latin America. Most, however, were unsuccessful in evading capture. Hiding out in Berchtesgaden, near the Austrian border, Sauckel surrendered in early May to an Office of Strategic Services (OSS) officer with the improbable name of Rudolph von Ripper. A member of the fading Austrian aristocracy, von Ripper is one of the more intriguing footnotes of the war. Avowedly anti-Nazi, his caricatures of Hitler and other satirical cartoons in the pre-war years provoked the Gestapo to imprison him in the Sachsenhausen-Oranienburg concentration camp on charges of treason. He later made his way to the United States, where he continued to work as an artist and became an American citizen. When *Time* magazine named Hitler "Man of the Year" for 1938, the traditional cover photograph was replaced with von Ripper's drawing of Hitler as a tiny figure, his back to the viewer, playing a massive organ as his murdered victims spin on a giant wheel.

After the US joined the war, von Ripper enlisted, entering the army as a corporal and ending the war as a captain. Wounded at least four times, he was a legendary figure; war correspondent Ernie Pyle called him "one of the most fabulous characters in [the] war theater." The US general Lucian Truscott described him as "the bravest man I've ever seen." Working in the OSS, von Ripper made his way into Salzburg in advance of the US Army, collecting intelligence on fleeing Nazi officials along the way. After one mission, he returned with six SS generals and three gauleiters, Sauckel among them.[1]

In the jail in Salzburg, Snow found the other Nazis he interviewed slicker, more ingratiating, and subtler than Sauckel, but a common thread ran through their statements. "All denied any personal guilt; there was no repentance in them, and—with the exception of the Goerings and Paul Schmidt—no criticism of Hitler," Snow noted. Sauckel was incredulous when shown photographs of the camps at Dachau and Buchenwald, and he was certain that Hitler knew nothing of it. As for the foreign workers, Sauckel claimed they were volunteers, better off than they would have been at home. The camps were "models of cleanliness and health." He had inspected them himself. "But of course," he added, "some enemies of the state had to be eliminated."[2]

Searching through the vast literature about the Second World War to learn how the Nazis moved millions of foreigners into Germany for forced labour, and how those workers were treated, I didn't give any thought to the Nuremberg trials. Like many, I associated them with the crimes of the Holocaust, not realizing the broader sweep of the charges heard in the first trial, known as the International Military

Tribunal, or the essential connectedness of all Nazi crimes. Reading British lawyer Philippe Sands's *East West Street*, which weaves the story of the genesis of the Nuremberg trials with his investigation of his own family's fate in the Holocaust, I realized that Wanda's wartime experience in Nazi Germany was included in post-war attempts to reckon with the Nazi war crimes. Sands focused his lens on Hans Frank, another of the Nuremberg defendants who, as the governor general of occupied Poland, oversaw the extermination of more than a million Jews from Galicia and Lwów (today, Lviv). The dead included members of the families of Sands's grandfather and two of the lawyers who played key roles in defining war crimes for the Nuremberg trial.

Sands's investigative journey was necessary because, like Wanda, his grandfather had "locked the first half of his life in a crypt." I felt chastened to realize that in my search for facts about Wanda's life I had forgotten about justice, a strange omission for a lawyer. The realization of the great injustice inflicted on Wanda and Casey surely motivated my curiosity about their lives. But I wasn't alone in this oversight. As Sands prepared for a speech on his work on war crimes against humanity and genocide that he was to give at the university in Lviv, he too realized that he had "never inquired too deeply as to what had happened at Nuremberg."

As the war came to an end, justice was much on the minds of Europeans and Russians, civilians and soldiers, and not just the Allied leadership. Before the Allies were able to create the legal tools to prosecute the Nazi leaders for their crimes, a period of lawlessness prevailed in Europe as outraged citizens, and sometimes soldiers, carried out more primitive forms of retribution against the Germans. As the Red Army marched through Germany, its soldiers exacted their revenge by looting German towns and villages and brutally raping thousands of German women. In France, during the "wild purge" — *l'épuration sauvage* — of 1944, groups linked to the French resistance killed as many as six thousand people considered traitors and collaborators. Women suspected of consorting with the Nazis were shorn of their hair, stripped naked, branded with swastikas, and paraded in front of their fellow citizens in disgrace.[3] In occupied territories, German nationals were expelled and sent to live in Germany as refugees themselves.

There were also lawful efforts to hold perpetrators criminally responsible. The first such trials took place in the Soviet Union in 1943, in the cities of Kharkov and Krasnodar. The Nazis' genocidal campaign against Jews had its beginnings in the occupied Soviet territories, where the Einsatzgruppen burned down villages and carried out mass murders by shooting or asphyxiation with exhaust fumes in "gas vans." In some areas they were aided by collaborators and local officials who had thrown in their lot with the Nazis. At Krasnodar, eleven Soviet citizens were tried for treason as collaborators. At Kharkov, four men—three Nazi officers and a Soviet collaborator—were tried, convicted, and executed for the torture and murder of thousands of mainly Jewish Ukrainians in the town during the Nazi occupation.[4] Both these trials were in the Soviet show-trial tradition, with the accused confessing their crimes and reciting their testimony as if from a script.[5] In Poland, the first trial specifically concerned with concentration camps was held in Lublin in late 1944, within days of the liberation of the Majdanek concentration camp.[6]

But the first, and most prominent, Nuremberg trial was a revolutionary and controversial attempt to hold perpetrators legally responsible for crimes of waging aggressive war and crimes committed against civilians before an independent, international tribunal created for that purpose alone. Prior to this, international law had no mechanism for the prosecution of war crimes, or even a consensus about how such crimes would be defined. But as news of Nazi atrocities reached Allied leaders in the early days of the war, they resolved to make the punishment of war crimes one of their objectives in the post-war period. In October 1941, Churchill joined Roosevelt in declaring publicly:

> The massacres of the French are an example of what
> Hitler's Nazis are doing in many other countries
> under their yoke. The atrocities committed in Poland,

Yugoslavia, Norway, Holland, Belgium, and particularly behind the German front in Russia, exceed anything that has been known since the darkest and most bestial ages of humanity. The punishment of these crimes should now be counted among the major goals of the war.[7]

In January 1942, representatives of nine occupied countries in Europe held a conference at St. James's Palace in London to discuss questions of punishment of Nazi criminal acts. In their January 13 declaration, they affirmed that "international solidarity is necessary to avoid the repression of these acts of violence simply by acts of vengeance on the part of the general public and in order to satisfy the sense of justice of the civilized world."[8] The declaration implied that some form of international action would be required to bring the alleged criminals to justice, but it stopped short of producing any concrete suggestions. Nor did the United Nations War Crimes Commission, established in 1943, have any concrete recommendations for the form of justice to be applied to the Nazi war criminals. Although the commission collected evidence on war crimes and criminals with a view to future action, it struggled to develop an operating definition of war crime, finally settling on "criminal action violating the laws and customs of wars" as set out in the Geneva and Hague Conventions.[9]

The creation of an international tribunal to prosecute war crimes was not a foregone conclusion. In a joint declaration following the Moscow Conference in December 1943, the three main Allied partners noted the reports of Nazi atrocities, massacres, and cold-blooded executions, and announced their intention to return the responsible German officers and party members to the countries where they committed their crimes, to be judged and punished according to the laws of those countries at the time of armistice. One of the atrocities listed in the statement was the "wholesale shooting of Polish officers," implying Nazi responsibility for the crime. Neither Churchill nor Roosevelt objected to its inclusion.[10]

Privately, some, like US treasury secretary Henry Morgenthau and Britain's lord chancellor, Lord Simon, preferred to "shoot the Nazi leaders without trial."[11] Churchill was also not in favour of public trials, which were uncontrollable and unpredictable. At first, he promoted courts of inquiry for the purpose of identifying those who would be executed; their guilt was presumed.[12] Such lawless solutions were ultimately rejected. During the last days of the war and the summer that followed, while the search for Nazi leaders was underway, representatives of the Allied powers established a framework for the prosecution of war criminals. The Charter of the International Military Tribunal would bring charges against defendants for three crimes: crimes against peace, war crimes, and crimes against humanity. It also introduced the concept of conspiracy as one possible element of each of these crimes. The charter established a tribunal, created a prosecution process, and appointed an array of prosecutors and judges to conduct "the just and prompt trial and punishment of the major war criminals of the European Axis."

The charter took jurisdiction over individuals, not states, and defendants would be held personally responsible for their acts, whether or not they were acting under orders from their superior or their government. The trial would create a record of Nazi atrocities and ensure that those responsible for them would be held accountable before the world.

Article 6 of the charter defined the crimes within the tribunal's jurisdiction. Article 6(c), which included "murder, extermination, enslavement, deportation, and other inhumane acts committed against any civilian population," suggested that Wanda was one of the victims of a crime against humanity. She could equally have been a victim of a war crime, defined in Article 6(b) to include "ill-treatment or deportation to slave labor or for any other purpose of civilian population of or in occupied territory." An indictment gave details of the criminal acts alleged in the charter. In the third count, war crimes included deportation for slave labour and specifically mentioned deportation from the "Eastern Countries."

Arguably, the same words describe what happened to Casey, but since the Soviets were prosecutors and judges in the tribunal and not defendants, the tribunal offered no reckoning for him or the hundreds of thousands of others deported to Siberia in the early days of the war or for the Polish soldiers executed at Katyń. In fact, as the chief prosecutors prepared for the trial, representatives of the Four Powers agreed to work together to prevent the defence from making "political attacks" against them. To prepare for such attacks, they agreed to divulge, in writing, their own wartime aggressions. The Soviet submission referred to several issues of concern, including the German-Soviet Non-Aggression Pact of 1939 and Soviet-Polish relations.[13] As for Katyń, the Soviets were not prepared to abandon their claim that the Nazis were responsible for the deaths of the Polish soldiers. The indictment alleged that "In September 1941, 11,000 Polish officers who were prisoners of war were killed in the Katyń Forest near Smolensk."

Manic activity filled the months that followed, as the infrastructure for a major trial in Nuremberg was created. The choice of location was both symbolic and practical. Nuremberg had been the site of Nazi gatherings held every September, a week-long event of meetings, parades, and huge rallies. During the 1935 event, the Reichstag passed the racist and anti-Semitic Nuremberg laws. Nuremberg was also one of the few places left in Germany with facilities capable of holding a trial of the scale anticipated. Although bombs had destroyed most of Nuremberg, the Palace of Justice, with over six hundred offices and an attached jail, remained standing. The Allies set about renovating the building, creating a courtroom with security features, advanced simultaneous-interpretation and filming technology, and facilities for the press. Miles and tonnes of paper were created, gathered, translated, collated, and bound; hundreds of judges, prosecutors, translators, and clerical assistants were assembled and somehow housed; and prisoners were secured and interrogated. The bright lights of American and British media arrived in town, among them Janet Flanner and Rebecca West for the *New Yorker*, John Dos Passos for *Life* magazine, and William Shirer for CBS.

In November 1945, less than seven months after the war ended, the four judges appointed by France, England, the United States, and the Soviet Union called the tribunal to attention to begin the trial of twenty-two of the Nazi leadership accused of war crimes. The English judges sat without their wigs, in the same plain gowns as their American colleagues, Rebecca West reported, "as a sign that this was a tribunal above all local tribunals." As for the Russian judges, they sat in military uniform "as a sign that this was no tribunal at all."[14] The chief prosecutor, Robert H. Jackson, advised that the defendants' own speeches, films, books, and records would prove their crimes. This was particularly so in the case of allegations of deportation to slave labour; according to Jackson, "on few other subjects is our evidence so abundant and so damaging."[15]

For three days in December 1945, Thomas Dodd, an American lawyer and former FBI agent, presented the evidence against Sauckel and Albert Speer, Hitler's minister of armaments and war production. The transcripts of those days consist entirely of Dodd reading from the exhibits filed in the record. Trial transcripts make for dry reading even when they record the oral testimony of witnesses; that disadvantage was compounded by the fact that no witnesses testified during the three days of the prosecution case against Sauckel. Rebecca West observed, as the months of the trial wore on, that the Nuremberg courtroom became a "citadel of boredom," the proceedings a form of "water-torture, boredom falling drop by drop on the same spot on the soul."[16]

Largely missing from the transcripts of the trial were the testimonies of forced labourers who would speak directly and simply about the methods used to detain and deport them and the living conditions in the labour camps. Their words would have been a powerful indictment of the Nazi labour policy and added force and even more weight to the documentary evidence. But the trial was not designed as a platform for the victims of Nazi oppression and atrocities, and their voices were absent. By the end of the trial, only thirty-three witnesses in total had testified for the prosecution; the defence called sixty-one, not including the nineteen accused who testified on their own behalf.[17] The proceedings strained under the burden of conflicting expectations and more evidence than could be assimilated by the most detailed and observant judge; the stories of the victims would have to wait.

But even with these limitations, the evidence was horrifying, and it proved that Sauckel was both responsible for and aware of the widespread atrocities and human rights abuses that took place as local officials rounded up workers and deprived them of food, proper housing, medical treatment, and their humanity as they toiled in German factories and farms. The Nazi foreign-labour policy, Dodd said, was one of "mass deportation and mass enslavement...carried out by force, by fraud, by terror, by arson, by means unrestrained by the laws of war and laws of humanity, or the considerations of mercy." This included "underfeeding and overworking foreign laborers, of subjecting them to every form of degradation, brutality, and inhumanity," requiring foreign workers and prisoners of war to "manufacture armaments and to engage in other operations of war directed against their own countries...[in] a flagrant violation of the laws of war and of the laws of humanity."

The court heard evidence about the reports Sauckel received from Alfred Rosenberg, reichminister for the occupied territories, detailing the transfer of eastern workers to Germany. In one, Rosenberg told Sauckel of an increase in "guerilla bands" in the region, due to the fact that the recruitment of workers was through "forced measures of mass deportation." He could not have been clearer about what those measures were: "men and women including youngsters from 15 years on up...picked up on the street, from the market places and village festivals and carried off," public beatings followed by "burning down of homesteads, and of whole villages in retribution" for the failure of the locals to cooperate in their deportation.[18]

Rosenberg inadvertently provided the voices of the victims of the Nazi roundups. Dodd read from the letters of the missing villagers mentioned in Rosenberg's communication to Sauckel, their words describing a grim reality with an emotional force missing from many of the other exhibits filed:

> At our place, new things have happened. People are being taken to Germany. On October 5 some people from the Kowbuski district were scheduled to go, but they did not want to and the village was set on fire. They threatened to do the same thing in Borowyischi, as not all who were scheduled to depart wanted to go. Thereupon three truckloads of Germans arrived and set fire to their houses. To Wrasnyischi 12 houses and in Borowyischi 3 houses were burned.

> On October 1 a new conscription of labor forces took place....The order came to supply 25 workers, but no one reported. All had fled. Then the German police came and began to ignite the houses of those who had fled. The fire burned furiously, since it had not rained for 2 months. In addition the grain stacks were in the barn yards. You can imagine what took place. The people who had hurried to the scene were forbidden to extinguish the flames, were beaten and arrested, so that six homesteads were burned down. The policemen meanwhile ignited other houses. The people fall on their knees and kiss their hands, but the policemen beat them with rubber truncheons and threaten to burn down the whole village. I do not know how this would have ended if Sapurkany had not intervened. He promised that there would be laborers by the next morning. During the fire the police went through the adjoining villages, seized the laborers, and brought them under arrest. Wherever they did not find any laborers, they detained the parents until the children appeared. That is how they raged throughout the night in Bielosersk...

The workers who had not yet appeared by then were to be shot. All schools were closed and the married teachers were sent to work here, while the unmarried ones go to work in Germany. They are now catching humans as the dogcatchers used to catch dogs. They are already hunting for 1 week and have not yet enough. The imprisoned workers are locked in the schoolhouse. They cannot even go to perform their natural functions, but have to do it like pigs in the same room. People from many villages went on a certain day to a pilgrimage to the Poczajow Monastery. They were all arrested, locked in, and will be sent to work. Among them there are lame, blind, and aged people.

Dodd also presented an order issued to SS officers in Ukraine in March 1943, showing that SS troops were authorized to use extreme measures in recruiting foreign labourers. The order acknowledged that while it would not always be possible to refrain from using force, it would sometimes be "necessary" to burn down villages. "As a rule," the order continued, "no more children will be shot."

Sauckel testified on his own behalf. He was a poor witness, prone to making speeches or defensively cutting off questions in an attempt to cast himself in the best possible light. The judges frequently intervened to try to get him to answer questions directly, without much success. He argued that his own conduct was legal and justified by his duties and the conditions that existed in Germany. If foreign workers were mistreated by police who rounded them up or in the trains that transported them, abused in the factories where they worked, or starved and besieged in the barracks where they put up with vermin and a poor diet, that was someone else's fault. He was not responsible for how others treated the workers; in fact, he did all he could to ensure their conditions were correct. He had issued directives that they be treated fairly, paid, and fed as well as German workers. If he heard any complaint, it was usually that there were not enough workers to sustain production. On the rare occasions that he heard of problems, he expressed his dissatisfaction and expected the problem to be corrected.

In the end, though, Sauckel was not able to explain away his own admission that millions of foreigners had been coerced to work in Germany, as reported by an anonymous secretary at a meeting of the Central Planning Board on March 1, 1944. Sauckel had been ordered to produce an additional 4,050,000 new workers that year, and there was great debate about the difficulty of that mission. While some of those present apparently clung to the idea that the millions of foreigners in Germany were there voluntarily, Sauckel disabused them of that idea. "Out of the five million workers who arrived in Germany," Sauckel said, "not even two hundred thousand came voluntarily."[19] Sauckel tried to deny making this observation, blaming it on a mistranscription, but he finally conceded in cross-examination that his offices were in contact with chiefs of the police, the SD (Sicherheitsdienst or Security Service), and the SS for the accomplishment of their tasks, "not for the recruitment of workers as such, but only to remove difficulties or disturbances in administration." Later, he agreed with one of the judges that in the face of resistance, the army would "help with the recruiting." The euphemisms—"disturbances in administration" and "help with the recruiting"—may have allowed Sauckel to distance himself from the actions of others and keep his conscience clear, but the meaning was obvious enough.

Film of Sauckel's final statement, on August 31, 1946, shows him standing in the prisoner's dock, a microphone before him and headphones over his ears. His voice is strong, but the papers shaking in his hands betray his fear. He shows none of the bravado he had exhibited early in the war, when he told a meeting of party officials that "if we lose this war, not only will they hang me, but they will also hang you. This can be taken for granted."[20] He again proclaims his innocence and his disgust with what he heard in the trial.

"I have been shaken to the very depths of my soul by the atrocities revealed in this trial. In all humility and reverence, I bow before the victims and the fallen of all nations, and before the misfortune and suffering of my own people, with whom alone I must measure my fate," he said. He maintained his own innocence and reiterated his belief that he had not acted outside the law, saying in part, "even high-ranking Frenchmen, Belgians, Poles, and also Russians have told me that they were supporting Germany with labor in order to protect Europe against a threatening communist system, and in order to prevent unemployment and mass suffering during the war." Even at the end, he saw no difference between the interests of Germany and those of the conquered people.

On October 1, 1946, almost one year after they began, the four judges pronounced their verdicts. They found that the German occupation authorities were in "flagrant violation" of the terms of Article 52 of the Hague Convention, which prohibited requisition of labour that would involve civilians in taking part in military operations against their own country, when they deported at least five million people to serve German industry and agriculture. The "conscription of labor was accomplished in many cases by drastic and violent methods," the tribunal accepted. "Manhunts took place in the streets, at motion picture houses, even at churches and at night in private houses."[21]

Nineteen of the defendants were convicted of one or more war crimes. Twelve of them were sentenced to death, including Sauckel (three received life in prison, and four lesser prison terms). After hearing his sentence, Sauckel continued his protestations of innocence. In his jail cell, a trembling Sauckel told the prison psychologist, Gustave Gilbert, that he did not consider the sentence fair. "I have never been cruel myself—I always wanted the best for the workers—but I am a man—and I can take it." Then, he broke into tears.

The psychiatrists who spoke with Sauckel during his imprisonment found a man of limited insight, a blindly loyal servant of Hitler who spoke in platitudes and clichés. Douglas Kelley's assessment was perhaps the most damning. He found that Sauckel had "neither the breadth of vision nor the depth of conscience to realize his guilt." He thought that Sauckel actually derived satisfaction from being one of the accused, which elevated him from the status of a second-rate Nazi to one of the elite.[22]

Just after one a.m. on October 16, 1946, the Nuremberg jailors began to carry out the death sentences of the ten remaining Nazi leaders—Goering had just taken his own life with a hidden vial of cyanide, and Martin Bormann, convicted in absentia, had reportedly committed suicide in May 1945—in the gymnasium of the prison. As his turn came, Sauckel claimed, for the last time, that he was innocent: "The sentence is wrong. God protect Germany and make Germany great again. Long live Germany! God protect my family."

The bodies of each of the men were laid out and photographed. Then, under cover of darkness, the corpses were loaded on two trucks and escorted to Dachau, where their remains were cremated. There would be no witnesses or graves to permit the celebration of the men as martyrs to the Nazi cause. Denied a burial, Sauckel's ashes were scattered over the River Isar in Munich.

Reckonings, according to the historian Mary Fulbrook, are more than representations of the past, but attempts to "rectify a perceived imbalance after a period of acute turmoil," to quell disquiet from unresolved conflicts, and where imposed by law, to impose punishments or measures for compensation or restitution. The impulse to reckon with the destruction and chaos imposed by the Nazis was understandable, and the need to impose order and the rule of law in the immediate post-war period was overwhelming. But the scale, the horror, and the barbarity of the crimes against the millions of people injured, killed, or enslaved by the Nazis meant that ordinary tools of law and criminal responsibility would be inadequate to bring justice to the war's victims. Given the challenges facing the Allies as they embarked on the competing post-war projects of reconstruction and reckoning, the audacity and efficiency of the Nuremberg trial is astonishing, despite its frailties.

To many observers, the charter and the tribunal rested on shaky foundations. Western legal systems generally do not prosecute crimes under legislation created after the event. The prosecutors and judges were not neutral in the usual sense of the term, and many considered that the trial was no better than "victors' justice." The Allies were also guilty of their own crimes. Not only were the Soviets brutal to eastern Europeans in the first part of the war and to the Germans as they marched west, but also the Allies savagely bombed German cities and killed hundreds of thousands of civilians. Members of the press expressed doubts about the optics of such a trial. Charles E. Wyzanski, writing in the *Atlantic*, suggested that although "the world is most impressed by the undeniable dignity and efficiency of the proceedings and by the horrible events recited in the testimony," there was a risk that the trial would come to be viewed as "an example of high politics masquerading as law."[23] Or as E.B. White put it more plainly: "Nobody, not even victors, should forget that when a man hangs from a tree it doesn't spell justice unless he helped write the law that hanged him."[24]

It is hard to maintain the high moral and legal ground when the form of justice a country administers to outsiders does not meet its own standards, but other options seem no more palatable. Imprison or execute the Nazi ringleaders with no transparent process? Allow them to move freely in society? Rebecca West was among those who pointed out the absolute necessity of ensuring the criminals were brought to justice for all to see:

> It was not only that common sense could predict that if the Nazis were allowed to go free the Germans would not have believed in the genuineness of the Allies' expressed disapproval of them, and that the good Germans would have been cast down in spirit, while the bad Germans would have wondered how long they need wait for the fun and jobbery to begin again. It was that, there in Germany, there was a call for punishment.

In recent years, historians and legal scholars have re-examined the objectives and foundations of the Nuremberg trials, placing them in a continuum of developments in international law dealing not just with war crimes but the law of war and prohibitions against waging aggressive war.[25] The tribunal was only the first of many imperfect efforts, over many decades, to come to grips with the greatest world conflict ever to occur. By documenting the atrocities of war, it began an evolution in our reckoning with mass violence and persecution that places millions of tragic stories in the forefront.

The public inquisition that took place in Nuremberg was necessary for a world coming to terms with the shocking events of the war, but it was not sufficient for all purposes. Mary Fulbrook points out that in the years immediately following the war, hundreds of smaller trials took place: the twelve other Nuremberg trials that focused on particular crime complexes or selected perpetrator groups; 358 trials held in the British zone of occupation, resulting in 1,085 convictions and 200 sentences of death carried out; and tens of thousands of other cases tried in East and West German courts and in Austria. Subsequent trials in Poland resulted in the execution of at least 193 perpetrators, including Rudolf Höss, former commandant of Auschwitz, who was executed there in April 1947; Amon Göth, former commandant of the Płaszów camp on the outskirts of Kraków; and Hans Biebow, former head of the ghetto administration of Litzmannstadt (Łódź).[26] And surprisingly, in Norway, more than 90,000 cases of collaboration were investigated and 46,000 people sentenced, in trials that were held as late as 1957. The search for justice for victims of Nazi war crimes is ongoing, even today. In February 2021, a ninety-five-year-old German woman, the former secretary to the commandant of the Stutthof camp near today's Gdansk, was charged with aiding and abetting mass murder.

Only now, as we come to the end of the stage that Mary Fulbrook describes as the era of the survivor, have the voices of the victims occupied centre stage in our attention. As Fulbrook points out, it is only many years after the fact that the full extent of the damage caused can be assessed and felt; not just the trauma of the atrocities and murders as they were experienced in the moment but also the significance of the losses suffered in the process, of a past, and a future that could not be. The distance of many decades, and the perspective of the survivors and, sometimes, their offspring, allows us to take one step further in comprehending the price paid by the innocent victims of war.

It's unlikely that Wanda had ever heard of Fritz Sauckel, or gave much thought to what happened in the Nuremberg trial. For her, the face of Nazi injustice was probably not among the Nuremberg defendants but in the soldiers who patrolled the streets of her town and took her from her home, in the German company who profited from her labour, and in the guards who kept watch over her and mistreated her. Those men were not being prosecuted and never would be. It might also have disturbed her that the Soviets, who had terrorized her family, deported other Poles from her homeland, and tried to eliminate her Polish identity by forcing on her an unwanted language, culture, and citizenship, sat not among the defendants but the judges. She could have been forgiven for any cynicism about the rule of law, having lived for so long in a lawless world. But she was a practical woman, and forgetting would have been of more use to her at that point than remembering. Her attention was focused on finding her own way out of the camps in Germany and into her uncertain future.

CHAPTER 9
WINDS OF CHANGE

"Homeless, hopeless, buffeted by propaganda, a quarter million DP's rot in exile rather than face the real or fancied terrors of home."

The lead in a November 1, 1946, article in *Maclean's* magazine offered a dismal view of the displaced still in exile more than a year after the war's end. Journalist Blair Fraser visited several camps in Italy and Austria, where he found "civilization's problem children...drifting across Europe like tumbleweed or settled in stolid apathy in voluntary concentration camps." The problem, according to Fraser, was that the displaced were awash in propaganda about the alleged hazards of returning to their home countries, which were now under Soviet control. The Poles in the camps who were afraid to return to Poland, he found, had been influenced by the "bitterly and militantly anti-Soviet" Polish Second Corps or the Polish Red Cross, "another London-Government organization with a bitter anti-Soviet slant," who supplied them with propaganda disguised as educational material. He thought that a small percentage of the displaced might face a real danger in returning home, but "for the great majority there is nothing to fear beyond the common hardships of life in a war-ravaged country under a police state."

With the impending windup of UNRRA, Fraser recognized that a solution to the problem needed to be found and expected that nations like Canada and the United States would eventually be required to take a stipulated quota of the displaced. He noted that some were in favour of pre-emptive action: "Some Canadian officials think the smart thing for Canada would be to go into the DP camps now and pick out the most desirable immigrants we can find—men with skills that we can use," he wrote. "Then we could apply these selected immigrants to our quota when the time comes."[1]

In Wildflecken, Kathryn Hulme reflected that 1947 was going to be the "despair year" for camp residents, "their year of door-watching with all eyes focused on the tight-shut portals of the United States while iron curtains clanked ominously all around."[2] Canadian officials active in international affairs were well aware of the crisis of the large number of displaced who either could not or would not be repatriated. The Canadian government had donated substantial funds to relief organizations like UNRRA. The idea that the government response would go beyond relief to resettlement was gaining currency in the House of Commons, as the public began asking their members of Parliament for help in bringing family members to Canada. The government was slow to respond to these pressures. Fears of a post-war recession lingered, and a shortage of ships to transport people from Europe to Canada meant that Canadian servicemen and their dependants received priority. To the general public, the plight of Europe's displaced was of little concern in comparison to the anxiety about a recovering economy and the need to make sure returning servicemen could find work.

The government began considering amending the Immigration Act. Earlier versions of the act gave birth to a "White Canada" immigration policy, in which cabinet had almost unlimited discretionary power to control the number, ethnic origins, and occupations of immigrants. In 1931 Canada had closed the door to all but American and British subjects with sufficient means to maintain themselves until they secured employment; farmers with sufficient means to farm in Canada; and the wives and minor children of Canadian residents. Immigration to Canada trickled to the lowest levels since the turn of the century.

The Senate Standing Committee on Immigration and Labour produced a report that condemned the government's "non-immigration policy" and recommended that Canada revise its legislation to allow for the selection of as many of the most desirable immigrants as the country could successfully absorb. It also encouraged Canada, as a "humane and Christian nation," to do its share toward helping the displaced and refugees still in Europe. The report gained the approval of the press and MPs and, behind the scenes, of ethnic organizations, labour and industrial lobby groups, and public servants. Gradually, the door to Canada was pried open. The first tentative step was a regulation passed on May 28, 1946, allowing residents of Canada to sponsor first-degree relatives in Europe as well as orphaned nieces and nephews under sixteen years of age. In January 1947, cabinet approved an Order-in-Council permitting the admission of workers for the sugar beet industry under pre-arranged contracts, and beet growers descended on the displaced persons camps in search of workers, preferably from the Baltic region. Cabinet also grudgingly approved two schemes that would bring Wanda and Casey—separately—to Canada in June 1947. These schemes would become notorious and controversial. Both Wanda and Casey came to Canada as unfree but necessary labourers in the first stage of a post-war immigration wave that would fuel economic booms in the decades to come.

On a warm summer evening at the end of August 1946, H.R. Hare, a Canadian civil servant with the Department of Agriculture and head of the "Canadian Polish Movement Unit," was the guest of honour at a formal dinner in Ancona, Italy, held by General Anders. After arriving in Rome a day earlier, Hare and his team were escorted into Ancona by a specially detailed dispatch rider and later driven to dinner in Anders's private car, which had been a gift from Stalin. Hare arrived at a villa decorated with large Polish and Canadian flags, and as he entered the officers' mess, an orchestra played "The Maple Leaf Forever" and Polish national music for his benefit.[3]

Hare was in Italy to oversee the recruitment of four thousand Polish soldiers who would be admitted to Canada as agricultural workers in a program developed over the summer. This would begin the process of dispersing the Anders Army out of Europe to new homes around the British Commonwealth. The Canadian government was conscious of its obligation to share the cost of war but entered into the scheme reluctantly. The British were spending approximately two million pounds per month to maintain the Polish troops stationed in Italy and England.[4] In March 1946, General Anders met with the British government in London and reluctantly agreed to demobilize the Polish forces. Under the arrangement, Poles would resettle into civilian life either in Britain or elsewhere in the Commonwealth.[5]

Even before the war ended, the Canadian government acknowledged Canada's "moral obligation" to recognize the position of Poles who had acquired the status of British subjects. Canadian officials did not have a high opinion of the Poles they had encountered in the displaced persons camps in Germany, and they would not have been anxious to welcome them. One army major, on observing the Poles in Schleswig-Holstein, reported that they were "most undesirable people as immigrants." He predicted that they would be a charge to the state, and the police forces "will have their work doubled." The Poles, he wrote, would be quite happy to be either "unemployed or in jail."[6]

Since the beginning of the war, Canada had faced an agricultural labour shortage as men enlisted in the armed forces or gravitated to the cities where construction and manufacturing offered better wages and working conditions. Labour programs organized the deployment of farm workers, including some of the 23,000 Japanese Canadians who were forcibly evacuated from their homes in British Columbia after the bombing of Pearl Harbor and interned in camps and farms across Canada, and up to four thousand of the over fifteen thousand German prisoners of war who were relocated to Canada from Europe for the war's duration. When the war ended, the feared labour surplus did not materialize. Canada needed workers. In May and June 1946, Canadian and British officials discussed the possible "exchange" of Polish soldiers with those German prisoners of war.

The four thousand single Polish men admitted to Canada as agricultural workers faced certain conditions. Canada would take no financial responsibility for them until they arrived in the country;

the British would have to arrange and pay for their transportation. The Canadians would screen the men, and their employment terms were set in advance: a minimum wage of $45 per month for a two-year term, with a maximum of sixty hours per week during the farming season and forty-eight hours per week the rest of the year. If they completed their two-year contract successfully, they would be permitted to remain in Canada.[7]

The government announced the plan in May 1946. Although the authorities had no intention of telling the men they were being exchanged for Germans, the press made no secret of it; newspaper headlines announced that Canada proposed to "Bring Workers into Canada to Replace Nazis."[8] Public reaction was not positive. The usual complaints appeared in letters to the government and the press, as well as some novel ones: there were not enough jobs for Canadians; if any immigrants were to be allowed into the country, they should be of British descent; the Poles should return to Poland to rebuild their own country; as followers of the Church of Rome, they would be "opposed to British rule in Canada" and provoke civil unrest; the Poles were likely to be anti-Semitic and might have been Nazi collaborators captured by the Allies. One letter to the prime minister described it as "one of the most ridiculous ideas that could possibly be put forward."

One prominent objector was the member of Parliament for Lethbridge, Alberta, John Blackmore, a Mormon, who had numerous questions about the political allegiance of the soldiers as well as their religious persuasion. "Are they Protestant, atheistic, Roman Catholic, or Judaistic?" he wondered. "I believe every member of this House realizes that any preponderance of any one of these among new immigrants would certainly be creating a new handicap to large bodies of the Canadian people."[9] The minister of agriculture's reply was dismissive, although not entirely accurate: "I personally will say that I will not enquire as to the religious denomination of any immigrant who wants to come to Canada provided he is a citizen worthy to be received into the country," he declared. "There is no discrimination against any immigrant coming into Canada on the basis of his religion, and there has not been from any time back." He ignored the recent experience of Jewish refugees who had been refused entry to Canada, including the 907 passengers on board the MS *St. Louis* who were turned away from Canada in June 1939.

In spite of these protests, the mission continued. A multi-department committee undertook the complex planning needed to recruit five thousand immigrants, and bureaucrats, doctors, and RCMP officers went to Italy to screen applicants. Hare discussed the program with headquarter officers and area commandants of the Polish Second Corps. He also had dinner with Polish officers at Cingoli, a town occupied by Casey's unit. The soldiers' intelligence impressed Hare. He also found that each military unit was "a great family, wherein the organization contains, not only officers and men, but wives and families who have no other place to live." He wrote that the men looked to Anders "as the God who led them out of depression and misery."

Of the more than 7,000 officers and men who applied, 2,902 were selected after medical, security, and labour screening; they arrived in Canada later that year. Casey wasn't in this first group. He left Italy at some point with the other remaining soldiers and joined the Polish Resettlement Corps in England. We don't know where he was stationed, but one of his photographs, of soldiers on motorcycles driving past troops, is of the Twelfth Podolski Lancers at "Camp Shobdon," near Leominster, Herefordshire. Maybe Casey thought he would make his home in England. But when the Canadians returned for more farm workers in 1947, Casey applied. Another 1,624 men were approved for immigration, bringing the total number to 4,526. Casey was discharged on June 11, 1947, which means he must have sailed with the last group from Southampton, on June 24, 1947. His discharge certificate from the Polish Resettlement Corps, signed at Godalming, Surrey, says he was discharged "on emigration to Canada." His military conduct was rated "good."

Among Canada's parliamentarians, possibly no one watched these developments in immigration reform more closely than Ludger Dionne, a businessman and MP from Saint-Georges, Quebec, a city in the Beauce region, about one hundred kilometres south of Quebec City.

Ludger Dionne was born in 1888 in Sainte-Hélène-de-Chester, roughly one hundred kilometres west of Saint-Georges. His father, Vinceslas (or Wenceslas), was a local entrepreneur who began life in a farming family in the Kamouraska region. Wenceslas established general stores in Sainte-Hélène-de-Chester and Saint-Paul-de-Chester, branching out as a supplier to the dairy industry: cheesecloth, butter boxes, separators, milk cans. As the sons came of age, the family opened more general stores in Stratford and Garthby, and in the early 1900s, two sons, Amédée and Arsène, moved to Saint-Georges to expand the dairy supply business into the Beauce region. Around 1918, Wenceslas and Arsène founded V. Dionne et Fils, to manufacture, import, and sell dairy supplies. The company grew quickly, eventually employing more than five hundred people in Ontario and Quebec.

The youngest son, Ludger, was also the smallest. Childhood illness and injury—polio, and an accident between a horse and a car—left him weakened and dependent on a cane. In early photos, he appears slight and frail; in one, the fully grown Ludger stands on a step behind his brothers to reach their height. These early setbacks did not diminish his ambition and work ethic. Ludger joined the family business after completing his education at colleges in Arthabaskaville and Victoriaville, followed by a period at St. Jerome's College in Kitchener, where he studied commerce and became fluent in English.

After the death of Wenceslas in 1930, Ludger Dionne embarked on a period of business expansion, beginning with the St. George Shoe Company. In the midst of the Depression, in an isolated and underpopulated region of Quebec, Dionne managed to create as many as three hundred jobs. As his profile as a successful businessman in Beauce grew, he involved himself in local politics. In 1935, he ran a closely contested race for mayor of Aubert-Gallion against the incumbent, Albert Dutil, whom he beat by just three votes.

He continued as mayor until 1943, concentrating on community infrastructure projects like roads, sidewalks, and bridges.

Dionne's most significant business interest, the Dionne Spinning Mills, came about almost by accident. Cheesecloth was a high-volume item for V. Dionne et Fils, and Dionne thought it would be more profitable for the company to produce the textile as well as sell it. He visited a mill in Massachusetts to learn more about the production of cheesecloth and was persuaded that there was a better option, one with a market bigger than the dairy industry. With his brother Arsène, he built a mill in Saint-Georges West, just down the street from the town's church and convent, where they would manufacture not cheesecloth but synthetic fibres, starting with spun rayon. Dionne Spinning Mills began operations in 1941 and was immediately successful. Encouraged, Dionne took on additional projects: the Beauce Heel Company and Dionne Veneer Mills in 1943, a mill expansion in 1944, and a second spinning mill expansion in 1945.[10]

Dionne faced just one problem: there were too few people in the area to supply the labour needed to carry out his ambitions, and even if workers wanted to move to Saint-Georges, there was nowhere for them to live. Not one to be deterred, Dionne came up with some creative solutions. First, he bought a bus to transport workers from neighbouring villages to the mill, an expensive and complicated strategy that he abandoned after a few years. He also built ten town-house-style apartments to rent to workers for $20 a month. But this would not accommodate anywhere near the numbers needed to staff the mill.

Many of the mill workers were single women, and they, Dionne reasoned, required a different type of accommodation. In 1943, he approached the nuns at the local convent, the Soeurs du Bon-Pasteur, with a business proposition. He would build a residence attached to their convent that could house his young female workers. The location would be convenient for them, just down the street from the mill, and the residence would sustain itself with the room and board the convent charged the women. Although the arrangement would be a step removed from their conventional role as educators, the nuns were inclined to agree with Dionne, who, after all, was one of Saint-Georges's most prominent citizens. The nuns obtained their cardinal's approval, and the massive building, capable of housing 225 women, opened on August 15, 1945. One business journalist, writing for the trade publication *Canadian Textile Journal*, was impressed: "The structure is attractive, with excellently appointed lounges, first-class dining rooms, extremely well-appointed kitchens and well-furnished bedrooms. It is doubtful if in any part of Canada there is superior accommodation for girls employed in manufacturing industries."[11]

But the young women of the Beauce region had other ideas, and turnover of female workers at the mill continued. Dionne claimed that in 1945 alone, more than five hundred young women left their jobs at the mill because of a lack of suitable housing in Saint-Georges.

Maybe the problem wasn't lack of housing. Women represented a large percentage of workers in the textile industry, but their average wages were lower than those for men in the same industry and lower than the average industrial wage for both men and women in Canada.[12] And, despite claims that the Foyer, as it was known, provided superior accommodation, life in a room in a convent might not have been as pleasant for a young woman as Dionne imagined. In the social and economic climate of 1940s Quebec, the Dionne Spinning Mill would never be more than temporary employment for a young woman on her way to another life. But Dionne was not yet ready to believe this.

In the midst of his feverish business activity in the early 1940s, Dionne somehow found time to advance his political future. In the 1945 federal election, he ran as the Liberal candidate for Beauce after Édouard Lacroix, a business rival who had served as the Liberal MP for twenty years, moved into provincial politics. Dionne's opponent was Édouard's brother Charles Lacroix, who ran as an independent candidate. Dionne won easily; the seat remained in Liberal hands, and he went to Ottawa as a backbencher in the Liberal government of Mackenzie King.

It's not clear when Dionne began to consider the displaced persons of Europe as a possible source of labour for his operation. Immigration to Quebec, especially to the Beauce region in the twentieth century, had never been high; and during the Depression and war years, it was almost nonexistent. But in October 1946, he began to lobby his colleagues in cabinet to gain support for his request to bring to Canada one hundred young women from the displaced persons camps of Europe to work in his mill. To advance his private business interests, Dionne needed an exemption from the regulation limiting immigration. Not only that, but he would carry out the selection of immigrants himself.

As a member of Parliament, he had access to the politicians who could give him the exemption he wanted. He wrote several cabinet ministers, claiming that he could not secure enough workers locally for his spinning mill. He claimed that one-third of the machinery in the mill was idle because of the lack of operators. He could not keep his young female workers, because, he wrote, "the people have too much money to spend." They would only work for a few months, leave, and collect unemployment benefits. If he could bring girls from Europe to work for him, he assured his colleagues, they would be accommodated in a building "which is just as up to date as the Lord Elgin Hotel in Ottawa."

His first attempts were unsuccessful. The deputy labour minister rebuffed him and welfare minister Paul Martin did not even bother to reply to his letter. But in late January 1947, the mill manager, John Adams, was able to meet with mines and resources minister John Glen (he was also responsible for immigration) through the intercession of the Liberal MP for Dorchester. Glen was more receptive, and on March 31, 1947, Dionne received a cabinet order permitting the admission of one hundred women from Europe to work at the Dionne Spinning Mill, at wages as required by the law of Quebec.[13]

Dionne moved quickly to make the necessary arrangements, enlisting the help of various cabinet ministers and External Affairs bureaucrats to smooth his way. His passport renewal was expedited, and visas and military letters of permission were requested on his behalf. The secretary of state for External Affairs, Louis St. Laurent, instructed his undersecretary, Lester Pearson, to "facilitate [Dionne's] travelling," including letters of introduction to embassy and consular officials in London, Paris, Brussels, and Berlin. Given that the government had no specific interest in Dionne's plan, at least not yet, he generated a remarkable level of official activity to ensure his success.

Before leaving for Europe with his wife, Emma, Dionne took care of one last detail. He contacted Sister de-St.-Égide, the mother superior at the convent. "I will come to see you before I leave for Europe to look for Ukrainian Catholics," he wrote. "I have obtained permission to import 100. I will need to house them as soon as possible in the residence."[14]

Randomly conceived, rife with conflict of interest and religious bias, dependent on a private citizen to carry out the government function of selecting immigrants, Dionne's plan should never have made it onto the cabinet table, let alone into a government order. In its own way, though, it pushed the envelope forward when it attracted the attention of Canadians to matters of immigration, inadvertently reinforcing the government's role in planning sensible immigration initiatives.

More importantly for Wanda, this poorly considered cabinet order altered the trajectory of her life. Just as Casey was preparing to leave England for Canada, Wanda's time in Germany was about to come to an end as well.

Ludger Dionne with one hundred Polish women in Frankfurt, Germany.
Life magazine, May 1947. (Walter Sanders/The LIFE Picture Collection/Shutterstock)

CHAPTER 10
ONE HUNDRED GIRLS AND A SCANDAL

"From slave labour to slave labour!" In the UNRRA area headquarters office in Aschaffenburg, Germany, Kathryn Hulme banged on the switchboard and shouted in disgust. A businessman and politician from Quebec was waiting for her in her office, a "dapper little man with a lisp and a limp and a great big briefcase in his hands," who wanted to visit several camps near Frankfurt in search of young women to work in his spinning mill in Canada. Certain that headquarters would never allow him access, she telephoned her director to confirm that she should turn the man away.

Hulme had been assistant director of the camp at Wildflecken during Wanda's residence. She knew better than most the circumstances that brought thousands of Poles to Germany—and the reasons they refused to return to Poland. She pulled out the UNRRA directive that prohibited unauthorized visits from emigration officials to displaced persons camps, no doubt written with this situation in mind. She couldn't believe that UNRRA would agree to the separation of the young women from their families, after so much effort had gone into reuniting them. If UNRRA headquarters was going to allow what Hulme called "industrial wolves" like Ludger Dionne to travel through the camps and "scoop their rivals on cheap labour," she wanted no part of it.[1]

But Dionne had made the right connections once he arrived in Europe, and UNRRA brass didn't share Hulme's objections. The Intergovernmental Committee on Refugees (IGCR) agreed to work with him, and it took administrative control of the process, obtaining for Dionne access to the camps that he would not otherwise have been permitted to enter. Once the barriers were removed, Dionne toured several camps with a Polish American chaplain, where he made an initial selection of 130 young women who would be screened at the UNRRA emigrant assembly centre at Sachsenhausen, Frankfurt.

Wanda first met Dionne at Wildflecken and was one of the lucky few who met with his approval and made it through the first round of vetting. In Frankfurt, the screening and registration team—three Polish staff members of a Catholic agency that worked with the IGCR, five members of the Canadian immigration team, and two Americans, including social worker Jessamine Fenner—were on hand to make sure the women were physically and mentally fit and qualified to enter Canada. Dionne and the Canadian consul and vice-consul for Germany watched over the entire process.

In the meantime, Dionne was frantically making arrangements for chartered flights to transport the women to Canada. Too impatient to wait for ships sailing to Canada with room enough for his workers, he spent over $40,000 on the flights, more than half a million dollars in 2022 Canadian currency. The question of who was ultimately responsible for the cost of the flights would linger over Dionne as news of the immigrant millworkers spread, but Dionne paid for it up front, leaving one to wonder: if the mill was that profitable, why not just pay his workers better wages? Or, like a gambler, was Dionne so deeply committed to his dreams of business expansion that reason abandoned him, leaving him to bet everything rather than walk away from the table?

In mid-May, Wanda and the other women Dionne had selected travelled from their camps to the assembly centre, where they stayed for two weeks while the final screening took place. On the first day, forty of them lined up before the office even opened, "looking as if their big moment had come, as if life was now to start anew...eager to be medically examined, eager to tell their life history, eager to talk with Mr. Dionne."[2] To Jessamine Fenner, they might have been forty average American girls, except for the fact that most of them "were brought to Germany as slave laborers by Hitler or fled before the Russian army. A large number were completely alone in the world."

Like almost everyone who encountered the young women, Fenner referred to them as girls, not women, and commented on their physical appearance. Although their clothes were "on the shabby side," some managed an attractive, even smart, appearance that "belied their arrival by truck from a displaced persons camp the day before and their present barrack style of living with limited facilities." Some were obviously of peasant stock, while others had the "poise and manner which indicated a less humble start in life."[3]

After a political screening by a Canadian official, the women went for medical examinations, which included chest X-rays and blood tests. Those who passed were sent on to one of the Canadian consuls for a final interview about their suitability for admission. Some of the women were excluded because of detected tuberculosis; others were outside the age limit, illiterate, or of "doubtful moral character." Fenner did not seem to be troubled that Dionne was the final arbiter of this latter qualification, "since he knew the mores of the town of St.-Georges and was the one who would bear the brunt later on if things went wrong."

Before leaving, the young women signed a contract that bound them to work for Dionne Spinning Mills for two years in exchange for the legal minimum wage in Quebec; wage increases and piece-rate earnings above that rate would be held back by Dionne until the end of the two-year term. Dionne later claimed the IGCR insisted on the two-year term for the protection of the women and that he knew he would not be able to insist on completion of the term if a worker wanted to leave.

On May 28, 1947, a warm early summer day in Frankfurt, Wanda, just twenty years old, left the assembly camp for the Frankfurt airport in an army truck, part of the first group of forty women to leave. "Resettled in Canada" was scrawled in red ink across her displaced person's registration record, reducing UNRRA's responsibility for hundreds of thousands by one person. On Wanda's flight were women who became her lifelong friends: Niusia (Anna) Psutka, at sixteen years old the youngest of the women in the group, and sisters Bronia (Bronislawa) and Róża Kieliszewska. None of them had ever flown before, and they knew little about their destination. In an astonishing act of courage and hope, nervous, excited, and some a bit frightened, they departed from Germany on a Transocean American flight destined for Bangor, Maine.

When they arrived in Bangor the next day, they were greeted by members of the local Polish community, who presented them with traditional gifts of bread (that they may never go hungry) and salt (to overcome the bitterness in life) followed by a more American tradition of soft drinks and cookies. Reporters and photographers were there to document the event, giving the women a hint of the spotlight that would shine on them in the coming months. Two nuns from the convent and the mill manager, James Adams, were also on hand to accompany the women on the final leg of their journey, 260 kilometres by bus to Saint-Georges.[4] In Saint-Georges, more reporters and photographers, including a film crew from the National Film Board, descended on the small town to record the arrival of the women and the reaction of the local community to their presence.

The second and third groups left for Quebec on May 29 and 31, with Dionne and his wife among the passengers on the final flight. By June 1, all the women were reunited in the Foyer in Saint-Georges. Before he left for Canada, Dionne took the time to write to the convent to tell the nuns what to expect:

> The young women I chose to bring to St.-Georges were
> recommended to me by the Polish priests who administer
> the sacraments to the refugees. For the hundred I have
> chosen, I left crying another thousand who wanted to
> come to Canada and end their lives of uncertainty.
> These refugees fear being sent back to their country
> to live under the domination of the Russians if no country

Polish women gather in front of the Dionne Spinning Mill,
Saint-Georges, Quebec.

(*Slavs Depart, Polish Workers Arrive*; 1947, National Film Board of Canada)

gives them asylum. There are many Polish priests who are
waiting to be deported to Siberia by the Russians.

The Russian agents in some of the camps are very
cagey. They have spread a rumour around the camp where
I chose 23 young women that I will send them to Canada
to turn them into prostitutes. Among the young women
there is one who has completed three years of training
to be a doctor. She speaks English and told me of the
fears of the other young women. I told her that in Canada
white slavery is against the law, and she conveyed this to
her friends. These people have lived so long in fear and
suffering that they have become distrustful. Nevertheless
they are ready to emigrate anywhere to avoid the Russian
yoke. Among themselves they agree that they could not do
worse than where they have been. Many spent the war in
German concentration camps.[5]

Wanda, her mother, and three unknown women before Wanda's departure
(Courtesy George Surdykowski)

It's easy to imagine the combination of excitement and appre-
hension Wanda felt as she set off on a flight to an unknown country,
without her family for the first time in her life, not knowing when or
if she would see them again. Comparing the photographs of the young
women in Saint-Georges with some of those taken at Wildflecken
reveals that at least one other woman who was with Wanda at the
Wildflecken school was also there, so she might not have felt completely alone. And in the confines of the Foyer, new friendships
developed quickly. Maybe the thrill of being one of the chosen women
and leaving behind the small, pinched life of the camp overcame any
anxiety she had about the future or whatever sadness she felt about a
past world that was lost to her forever. Before leaving Germany, she
had posed with two other girls and two older women, one of them
her mother, for one last picture. They're seated on a bench in front of
some small trees, with a couple of large buildings in the background.
The young women are all smiling, and Wanda looks happy, but Helena
frowns, staring at the camera with a look of dread in her eyes.

#

While Dionne was busy in Europe, news of his trip spread in Canada, and opposition members began to press the government for details. On April 22, J.A. Glen, the minister responsible for immigration, was asked about a report in that morning's *Ottawa Citizen* that "a new immigration policy may come soon," and that the member for Beauce was in Europe, with the government's permission, to recruit workers for his textile mill. Glen replied that a new policy for immigration would be announced in due course. On the subject of Dionne's trip, the minister of labour, Humphrey Mitchell, added, "There is no secret about it." Dionne had received permission, in view of the labour shortage in the area, to recruit one hundred workers for his mill. Mitchell suggested the permission was granted "under the normal regulations," without offering any details about what those regulations might be.[6] Over the next few days, Mitchell tabled the specific Order-in-Council that approved Dionne's request and offered some details about the application. He still had no knowledge, however, of the terms of the contract between Dionne and the women.[7]

Prime Minister Mackenzie King finally announced the government's long-anticipated immigration policy on May 1, 1947. The policy's stated intention was to foster Canada's growth through immigration, but it left room for the government to continue its discriminatory practices. Although it supported an expansion of the numbers and groups to be admitted, changes would be related to the "absorptive capacity" of the economy. The 1923 Chinese Immigration Act, which barred almost all Chinese immigrants from entering Canada, would be repealed, but large-scale immigration from Asia would not take place, since it would "change the fundamental composition of the Canadian population." Preferred groups under the old policy would continue to receive priority.[8]

The policy also recognized a moral obligation toward refugees and displaced persons before any international resettlement agreement was reached. The first steps toward the early admission of some thousands of the displaced began with an Order-in-Council on June 6, 1947, authorizing the admission of five thousand non-sponsored people. Teams of immigration officials spread out across Germany to interview the displaced, looking for able-bodied men and women who could do the jobs that were unfilled in the Canadian economy. By July, the government had received requests for more than five thousand immigrants, mainly from the lumber, pulp and paper, and mining industries in what would be known as a "bulk labour" program.[9] Subsequent Orders-in-Council between July 1947 and October 1948 would result in the admission of another forty-five thousand.[10]

Any goodwill the more generous immigration policy generated vanished as more revelations about the Dionne affair came to light. "Help Wanted: Female" appeared in *Time* magazine on May 19, 1947, opening up the story to an international audience. The reporter described Dionne as "a religious man who goes to Mass every morning [who] also believes in the letter of the law," which included keeping his wages for the women to the legal minimum of $9.60 for a forty-hour week. (In fact, the women would earn just $3.60 a week after they paid their room and board to the nuns.) The reporter observed that both the Canadian press and the labour unions were divided over whether Dionne's scheme was a charitable act or a "great scandal" but noted that "among the 12,000 DPs in Camp Wildflecken, near Fulda, Germany, the idea sounds fine."

Another piece, a June 2, 1947, *Life* article by journalist Will Lang, described Dionne as a "tight-lipped little man with an abiding belief in old-fashioned virtue." Married, he had lost three children, and he took a fatherly interest in the young women whom he would "raise" with the help of the nuns in Saint-Georges. Although Dionne denied reports that he was demanding only virgins, the morals of the women were not irrelevant. He told Lang that one of his interview questions was, "You don't like to run around nights, do you?" In the residence at the convent, this would be impossible under the watchful eyes of the nuns and a strictly enforced early curfew.[11]

More specific information emerged on May 22, when the *Globe and Mail* interviewed Dionne in Frankfurt. He said that the one hundred

Polish women and nuns gather in front of the convent of
Soeurs du Bon Pasteur, Saint-Georges, Quebec.

(*Slavs Depart, Polish Workers Arrive*; 1947, National Film Board of Canada)

women chosen had been given permits issued by the Department of
Immigration and would be able to apply for citizenship after five years
in Canada. Their hours of work would be a six-day, forty-five-hour
week that would be paid at the minimum level set by the government,
with the difference between that amount and the higher average wage
at the mill to be paid to the individual worker at the completion of the
contract. Most of the cost of their flight would be borne by the mill,
with a portion paid by the IGCR. The women would live in the dormi-
tory attached to the convent near the mill, where the forty nuns at the
convent would "supervise" them. Strangely, Dionne's main concern
for the women was that "lacking the finery of their Canadian sisters,"
they would feel self-conscious during their first few weeks in Canada.
He hoped to alleviate that by making "modern clothing" available to
them at cost or below-cost prices.[12]

This led to further questions in the House of Commons on May 26,
when answers from Labour Minister Humphrey Mitchell only muddied

the waters. He produced information from the company's lawyer to the effect that none of the "girls" in the mill were employed at less than twenty-five cents per hour and that the average rate of pay was thirty-five cents. He also quoted from a letter from Dionne stating his intention to pay for their transportation but to include a contract term that would require them to repay this cost at a rate of about 25 percent of their weekly earnings. When asked whether this term would contravene the legislation that prevented the importing of labour, Mitchell replied that he did not know.

Much of the English-language press was sharply critical of Dionne and of the cabinet order that effectively authorized him to exercise the function of the government in immigration matters. The *Montreal Gazette* found it unfortunate that the only immigration immediately following the prime minister's statement "should be a shocking perversion of the selective policy so eloquently outlined by the Prime Minister."[13] As for Dionne, he "is not a humanitarian; he is exploiting the misery of the unfortunate," the paper said, taking advantage of the tragedy of war to meet his own company's needs. The *Globe and Mail* described the mission as "policy at bankrupt level," violating the spirit of the Alien Labour Act, which made it "unlawful for any person...to prepay the transportation of or in any way to assist, encourage or solicit the importation or immigration of any alien or foreigner into Canada under contract or agreement...to perform labour or service of any kind in Canada." It claimed the scheme of indentured labour under which the women were coming to Canada was a "modified form of slavery," a view shared by the director of the Textile Workers Union, who commented that the women were being placed in "industrial slavery."[14] The French-language Quebec press, more sympathetic to the Liberal government and thus ready to defend it, was more inclined to see Dionne's actions favourably and to describe him as a humanitarian and a victim of an unfair political attack.[15]

The controversy came to a head in the House of Commons on June 2, 1947, before Dionne had returned from Europe. While the debate originated with concerns about the government authorizing Dionne to recruit foreign workers, it opened up a number of sore spots in the Canadian political conscience: the lack of Canadian response to the post-war conditions of displaced persons; the absence of government policy or action on immigration; and the labour situation in Canada. It also raised concerns about Dionne's contract with the women and his conflict of interest.

M.J. Coldwell, the leader of one of the opposition parties, the Co-operative Commonwealth Federation (CCF), argued that Dionne's scheme contravened the government's policy against individuals importing labour, quoting from the mill manager's statement, reported in the *Montreal Gazette*, that "after the girls have paid back their fares, approximately $300 each, they are free to leave at any time." (The contract had not yet been disclosed to the opposition members, so the only information about its terms was what the press had reported.) If the women were in fact responsible for repayment of their airfare, this was indentured servitude and a "violation of human rights and fundamental freedoms; it is a violation of the principles we approved when we signed the charter of the United Nations." Coldwell also wondered what might happen if one of the women should have to be deported. Where would she be sent? And had the Polish government been notified that the women were in Canada?

Other members of the CCF weighed in. One pointed out that the only emergency being addressed by the Dionne scheme was his own need for workers and not the desperate condition of the displaced persons. Still others were concerned about Dionne receiving preferential treatment, when they had been unable to help numerous constituents who approached them about getting their relatives and friends out of the camps in Europe. Clarence Gillis, the CCF member for Cape Breton South, called the arrangement "a fire sale on human misery." Gladys Strum, the CCF member for Qu'Appelle, Saskatchewan, thought the scheme sounded like something out of "*Uncle Tom's Cabin*, which remind[s] one of the old slave markets."

Some members supported Dionne. Anthony Hlynka, the Social Credit member for Vegreville, Alberta, had travelled through Europe for several months, where he became aware of the plight of the displaced, "one of the most tragic situations that has ever faced the defenceless and homeless people of Europe." He was glad that there were businessmen who wanted to bring in some of them, before the "best type of people" were taken by other countries. No one who spoke was opposed to the admission of displaced persons on humanitarian grounds or to an increase in immigration to provide the labour needed for Canada's economy, but the consensus was that this should be done by way of transparent regulations that did not leave the immigration process to the whims of individual employers or industries.

The three government ministers responding to these criticisms focused on Dionne's humanitarian motives and, sidestepping the question of who should be responsible for providing passage to immigrants from displaced persons camps, claimed it was only to the benefit of the women that Dionne had found a way to get them to Canada. Secretary of State for External Affairs Louis St. Laurent claimed there was nothing wrong with allowing Dionne to go to Europe to choose his workers. The process was under the control of the immigration branch, which carried out the usual screening. Shouldn't people be pleased that at least one hundred of the displaced no longer had to tolerate the "agonies" of the camps in Europe? As someone who was familiar with Saint-Georges, "a little country village," he knew that Dionne had established industries so that the people of the region did not have to leave to find employment.

At one point in the debate, the government tendered a copy of the contract it claimed Dionne had made with the women. It contained no requirement that the women repay their passage to Dionne, but it did allow the company to deposit the difference between the minimum wage and the "current wages" into an account that would be payable after the two-year term of the contract had elapsed, earlier if both parties agreed to terminate it. John Diefenbaker, Conservative member for Lake Centre, Saskatchewan, methodically went through Dionne's public statements and communications to cabinet ministers, pointing out that this was not what Dionne had originally proposed. When the Order-in-Council was approved, he had clearly intended to hold back 25 percent of the women's earnings to reimburse himself for the cost of their transportation. The government had consented to and approved an order that the women Dionne recruited would be indentured servants, and the contract that miraculously appeared the afternoon of the debate could not alter that truth. Diefenbaker called Dionne's mission a "makeshift system designed apparently to meet the needs of one employer in this country," and argued that the Polish women came to Canada with their "freedom two years delayed, a freedom they must buy with the sweat of their brows."

The debate ended with Gladys Strum summarizing what all present had either said already or must have been thinking: that Canada had a moral obligation to the displaced, which should not be left to private individuals or businesses. It was Canada who should provide the transportation and establish immigration and citizenship rights for people who would be grateful "not to the honourable member for Beauce, but to Canada...because she has met her obligations."[16]

It was probably no more than a coincidence that the first Order-in-Council authorizing the admission of five thousand displaced persons was signed three days later, on June 5, 1947. While Dionne was in Europe, the government and public service were working out a selection policy for new immigrants, and such documents take time to get to the cabinet table.[17] But it's also true that the government knew what it had to do; it just hadn't gotten around to doing it. After the debate, it had no excuses for inaction.

Dionne's appearance to answer his critics in the House of Commons on June 13 was something of an anticlimax. First, he educated his fellow members about the economics of the textile industry in Quebec. He was chronically short of female help not because of low wages but because the young women who worked for him were doing it for pin money and would leave in the spring to help with the maple syrup and crops. They were not "industrially minded," looking for a career. Any disruption in his production affected not just him but the industry generally. When the textile mills he supplied went to the US for yarn, eventually the Canadian taxpayer paid because, thanks to wartime price controls, the government subsidized the cost of US yarns. The country had an interest in the steady supply of labour to Dionne's mill, he argued. "I cannot understand why I should be blamed for trying to improve the conditions in my mill, and at the same time to improve the conditions in other mills in Canada," he said.

Dionne denied underpaying. They would receive twenty-five cents an hour for the first month, increasing to thirty cents the second month. Once they gained experience, they would be paid on piecework and could make from $16 to $25 a week. Their room and board was only $5.50 to $6 a week. Those wages compared well to those paid in Ontario, he thought, where the cost of living was so much higher. Dionne also pointed out that it cost him $100 to train each woman; given the turnover of 550 women in one year, the cost to the mill was $55,000. "Do you not think that an employer who knows his business would prefer to give this $55,000 to his employees rather than lose it in inefficiency and be always operating with learners?" he asked.

Dionne admitted that his motive was business, but when he witnessed "the great human distress it finally ended in a humanitarian action." He painted a portrait of conditions in Europe, where refugees were living "under the shadow of hunger, despair and violence" and "dying daily in these camps." He had assumed the guardianship of these "war-torn refugees...who seem to be very happy to have something to eat when they are hungry and enjoy freedom." He was proud of what he had done, and he would do it again if necessary.[18]

A *Globe and Mail* editorial found little of substance in Dionne's speech. The government had delegated authority to a businessman to create a private immigration scheme and did not even know the terms of the contract he proposed. The government was willing to permit the women to be brought to Canada as indentured servants, no matter what was contained in the contract ultimately produced by Dionne.[19] A *Maclean's* editorial supported the opening of Canada's borders to the displaced of Europe, but employers, it argued, should not have "carte blanche to import indentured workers on terms the Government doesn't even know."[20]

Away from the spotlight, the young women were busy establishing friendships among themselves in Saint-Georges and trying to have the kind of life the young Québécoise women among them took for granted. After years in threadbare clothing, either donated or handed down, they spent some of their wages on luxuries they had never had—stockings, makeup, clothing. Photos show them posing on a wintry street, garbed in new coats and boots, their hats obviously chosen for style rather than warmth. In the summer, they posed in bathing suits, leaning against some rocks in the river, or in a park. They look like women who have always been accustomed to strolling freely down the street or lounging around, swimming and picnicking with friends.

To the young women, the attention they attracted must have been perplexing and annoying. They found themselves objects of curiosity to the press and the local populace and political tools for a variety of special interests. A Beauceville newspaper reported on June 12, "certains automobilistes sont une vrai menace publique." Young men had taken to driving back and forth in front of the Foyer, honking their horns at the residents and following them as they walked on the street.[21] A journalist and member of the communist Polish Democratic Association (PSD), Władysław Dutkiewicz, established contact with some of the women to learn about their treatment. When a couple of them complained to him, he encouraged them to flee, telling them they should "escape that prison house" and come to Toronto, where they could earn as much as $20 to $30 a day. Bizarrely, he also published their names and addresses and encouraged his readers to write to them.[22] One reporter seemed to find it relevant that, several months after their arrival in Canada, none of the young women had gotten married or found a boyfriend.[23]

In spite of all the speculation, none of these reports say much about the daily lives of the Polish women in Saint-Georges or their own feelings about their new lives. Newspaper accounts, mostly written by men, focused on the political controversies and showed little curiosity about or understanding of the young women as individuals. An exception to this was a visit from Jessamine Fenner, who had met them during their screening in Frankfurt. Aware of the public attention the women had received since their arrival, she thought it seemed important to tell their story "from the inside" and to bring it up to date. Fenner visited with the women in Saint-Georges over several days. She spoke with individuals and groups, went to the Foyer on Saturday night to watch a movie with them, took some of them for a Sunday drive, shared their meals, and toured the factory. The mill, she reported, was "new and clean and modern, even if noisy." Some of the women reported that the work was hard and life was limited, "but at least we are out," meaning the camps. They worked in two shifts, eight hours a day for five days a week and a half-day shift on Saturdays. Since the Foyer was only a couple of blocks from the mill, they went home for lunch.

Their complaints were consistent and not especially damning: the food was boring, and the rules in the Foyer were strict. But Fenner was confident that Dionne would not try to retain anyone who wanted to leave, and ten of the women had already left by November 1. Still, she felt the women had a moral responsibility to complete the contract, and she thought most of them would, despite "some present discomfort."[24]

It's unclear how Fenner, an American who had been working with displaced persons in Germany at the end of the war, was prompted to make her way to Quebec to see the women. Her article was published in a January 1948 issue of *The Survey*, an American social work journal. Who sponsored her trip? She disclosed that Dionne had written to her in October 1947, responding to many of the criticisms that had been levied against him. Whether she approached him, or he invited her in the hope of dispelling some of the negative publicity, is unknown. In the end, she supported his view of the situation. She didn't doubt that Dionne's purpose was to help the displaced and secure labour for his mill. The Quebec wage scale wasn't defensible, but at least the women would have a chance at life in a free country, with better living conditions than they had enjoyed. A letter she had received from the

Two Polish women at work in the Dionne Spinning Mill.

(Slavs Depart, Polish Workers Arrive; 1947, National Film Board of Canada)

Polish American chaplain in Frankfurt bolstered her opinion. He wrote that the criticism of Dionne showed how little people understood the situation of the displaced in Europe. "Anything, just anything, will be a little better than what awaited these girls in Germany," he told her. "Only by comparison can one fully appreciate what Mr. Dionne has done."

The negative publicity as well as the Canadian Polish Congress and communist Polish Democratic Association's complaints to the labour minister about mistreatment of the women, prompted the government to do some damage control. It appointed Victor Podoski, a former diplomat associated with the Polish Foreign Office from 1921 to 1945, to travel to Saint-Georges to interview the young women and report on their treatment. Podoski observed the working and living conditions of the women, and he spoke with each of them at least once. He also interviewed Dionne and other members of the mill staff, the Polish priest who attended the women, and a number of local people, including the parish priest. He released his report on

September 23, 1947. Podoski was not persuaded of any deficiencies in the treatment of the young women. Referring to the allegations of "conditions of virtual bondage," he thought the problem arose through the emotional but well-meaning reaction of an uninformed group, and the "malice of some (a few) whose aim it is always to create unrest and stir up trouble." He concluded, "my own conviction is that the labour conditions of the Polish girls are quite satisfactory, that living conditions are very good, and that the treatment is absolutely fair and truly Christian." He observed that the security surrounding the young women was intense, but, he noted, Dionne felt a grave responsibility for their well-being. He was satisfied with their living conditions and wrote that he would not wish for better for his own daughter.[25]

But things for the women may not have been quite as rosy as Podoski's conclusions suggested. On the question of repayment of travel costs, Podoski received information that Dionne had actually paid over $50,000 in airfare and recovered $20,000 from the IGCR, the equivalent of what the IGCR would have paid for the women to travel by ship. The remaining cost per person worked out to $338. If the women remained until the end of their contract, they would have as much as $500 in their withheld pay to be turned over to them. Contrary to what had been reported, Podoski understood that if the women left before the end of the term of their contracts, Dionne was entitled to keep the withheld pay, indirectly recovering at least part of his transportation costs. It seems obvious that this provision was a form of insurance for Dionne. For the women, it was a form of coercion to maintain their part of the bargain.

Podoski accepted the need for Dionne's paternalistic treatment of the women, which he saw as necessary to help them take their first steps in Canadian life and protect them from danger. But he also noted some oppressive practices carried out under the guise of protection. According to the women, uniformed police officers often stood outside the mill when they left and sometimes followed them to the Foyer or from the Foyer to the stores. Understandably, this left them feeling nervous. When questioned about it, the chief of police speculated that what looked like "following" might merely have been his men taking their usual route from headquarters to the centre of town. But Dionne admitted that the police would stand outside the mill "to discourage young men of improper conduct to invite girls into their cars and take them to the woods or to the cabins." Podoski had been told of such attempts and, he wrote, some of the women had themselves asked for protection.

Podoski's report seemed to mollify those still paying attention to the issue. Columnist Richard Needham wrote, approvingly, that although the girls were "sternly protected against contact with strangers who may have a bad influence on their behaviour and morals...it must be remembered that these girls have no fathers and mothers to look after them; they consequently would seem to need special attention."[26]

In Warsaw, the chargé d'affaires of the Canadian Legation, Ken Kirkwood, was just settling into his new role when he was summoned to a meeting with a Polish foreign affairs official on May 27, 1947. The purpose of the meeting was to advise him of an impending protest over the Dionne affair, which, according to the note handed to Kirkwood, involved one hundred Polish girls described (incorrectly) as between thirteen and sixteen years of age. The girls were Polish citizens, under the protection of the Polish government, which was working toward repatriation of all Polish subjects; their ages would offend child labour laws anywhere; and the Canadian government had made no effort to inform the Polish government of its plans. The official protest that followed on June 3 told the Canadian government that Polish citizens now living abroad were needed to take an active part in rebuilding Poland and "should not be regarded as a human reservoir upon which a foreign country could draw without the approval of the Polish government." Any decisions regarding resettlement of Polish citizens should be made "only on the basis of bilateral agreements with the Polish government."[27]

For the next year, External Affairs officials in Ottawa and Poland would be occupied with defending claims about the mistreatment of the Polish women in Saint-Georges while simultaneously trying to maintain a cordial diplomatic relationship with Poland's emerging communist government. The first step was a polite but firm response to the Polish protest; Secretary of State for External Affairs Louis St. Laurent expressed the government's sympathy for the Polish desire to repatriate its citizens and affirmed its policy to encourage the voluntary repatriation of displaced persons to their countries of origin. There was no contradiction between this policy and Canada's willingness to admit those who came to Canada voluntarily and who were free to return to their homes if they wished, he argued. Concerns about whether a choice to emigrate was freely made should be directed to the authorities responsible for administering the displaced persons camps. St. Laurent did not agree that the Canadian government was obliged to consult with or obtain the consent of the Polish government before admitting Polish nationals to Canada, a position it took with respect to any other country.

The Polish government chose another line of attack in the fall of 1947, which took much longer to resolve. On September 29 the Polish chargé d'affaires in Ottawa, Z. Bielski, made an official inquiry about the living conditions of the Polish women in Saint-Georges, repeating many of the charges that had been raised and addressed in the House of Commons, the press, and Victor Podoski's report. The women were paid less than the minimum wage; any surplus they were entitled to for piecework was withheld from them; the women were not free to move about during their leisure hours and were prevented from learning English; and most damaging, the selection of the women preferred those who were "the most docile kinds of workers, if possible illiterate," who would be helpless and at the mercy of their new employer.

Given that Podoski was associated with the pre-war Polish government, his report would not have been given much credit by the new Soviet-backed government. From Warsaw, Kirkland reported the renewal of a "vitriolic press campaign" about the Dionne workers in September and October 1947. Scores of articles had appeared in the press throughout Poland, many of them including the word *slave*.

The headlines were outrageous — "Grim Mediævelism in Canada"; "Bestial 'Slave-Merchant' Jails and Still Tortures Polish Girls" (*Polish Word*, Wrocław); "The Canadian Hitlerian and the Polish Slave Girls" (*Popular Kurier*, Łódź) — and not taken seriously by informed Poles, but Kirkwood thought they may have been intended as a message to Poles remaining in the displaced persons camps about their fate, should they decide not to return to Poland. He thought the source of the campaign may have been the Polish Congress in Canada, and while it was unlikely the Polish government initiated it, that didn't mean it hadn't given its blessing. As well, he considered that a smear campaign might be only "one facet of the Communists' general anti-Western and anti-capitalist propaganda," unfortunately deployed against one of Poland's "benevolent friends."

Similar allegations had appeared even in the Soviet press. In June, the chargé d'affaires in Moscow was advised of a number of articles, such as one in *New Times* entitled "The Slave Market in Canada." Another item in *Vechernyaya Moskva* was a general critique of the Allied plans to facilitate the immigration of displaced persons, with special attention to the Dionne affair, whose workers were "doomed to slavery sanctified by law." An open letter to the editor of the *Toronto Daily Star* by a prominent Soviet trade unionist, Elena Kononenko, published in the Soviet labour newspaper *Trud*, described the women as "beasts of burden" who had been sent to Canada in a "monstrous transaction," comparing Dionne to Simon Legree of *Uncle Tom's Cabin*.

The Bielski letter was sent to Dionne for his input, and he in turn gave it to the Polish women for their reaction. Dionne had little to add to what he had already said in his House of Commons speech. With respect to their finances, he said only that when the women were short of money and asked for it, they got it "even if they have no more reserve left in our books. In other words, I try to treat these little girls as I would like to be treated if I was in their place."

One of the women, Stefania Zacharska, wrote a lengthy and indignant response, reportedly on behalf of all the women. It was clear that she regarded Bielski, a Communist representative, with suspicion and mistrust. While in Germany, the women had already resisted the efforts of the Soviet-backed government to lure them back to Poland, and to them, Bielski was likely no more than just another Soviet lackey whose motives had nothing to do with their actual well-being. They may have found his interest in their situation somewhat threatening.

One of the External Affairs officials found her remarks about Bielski "scurrilous," and the department made no effort to refer to them in its eventual reply to the inquiry. But after months of silence from the Polish women while they were under the microscope, Zacharska took the opportunity to show that they were not at all the "little girls" Dionne thought they were, or as the press portrayed them, but women with their own opinions about their best interests. She wrote that their compensation was just as agreed in Germany and not lower than that paid to Canadian girls. No one restricted how they spent their time; "don't forget that we are grown up and nobody can order us around nor dispose of our time," she chided him.

The women were "stung most of all by the assertion that girls who came to Canada were selected from the lowest class." This was hurtful and untrue. Zacharska could only wonder at a man who, "pretending before strangers to be a Pole, [would] humiliate Poland at the same time in the eyes of the world." If they were so uneducated and helpless, why was he interested in them? She felt it was her duty to express gratitude to Dionne, "who is constantly being reproached for having brought us over to Canada." She ended the letter with a dig at the motives of the current Polish government and a plea. "Why didn't you take some interest in us in 1939, when so many of our brothers perished in chains in Siberia and 12,000 in Katyń?" she asked. "Please let us alone. As from today, we absolutely release all improvised guardians of any responsibility in regard to us, which they have taken upon themselves, we don't know upon what grounds."[28]

Bureaucrats had grown weary of what they viewed as a self-inflicted wound that they were called in to treat. Lester Pearson, soon to enter politics himself, probably spoke for all his public service colleagues when he wrote that he hoped the government would not get involved in "further immigration arrangements of this kind."

Privately, in discussions with his colleagues, his views were probably more forcefully expressed.

It took over three months for St. Laurent to reply to the Bielski inquiry. In his letter, he reiterated all the information that had already appeared publicly about the terms of the contract between Dionne and the women and their living conditions at the Foyer. He advised that the women had been selected with the assistance of the National Catholic Welfare Conference in Frankfurt, which had been authorized to act by the IGCR. The government did not believe that these reputable organizations would have permitted the use of the selection criteria Bielski suggested.

Lester Pearson sent a copy of St. Laurent's reply to Bielski's inquiry to Dionne but requested that it be kept confidential: "Mr. St. Laurent has decided that it would not be advisable to revive interest in the press in this matter and we do not propose to publish this note or to issue a press release on the subject unless renewed press attacks in Poland make this advisable." Given the request for confidentiality, it's unclear whether Dionne shared it with the Polish women. If not, that is unfortunate. They would have been most pleased by St. Laurent's defence of their dignity in his undiplomatic response to Bielski's allegations about the selection criteria: "I can only assume that this unsupported allegation was transmitted in ignorance of the facts."

CHAPTER 11

FREE BUT NOT FREE

In the end, Dionne's foreign-labour experiment was thwarted not by the censure of the Canadian public, or the international tensions he created between Canada and the new government of Poland, but by the very thing that led him to Europe in search of workers in the first place: his unwillingness to pay his workers a decent wage.

"Union Says, 'Welcome, Girls,' Rushes to Organize Them."[1] Dionne's recruiting mission got the attention of Canadian labour unions, and the Textile Workers Union (TWU) soon joined the reporters, photographers, and curious onlookers who descended on Saint-Georges. The TWU began an organizing drive, distributing flyers and trying to speak with the Dionne workers. "Break the Chains of Slavery," one flyer proclaimed. "A union in your factory means better wages…job security…rules for grievances….To gain these conditions in your workplace, join the Textile Workers Union."[2] One afternoon, roughly two hundred demonstrators assembled outside the mill, carrying pickets and handing out flyers with slogans written in French, English, and Polish: "Twelve dollars a week is not a decent wage" and "French and Polish workers unite for decent wages, shorter hours, better working conditions, job security."[3] Members of the syndicats catholiques (a collective of Catholic unions in Quebec, affiliated with the Confédération des travailleurs catholiques du Canada) showed up, possibly hoping to crowd out their competition by renting all the meeting rooms in the town.[4]

Dionne quickly responded. On his return from Europe, he told the
Montreal Herald that "those unions have no right to be criticizing me."
They had shown no interest in helping find the labour he asked for,
and they failed to see that if his production increased, other factories
would benefit. He also claimed that the TWU "can't get to first base"
in his mill, because two years earlier the Catholic union had made
an agreement with the mill that still stood.[5] Dionne may have been
grandstanding. If the Catholic union was the bargaining agent, where
was the collective agreement? The mill manager, James Adams, told
the *Toronto Star* that two years earlier it had called on the Catholic
union to organize the plant, but it failed because the workers didn't
want to pay the dues. "They see no need of it because of their good
working conditions," he claimed. He added that the TWU had shown
no interest in the mill before the Polish workers arrived and said he
didn't think they would have any success with the Dionne workers.[6]

When Jessamine Fenner visited the Polish women a few months
after their arrival in Quebec, she interviewed a public relations officer
for the TWU. The union's attacks on Dionne had been "so violent"
that she wanted to know if it really believed there were one hundred
"slave labourers" in Saint-Georges. The union representative told
her that the union didn't believe that there was a labour shortage
in rural Quebec. Instead, wages were too low to retain workers.
If Dionne paid his employees a fair wage, he would not have had to
go to Europe for more workers. As for the Polish workers, the union
accepted that the women were likely better off than they would have
been in a displaced persons camp. The living conditions in the Foyer
seemed satisfactory, and the conditions in the mill were normal. It
feared that by importing workers, Dionne (and other businesses that
followed his example) would artificially depress wages in the region.
Fenner thought this meant that the union concern was not so much
for the "tough deal" the women had made as with wages generally,
as if these were mutually exclusive. But the union clearly understood
the position the women were in: "With his Poles [Dionne] will have
secured a sizable nucleus of workers who will be a future stable group
because of the handicap of language, lack of acquaintances elsewhere,

and an inability to get better jobs even at the end of two years. They are free but are they free?"

The answer to the last question became evident within a year. By August 1947, the mill entered into negotiations with the Fédération nationale catholique de textile. If Dionne thought he would enjoy some gentlemanly negotiations with a Catholic union, he was badly mistaken. Bargaining centred on the wages paid to the mill workers, with the union seeking a fifteen-cents-an-hour increase, the same as it had won for its members in recent strikes at Dominion Textile. This increase would still leave the wages below the provincial average, but Dionne refused. The parties could not reach an agreement, and they moved on to mediation. The mediator recommended an increase of seven cents an hour, but Dionne refused to implement even this suggestion. With no further progress likely, the union called for a strike at the Dionne Spinning Mill. Of the 350 mill workers, 150 were members of the union, and 142 of them voted to stop work.[7] Production ground to a halt on July 19, 1948, just over a year after Wanda arrived in Saint-Georges.

The strike escalated tensions between Dionne and the union—and, as the citizens of Saint-Georges took sides, in the town in general. There were acts of sabotage at the mill, windows and streetlights were broken, and non-union members were prevented from entering the mill by picketers. The union denied responsibility for pushing the mill manager's car into the river. Dionne obtained an injunction against picketing, and he sued the union for damages. The police were called in at the end of September, when Dionne claimed that the union was preventing workers from returning to work. Twenty officers appeared on September 24 to escort the non-striking workers into the mill. The strike ended soon afterward, when the Quebec labour minister finally brokered a deal that included a wage increase of only 5 percent and a provision that preference in rehiring was to go to residents of the town, including the Polish workers.[8]

But by the end of the strike, only eighteen of the Polish women remained, and the number declined further in the fall of 1948. By November, Sister St.-Égide reported, "The strike declared at Dionne

Spinning Mill on July 19, lasting 70 days, dispersed fifty of the Polish women. They are now for the most part in Toronto and Montréal. One of them, Zdzislawa Solecka, was adopted by Mr. and Mrs. Jules Baillargeon of Saint-Georges. Ten remain in the residence."[9]

What did the Polish women make of this? For a long feature article in the *Montreal Standard* magazine, Mavis Gallant, then a journalist and later an acclaimed literary figure, interviewed some of the forty-seven women who remained in Saint-Georges during the strike. Some of the women had departed with Dionne's consent, she wrote, but many more simply packed up and left for textile mills around Montréal, or other industries in Toronto, western Ontario, and as far west as Alberta. A few had married, and four more had gone to the United States. Of those still in Saint-Georges, only a few intended to work out the remaining months of their contract; they were simply not happy.

In the media circus that followed their arrival in Canada, almost no one had taken the time to listen to the young women and understand their experience. Reporters, investigators, and even union organizers commented on their appearance, made assumptions about their lives, and saw their existence through the filter of paternalism. Their Polish compatriots were no better, as Gallant observed: "Poles from all over Canada, left, right, centre and crackpot, descended on the little town." Hysterical stories appeared in the communist Polish-language press about the "bondage" in which the girls were kept, and "Polish national groups warned them about a thousand things, told them what to say, cajoled them, threatened them, and mostly just pestered." According to the village priest, representatives of the far-right "violently nationalistic" Polish Congress in Montréal contributed to the isolation of the girls, instructing them "to go out with Polish boys only and to marry Poles," holding out the hope that a return to Poland would be possible once Poland was liberated from the Russians.

After all this, the women were not inclined to trust outsiders. Even the Polish priest who heard their confessions struggled to connect with them. At first, Mavis Gallant may have appeared to the women as just another journalist who wanted something from them, but she paid close attention to where they lived, how they spent their time, and what they said, and in her essay, their voices were finally heard. She found a group of dispirited young women who weren't members of the union—reportedly because they weren't Canadian citizens—and didn't really understand what the strike was about but were alarmed because they couldn't work. They told her that they had signed some documents, but when a union meeting was called, the nuns discouraged them from attending, telling them, "such meetings were for Canadians, not Poles." They were in an extremely vulnerable position. Without work, they had no earnings and were unsure if they would end up owing money to Dionne, who was paying for their room and board out of their funds. When some of the women asked permission to find other work during the strike, they were refused. With no work and nothing to do, they were "nearly beside themselves with boredom."

Gallant found that money was a prominent concern; to the women, money meant security. They were aware that their wages were less than were paid elsewhere and had an understandable desire to earn more. To make matters worse, just before the strike was called, the mill had been running only three or four days a week, and their low pay barely covered their room and board. One woman reported making about $16 in an average week; from this, she paid $7.50 to the Foyer, and the company held back $4 for her "fund," leaving her with only $4.50 for the week. The company told Gallant that if the women needed money, it would advance it from the held-back funds or give them a loan if their need exceeded their savings.

The accounting of their "funds" seemed to be a mystery to the women, which must have contributed to their anxiety as the strike wore on. If they wanted to send a parcel to relatives in Europe, they had to ask for an advance from the office and sign for it. The nuns retained their identity documents for safekeeping, which bothered the women. They knew they would need them if they wanted to leave. Dionne told Gallant they could have their documents whenever they wanted; they were "kept away from them for their own good," a phrase Gallant heard often in Saint-Georges. She spoke with an official at the plant, who told her the women could have the visas, "but they must have a good reason."

It seems clear that, by the time of the strike, Dionne was not inclined to lose any more of his Polish workers. Some had already left before then; the women told Gallant that, at first, Dionne would release anyone who had a good job to go to, but they believed that now he had lost half of his group of workers, he wouldn't let any more of them go.

"Dionne more or less confirms this," Gallant wrote. He said, "It cost me $35,000 to bring them here.... They don't have to pay me back in money but morally they owe me something. I should get some return on the investment."

The workers' unhappiness was partly due to the narrowness of life in Saint-Georges, a small town of only 9,500 people. Roughly six years earlier, it had been a "sleepy Quebec village" with virtually no industry. For energetic young single women there was not much to do: three movie theatres, a few stores, and several hotels. The clergy had banned dancing (except square dancing).

In the Foyer, the women had a curfew of 11:00 p.m. Any socializing was done in the large reception room with glass doors, "furnished in the rather cheerless manner of most Quebec convent *parloirs*." The nuns closely questioned all visitors. Even Gallant was refused admission. "On my first visit, for instance, the Sister presiding at the door refused to accept a press pass as a credential, and took the entire wallet away twice to be examined by her superiors," she wrote. "I was not allowed upstairs until I returned with a company official. The Sister explained to him that she thought I might be a communist spy."

The women resented the supervision and scrutiny. They disliked having their morals a subject of conversation and bearing the unwanted attention of local young men who came to see them or drove by in cars shouting outside the Foyer. The nuns and Dionne unduly restricted their contact with local people; one family invited several women to Christmas dinner, but Dionne refused to permit it. A young woman attempted to visit some of the women at the Foyer, but the sisters put her out.

In the community, Gallant observed an attitude toward the women of "curiosity, pity, and a very slight hostility." In the spinning mill in particular, the arrival of the women was met at first with "tremendous hostility." Dionne realized the Canadian workers felt the Polish women had been brought in to keep wages down. "I never had trouble with the union until they came," he insisted to Gallant. The community eventually adjusted to their presence but felt the women were too isolated from their surroundings. They wondered if it would have been better if the women had boarded with local families. To company officials, this was out of the question. They claimed "the girls would have been lonesome, that they couldn't have been properly supervised." Although some of the women had made friends, for the most part, "after 14 months, the girls are still being stared at."

Some of the isolation may have been self-imposed. It seems likely that most decided early on that they would not stay in Saint-Georges. Few attended the French lessons offered, and they made little other effort to learn the language. Gallant explained, "Some of them have reasoned it out this way: Canada consists of nine provinces, and French is spoken in only one. In the province where you speak French you get lower wages. So why learn French?" They also noticed that English was the "managerial language, even in their community." If they were going to move to another Canadian city for work, English would be more useful to them.

Because so many of the women complained about the food in the Foyer, Gallant shared a meal with them. The food "by ordinary Canadian standards," she said, "is not good." The meal, which was cold, consisted of "meat of an unusual flavor and consistency...two very dry potatoes and a soggy mass of chopped lettuce. Dessert was a gluey blancmange baked over another indefinable substance. There was also tea with no milk or sugar and bread with no butter." Gallant thought that although no Canadian housewife would serve such a meal, it was undoubtedly better than the food in a displaced persons camp. Maybe. It was certainly better than what the women had in the Nazi labour camps; but the displaced persons camps, with their emphasis on minimum calories, and availability of Red Cross packages and black market supplies from local farms, probably offered a diet at least as appealing and nutritious as the nuns provided.

To Gallant, Dionne appeared to be hurt because the women were ungrateful, and he was "like a harassed father with a recalcitrant band of daughters on his hands." Although he made efforts to keep the women occupied during the strike with various outings, "it did nothing to settle the basic problem, which is that the girls are not living normally in the community." She found Dionne's "excessive paternalism" toward the women to be characteristic of the way he ran his business, but this failed to take into account "that it was psychologically all wrong for [them]." The problem, in Gallant's view, was that in Saint-Georges, they were "continuing the separate unnatural group life of a camp. They have seen nothing except the industrial town they live in and the not too prosperous farms of the Beauce county."[10]

Maria Palucha and Sophie Kojro, who left Saint-Georges in October 1947, probably would have agreed with Gallant. The *Globe and Mail* spoke to them in Toronto, where they were living in a boarding house run by a Polish family, looking for work and taking English and shorthand classes at Harbord Collegiate. Both in their early twenties, they already knew what it meant to lose their freedom during the occupation of Poland, but they "didn't expect the rules at St.-Georges to be so strict." Maria Palucha had picked up enough English in Germany to be a spokesperson for the women when they arrived, and she wanted to learn it properly, which she couldn't do in Quebec. They were delighted with Toronto, "which seems to have everything"—opportunities to learn, and the company of their own "country folk" there.[11]

Ghislaine Baillargeon (the name Zdzislawa Solecka took upon her adoption) later recalled that Dionne finally released all the women from their contracts at the urging of the government. By the end of the strike, he would have reached the point of diminishing returns as the women had no income to pay their room and board, and their held-back funds were running out. Eventually, Dionne would be out of pocket if he kept them on in the convent. Baillargeon claimed that although none of the women reimbursed Dionne for their transportation costs, neither did they receive any money from the 25 percent of their wages that were held back as "savings." In the end, they were paid no more than minimum wage for their labour.[12]

After spending some time with the women, Mavis Gallant considered what their experience revealed about Canada's immigration program. Although the women were happy to be in Canada, they seemed disconnected from their new country. She thought this was partly because it was not Canada that brought them here, but a businessman. In some ways, Canada was merely an abstraction to the women, a place to earn money. Their relationship with their new home was almost entirely mercenary. This wasn't surprising; their lives for nearly ten years had left them mistrustful of the world, and they were now "interested only in themselves, their own welfare, their own future."

Gallant thought it important for the government to take the lead in immigration and not leave such matters to private citizens. Echoing Gladys Strum's speech in the House of Commons over a year earlier, she wrote, "No one has tried to make them feel they have a stake in the future of Canada. If our much-publicized Citizens Department is doing anything it does not show in Beauce. As citizens they may not all turn out to be total losses, but as a system of populating the country it means everyone loses, including the people of Canada."[13]

Gallant was right to notice the peculiar absence of the Canadian government from the lives of the young women in Canada, with its only intervention the appointment of an older Polish man to investigate and assure the public that the women were not being mistreated. They didn't choose Canada. They chose to leave Germany, and they took the first offer that came along, more arranged marriage than love match. They knew they were being used by Dionne, and they were using him in return.

The time would come when Canada would be home for most of them, and they would live the lives they chose; it just wouldn't be in Saint-Georges.

On a fall day when the maples were at their peak of colour, I drove with a friend from Quebec City to Saint-Georges, heading south along the Chaudière River. As we entered the city, we encountered a tranquil rural scene. Trees rose up the hills on both sides of the river valley and obscured the houses behind their leaves; a few buildings rising above the trees dominated the scene. On the west side is the city's most impressive building, L'Église de Saint-Georges, its steeple towering over the entire city. Directly behind the church is the Centre culturel Marie-Fitzbach, named for the founder of the Soeurs du Bon-Pasteur, and once the home of the convent and primary school where Wanda lived when she arrived in Canada.

Our first stop was the imposing church for which the city was named. At the entrance to the church stood a statue of St. George slaying the dragon. Made of wood, plated in bronze, and finished with gold leaf, it is a hint of what lies inside the church. It was built in 1902 and known as one of the most beautiful churches in Quebec, its opulent interior symbolizing the importance of the Catholic Church in that era. Although Saint-Georges had only about 3,500 residents in the early part of the century, the church can seat 2,200 people. Alone inside, we climbed the stairs to one of the balconies—both of them six rows deep—to take in the full view. On the main level, six columns of wooden pews, thirty rows deep, face the altar. The ends of the pews are hand carved with shell designs and curved edges. The twenty-four columns that support the structure are adorned with carved and painted mouldings and religious icons. Massive crystal chandeliers hang from the vaulted ceiling, which is decorated with gold-painted medallions. The frames for the Stations of the Cross are covered in gold leaf. A large brass censer looms over the altar, and at the other end of the church, a massive organ dominates its own balcony. On the main level, five confessionals suggest as many priests in residence at one time to hear confession.

It is doubtful the church resembled the one Wanda would have attended as a young girl. In Polesie, where Wanda grew up, the

Catholic churches would have been small buildings made of wood. In Opaĺ, where the Polish Catholics were a minority, there would have been no money for such an opulent building. But even so, of all the places in Saint-Georges, Wanda might have felt most at home here. A church is a place of sanctuary, an escape from life as a factory worker, where she would be equal to all others. She would have recognized the Latin Mass, more familiar to her than the French she heard everywhere else. And she, too, had a taste for elaborate ornamentation that would be evident in her future home. In that modest bungalow a small crystal chandelier would hang over her kitchen table, and the coffee table in the living room would consist of a marble base with a glass top supported by carved gold legs, reminiscent of the arches in the church. The majesty of the surroundings may have comforted her.

Outside the church, in what must have been the original cemetery, is a large granite monument marking the graves of the Dionne family: father Vinceslas, mother Marie, and five of their twelve children—Uleric, Arsène, Amédée, Marie, and Ludger—along with their spouses, including Ludger's wife, Emma Veilleux. We spent some time exploring the property. Next door to the church was where the original convent once occupied by the Soeurs du Bon-Pasteur had been in 1880. A four-storey brick building was constructed in 1923 and served as a school. In 1995, the nuns transferred the former school building to the City of Saint-Georges for use as a cultural centre. They retained the residence, which they continued to operate until 2004, not for Dionne employees, but as a retirement home. In 2010, the Soeurs du Bon-Pasteur finally departed from Saint-Georges. The city acquired the residence but decided it would be too expensive to renovate, especially given the asbestos used in its construction, so it was destroyed several years later.

The remaining building has found a new purpose as the Centre Culturel for the people of Saint-Georges, housing a library, an art gallery, and a small museum. A chapel, with its own two confessionals, was restored to a condition that is likely more beautiful than the original. The tall casement windows, in their original state, offered a stunning view of the river valley and its colourful trees on one side, and the church and cemetery on the other. A large plaque outside the centre commemorates the arrival and installation of the young Polish women in 1947 and their departure, many after the strike at the mill.

We stopped by the Société historique Sartigan, located on the same floor as the art gallery. The woman who worked in the office welcomed us inside and agreed to help us locate the records about the young Polish immigrants, which she located in some binders on the upper shelves. Other women trickled in, apparently volunteers, and she explained that we were looking for information about Ludger Dionne and "les Polonaises." All of them knew who she meant and tried to remember if any of the Polish women remained in the area. They thought there might have been one, but no, "elle est décédée." But what about another one, who lived with the nuns? What was her name? Stefania? And her last name? They didn't know.

The spinning mill, once just down the street from the residence, is no longer in existence. After Dionne's death in 1962, two of his nephews, Jean-Guy and Vianney Dionne, purchased the business with a third partner under a company named Industries Dionne Inc.[14] The business expanded throughout the next two decades, but it ultimately fell victim to the same global forces that decimated the rest of the Quebec textile industry. The company was sold to Dominion Textile in 1990, which in turn sold its yarn division to Cavalier Textiles in 1994. As clothing imports increased, the company lost its market share, and it was forced to close the spinning mill in Saint-Georges in 2004. One hundred and thirty employees who remained at the mill lost their jobs, and the building that had been erected in 1940 was torn down. An IGA grocery store now sits on the site.[15]

Until his death, Dionne devoted himself to his businesses, prospering but living modestly in the family home in Saint-Georges. The strike, and the ill-fated experiment with the Polish women, did nothing for his political career, though. The voters got to know Dionne better through the publicity surrounding those events, and they didn't like what they saw. In the federal election of 1949, when Louis St. Laurent's Liberals made gains in Canada, winning a record-breaking 190 seats in the House of Commons, Dionne lost his seat to an independent candidate by a mere 222 votes. He made one attempt at re-election, in 1957, but was defeated again, this time by 825 votes.

In 1997, twenty-three of the Polish women met again in Saint-Georges at the invitation of the Dionne family to celebrate the fiftieth anniversary of their arrival in Canada. Wanda and her friends did not attend. They may not have known about it, but I doubt Wanda would have had much desire to go even if she had. One of the women, Olga Krol, contributed a homespun poem in memory of their time in Quebec, more bitter than sweet. She recalled the life in the convent, which was "oh so strict, my God!" But they were not homesick; they had each other. She remembered Niusia playing the accordion, the same accordion we sometimes heard her play, when the girls would dance with each other.[16] She mentioned the strike, after which the remaining women scattered across the country to find work once again in factories.

Saint-Georges grew from nine thousand residents in 1947 to its present population of thirty-one thousand as other small industries moved into town. On today's north–south autoroute, it is close enough for many to commute to Quebec City. As it has everywhere in the province, secularization has come to the Beauce region; the Church of Saint-Georges offers only one Sunday Mass, with another Mass on Saturday evening. The city has claimed its place in the modern world, creating an impressive art installation on the east shore of the river. For the last few years, it has sponsored an international outdoor sculpture competition, filling the riverside park with numerous stone and metal sculptures. Paths line the river, and footbridges cross over to the small island that contains some of the sculptures. In its present size and state, the city might have held more appeal to keep the young women there once their contracts had ended. But by 1948, Wanda and her friends had seen enough.

In the midst of the strike, Wanda, along with Niusia and three other friends—Bronia, Róża, and an unnamed woman who had been in school with Wanda in Wildflecken—all left Quebec for Kitchener, Ontario. Kitchener had had a large Polish community since the middle of the nineteenth century, most of the immigrants having escaped

Wanda and friends in Victoria Park in Kitchener
(Courtesy George Surdykowski)

the eastern borderlands during the partition years to find a better
life in Canada, and one of Wanda's friends might have had a relative
or family friend there. Their first stop on arriving might have been
the Polish church, Sacred Heart, where the priest would have helped
them find a place to stay and make connections to find work. Like
their decision to go to Saint-Georges from the displaced persons camp,
the choice to leave Quebec for Kitchener was an act of faith, a leap
into the unknown, guided by the confidence that comes with having
survived the worst that strangers could inflict on them. By the fall,
the women were established in the city, getting accustomed to the
English-speaking world and taking their first steps as independent
women, obliged to no one and free to do as they pleased. In September
1948, Wanda recorded her independence in a photograph, standing
with two friends before a monument in Victoria Park in Kitchener.

The presence of the plaque about the Polish women in front of the
former convent suggests that the people of Saint-Georges look back on

this episode as a demonstration that the community embraced these refugees from war-torn Europe, a source of pride for today's citizens of the city. The departure of the women, and Dionne's own political demise, suggests that this might not have been so seventy years ago, but the passage of time has allowed the city to burnish its memory of the events. Given the subsequent increase in immigration to Canada and her own family's admission into the United States a few years later, Wanda must have realized that she need not have gone through such a difficult and sometimes demeaning process to make her way to a new country. But her decision set her on the path of a life that she loved, in a country where she could make a home and a family, and live without fear. It could be that her exile was a welcome liberation from the past, and not just a burden.

Wanda also left Saint-Georges with an unexpected gift. In the midst of her strange and isolated life at the convent and the mill, Wanda found one thing that would sustain her for the rest of her life, an advantage that few other immigrants possessed—the friendship of other women who had been through the same experience as she had, for whom no explanation of her past was necessary. They were with her in Quebec at the beginning and through all of life's trials, and they were there for Wanda at her end over fifty years later.

I recall only one occasion, on a warm summer day in her kitchen, when Wanda spoke of her life as a young woman making her way with her friends in their new lives in Kitchener. Her friend Niusia was there that day, and George and I had joined the two women for the afternoon. Niusia had driven to Kitchener from Connecticut in her big Lincoln for a visit, as she did more often since Casey's death ten years earlier. She was still single, and she came and went as she pleased. The arrangement suited both women.

As Niusia loaded a cigarette into its holder and settled in for some conversation, she unfolded a fifty-year-old copy of *Life* magazine and spread it on the table, its musty basement smell competing with the aroma of coffee and sweets that Wanda had put on the table. The June 2, 1947, edition had a photo of actress Jane Greer on the cover, glamorous in a blouse patterned with images from playing cards. Greer's hair curls softly over her cheekbones, and her vibrant lipstick and sharply arched brows adds to her aura of feminine beauty. The cover story reports that Greer had her debut modelling a Women's Army Corps uniform in the June 8, 1942, issue of *Life* at the tender age of twenty—Wanda's age in June 1947. Another photo essay in the magazine might have appealed to twenty-year-old Wanda. "White Dresses," a "fashion" item, portrays a series of white dresses representing the stages in the life of a young American girl: first Communion, prom, coming out, graduation, and marriage. The dresses are extravagant visions of elegance, all lace and frills and satin. Wanda admired fashion—she was often garbed in skirts or dresses that set off her figure—and she would have loved these. But the prices would have shocked her: $150 for a wedding gown, and $450 for a luminous white "coming out" dress.

Niusia, still boyish in her seventies with her hair cut in a short bob and her clothing a practical shirt and pants combo, was certainly not interested in either of these frivolous items. Niusia had brought this copy of *Life* magazine because it carried the story of the young women's journey to Canada, and she couldn't wait to share it. She opened the magazine to the article at page 45: "100 Girls and a Dionne—Canadian Manufacturer Recruits Virtuous Polish Girls for Hard Work and a Moral Life in His Big Factory." The journalist Will Lang was in Frankfurt to interview Ludger Dionne and photograph the young women before they left for their new life in Canada. "Look! Here is how we got to Canada," Niusia said.

Wanda and Niusia stared at the photos of their world fifty years earlier, a distant lifetime ago, and thrilled to the idea of their brief celebrity. But they were not interested in Dionne or the time they spent working in his factory. They talked instead about life after Quebec, their real life, which finally started once they arrived in Kitchener with their friends who were also among the lucky one hundred young women.

"Remember, Wanda, when we bought the chicken? We wanted to cook a chicken and so we did what we knew." Niusia looked up at

Wanda, grinning. "We bought a live chicken at the market and brought it home to our apartment. Imagine! Killing a chicken in an apartment! But we didn't know, this was the only way we knew." Niusia chuckled. Wanda smiled a little sheepishly, disapproving their backward peasant ways. She would never have permitted a live chicken in her kitchen.

Wanda and Niusia looked at the photos of the strange world they once inhabited and turned to the Dionne story. It was a stark departure from the idealized images of women depicted elsewhere in the magazine, where they were either consumers of appliances, recipes, and fashion — homemakers — or objects of beauty, valued for their face and figure. One picture showed a convoy of trucks departing for the Frankfurt airport, the women standing in the open backs, a chilling reminder of their earlier journeys to the labour camps. In another, family members weep at the loss of their daughters or sisters. In a third picture, the caption reads, almost in the style of a game show, "the prettiest recruit is 17 year-old Janina. Once a slave laborer for the Nazis, she has managed to collect eight dresses, only one pair of shoes."

The two women spent a long time inspecting the lead photo, which featured Ludger Dionne standing in front of all the girls under a sign saying "Emigrant Assembly Centre, UNRRA 533." The sun casts shadows on the cobblestone and causes some of the girls to squint. Dionne, looking distinguished in a three-piece suit, holds a cane in his right hand and gazes directly at the camera with the sombre expression of a businessman who has completed an important transaction. Behind him, the young women stand in rows, arms locked together. Most of them are smiling. Some appear in Scout uniforms, although most wear similar dresses or skirts and blouses. Their shoes are all the same, oxfords with laces. Their legs are bare or they wear socks. Their hair has been carefully styled, pulled back and up with pins.

Wanda and Niusia struggled to find themselves in the picture. Niusia had pointed to one face in the crowd, and said, "That's you, Wanda." Wanda peered at the photo and frowned, shaking her head. More than fifty years later, Wanda had not forgotten that day, and her answer hinted at the multitude of other details of the past she must have carried with her, unspoken. "I don't think so," she said. "I never had a dress that looked like that."

CHAPTER 12
JOURNEY'S END

The RMS *Aquitania* was one of the jewels of the Cunard Line, a passenger vessel luxuriously appointed for the comfort of wealthy passengers sailing from Great Britain across the Atlantic or, when the transatlantic business was slow, on Mediterranean cruises. Ready for the scrapyard in 1939, the elderly ship instead found new life in the war as a troop ship for Allied servicemen. Painted battleship grey and retrofitted to increase its passenger capacity to as many as 7,400, the *Aquitania* safely moved over 400,000 troops across half a million miles during the war years. Before it was finally retired from service in 1949, the ship stopped regularly in the Halifax harbour, bringing homecoming troops and war brides to Canada.

On three separate voyages in May and June 1947, the *Aquitania*'s passenger list included 1,624 young Polish servicemen who arrived at an unforeseen destination after an eight-year odyssey from the gulags of Siberia across the Soviet Union, Central Asia, the Middle East, Italy, and England. This was no triumphant return of the hero to Ithaca, as the young men might have dreamt of, but an entry to a new world that only grudgingly admitted them to its shores and even then, only because they could be put to good use.

In the early hours of Sunday, June 29, the middle of a warm and sunny weekend in the southern Maritimes, the last of the Polish servicemen sailed into Halifax harbour. They did not arrive unnoticed. If not quite given a hero's welcome, they were nonetheless warmly greeted by a small group of interested parties: a reporter, Henry Prysky, who had been following their story for the Halifax newspapers; a bureaucrat with the federal Department of Labour, who had been involved in recruiting the men; representatives of the Canadian Polish Congress, who distributed Polish newspapers to the group; and the Royal Canadian Mounted Police, who processed the men before releasing them to find their way to their final destinations.[1]

Twenty-seven-year-old Kazimierz Surdykowski was one of the 328 Polish soldiers aboard the ship. He would make the final leg of his seven-year journey on a train from Halifax to Toronto, from where he would be sent on to a farm in southern Ontario. It must have been soon after his arrival that he became known as Casey, his name cut down to size, the strange consonants removed for his new life in the English-speaking world.

Casey's adjustment to his new home would have taken a much different path than Wanda's. On a farm near Stratford, his daily life was isolated, his work solitary. He may have learned some basic English while stationed in England, but he probably had trouble speaking with his employer or banking or shopping. The government provided the veterans with English–Polish dictionaries and in some cases arranged for English classes, but for the most part they were on their own. Occasionally, they received government newsletters written in English, French, and Polish, giving them information about their rights and some news about their fellow veterans. For the most part, though, the close contact and communal life he had shared with his fellow soldiers for the last five years was over.

Of the nearly five thousand Polish soldiers who came to Canada in 1946 and 1947, most ended up on the prairies, but nearly two thousand went to Ontario. The conditions on the farms varied widely. Some had to sleep in barns, and the work hours were longer than legally permitted. One of the most widespread complaints was the low wages. The contract prescribed a minimum payment of $45 per month. The average paid to the veterans in southern Ontario was $53, but this was still well below the average wage for Ontario farm workers, who earned approximately $70 per month, including board.[2]

The veterans faced none of the circus-like atmosphere that surrounded the Polish women who worked at the mill in Saint-Georges.
Although the press paid attention to the progress of the soldiers, it
was mostly concerned with their conduct, incidents of tuberculosis
or sexually transmitted diseases, and whether or not the men had
abandoned their contracts. Some critics, like the editor of the *Calgary
Albertan* newspaper, claimed that numerous men had walked off the
job, taking other jobs in the city with higher wages. In fact, two-thirds
of the men remained with the farmer to whom they were first con-
tracted, even though they had the opportunity to change employers
after one year. There was a small group of "problem" cases: fifty-two
men, or just over 1 percent of the group of veterans, left the farm they
worked on to get other work without the permission of the farmer
or the Department of Labour. Although a few were so troublesome
that the government considered taking action, none of the men were
deported.

Still, the possibility or threat of deportation hung over the men,
repeated in the government newsletters and resorted to by farmers
looking to keep their workers in line. The men were in no doubt that
their positions were precarious until they were released from their
contracts and eligible for permanent residency in Canada. The official
line was that the men should be grateful for the chance that had
been offered to them. In his letter to the veterans in late December
1947, the deputy minister of labour, Arthur MacNamara, reminded
them of their obligations: "Because of the urgent need for food, the
British Government was prepared not only to make shipping available
for you when it was not obtainable by others but also to help finance
your journey to Canada. As you will understand, your obligation is a
serious one." The men, he wrote, should be grateful not just to the
government but also to the farmers who paid them, providing "an
important means of your coming to Canada before others were able
to come," and helping them to quickly adjust "to Canadian life and
conditions."[3]

Some Canadian officials were uneasy about the terms offered to
the veterans. Canada's high commissioner in London, Norman

Robertson, confessed that he had "some qualms about the reason-ableness and justice of the two-year term of indenture required from immigrants under this scheme, particularly since I have learned that quite a number of Polish ex-soldiers from the United Kingdom have been accepted as ordinary immigrants who are free from any such contractual restrictions on their employment after arriving in Canada." Similarly, those veterans who remained in the United Kingdom faced no requirement of a term of indenture before being accepted as permanent residents. Casey could have stayed in England, but something in his experience must have convinced him he was bet-ter off taking his chances in Canada, even under the onerous terms that were offered to him.

On farms across the country, the men worked off their two-year terms. Sometimes the conditions were hazardous. Several died in farm accidents. At least one had to be removed from his employment after his employer beat him. The farmer involved was convicted of a criminal offence, prompting the Saskatchewan government to initiate an inquiry into the treatment of Polish veterans working on the province's farms. The majority of soldiers fulfilled their commitments, but almost none of them chose to remain as farm workers after the end of their contracts. They had other, better options. They moved to cities where they could find work in the booming manufacturing sector, which, as it turned out, needed hard workers.

On the heels of the government plan to bring the Polish veterans to Canada, the floodgates of immigration opened. After the first Order-in-Council in June 1947, authorizing the entry of an initial five thousand unsponsored immigrants, several similar orders were issued in the next fifteen months, adding another forty-five thousand people, many of whom would bring family members to Canada. Many others came to Canada under "bulk labour" programs, in which employers travelled to Europe with immigration officials to hire workers from the displaced persons camps. In May 1947, three Ontario pulp and paper companies reached an agreement with the federal government to bring in 1,400 workers under a guaranteed contract for a minimum of ten months. Mining companies and clothing manufacturers made similar requests. Between 1947 and 1951, Canada admitted more than 160,000 displaced persons.

Like the arrival of the one hundred young Polish women, the bulk-labour schemes provoked negative reactions. Some Canadians found the contracts offensive to notions of fairness; a May 27, 1947, *Globe and Mail* editorial criticized the government for allowing employers "to recruit labour on a plan of semi-servitude utterly at variance with Canadian notions of human rights and freedoms." The eminent Canadian diplomat John Holmes was troubled by the image of Department of Labour teams roaming Europe, no more than "itinerant headhunters" looking for able-bodied immigrants "like good beef cattle, with a preference for strong young men who could do manual labour and would not be encumbered by aging relatives."[4]

Others were concerned about jeopardizing the livelihoods of Canadians, not realizing the changes looming over Canada's post-war economy. Rather than threatening the employment of existing Canadians, the first wave of post-war immigrants helped to fuel Canada's burgeoning mining and manufacturing sectors. The result was not just a shift in the demographics of a country that held only 12.5 million people in 1947, but the beginning of Canada's perception of itself as a humanitarian country open to immigrants of diverse groups.[5]

Reporting on the arrival of the first group of Polish soldiers in November 1946, a news item in the *Edmonton Journal* offered a "five point plan" for their speedy assimilation into Canadian society:

1. Teach them English.
2. Offer education facilities.
3. Provide entertainment.
4. Encourage them to mix with Canadians.
5. Go slow in forming Polish societies.[6]

The writer was concerned about the Poles "brooding" over Poland's troubles and congregating in Polish societies that would keep them from engaging in Canadian life. One official was quoted as saying, "We want them made into Canadians in the quickest possible time." At the heart of the plan was the suggestion that the men should shed their pasts and their culture and enter mainstream Canadian society as if they were no different from Canadians whose English-speaking ancestors had colonized the country.

That the veterans may have had cause to brood over more than Poland's "troubles" did not seem to occur to many observers. News reports showed a distinct lack of curiosity about who the veterans were or the experiences that led them to accept immigration to Canada on the most unfavourable terms rather than return to post-war Poland. Too many journalists treated them as if they were no different than Canadian veterans returning home after their period of service.

But Canada was not home to Casey and the other Polish service-men. The move to Canada marked the second period of exile in Casey's short life, this time a permanent one. Exile is not a voluntary state, born out of a conscious decision to follow a new path and make a new home. It doesn't carry with it the hope of an immigrant, moving from home in search of opportunity yet still retaining the prospect of a return to home if one chooses. The exile who arrives in a new country, even one that is welcoming, will not immediately regard it as home or abandon memory of home and take on the cloak of another identity. The trauma and humiliation of the last seven years surely created psychic wounds that Casey would have to heal or suppress before he could think of Canada as offering the possibility of liberation from the burden of the past.

The Bosnian American writer Aleksandar Hemon has written about the unique existential crisis of the exile, who has lost the continuous narrative of life that most of us enjoy. All the landmarks of the past—the schools they attended, the paths they walked with friends, the places where they enjoyed secret pleasures or discoveries—have disappeared, removing a part of their identity with them: "If you somehow vanished, your fellow citizens could have collectively reconstructed you from their collective memory and the gossip accrued over the years," Hemon observes. "Your sense of who you were, your deepest identity, was determined by your position in a human network, whose physical corollary was the architecture of the city."[7] Without that human and physical network to ground him, the exile must try to construct new networks and establish identity in an alien landscape.

Not everyone can assimilate after such a loss. Some simply continue as if they had never left home, essentially creating a theatre in which they act out a life that no longer exists. In his memoir *Two Cities*, Polish writer Adam Zagajewski chronicled his family's expulsion from Lwów at end of the war, when the borders shifted and ethnic Poles were sent away. When they ended up in Gliwice, it was not so much that they were emigrants who had left their country but that their country had simply shifted to the west, "and they along with it." Some of the oldest among them passed their days not in Gliwice but in a Lwów that existed in their minds, pretending that nothing had changed.[8]

But before assimilation and identity, before healing from the wounds of war, Casey and his fellow soldiers had the more urgent task of survival. With no families to support them, little or no knowledge of the language or culture in this new country, no money other than what they earned on the farms, and no social network, their futures must still have seemed untenable. Unlike Wanda and the other Polish women at the Dionne factory, they were alone and likely very lonely. The most direct means to making their way in this new world was the very thing the *Edmonton Journal* writer found undesirable: the support and companionship of their countrymen, who were all struggling to make a life in a strange new place.

Casey's new home in Stratford was a short distance from Kitchener, which had been home to a sizable Polish community since the turn of the century. He worked first as a mechanic and later found a job building tires at BFGoodrich. This was heavy and dirty work, carried out amidst the fumes of extruded rubber and the dust of the talc that

Casey (left) at work in the BFGoodrich factory during the 1970s
(Courtesy George Surdykowski)

was used to keep the rubber from sticking to itself. A photo of Casey at work, standing with two other men on the factory floor, shows him in his work clothes—pants, a plaid shirt, and a cap on his head—and smiling as much as he did in any other picture. After everything he'd been through, the certainty and predictability of work may have been satisfying.

In Kitchener he found a Polish church and a Polish veterans' branch of the Canadian Legion, which was established shortly after the war ended. One evening, Casey attended a dance at the Polish church. There, he met a young woman who had lived only eighty kilometres away from him in their youth in Poland. The shy and retiring Casey was immediately attracted to the outgoing and fun-loving Wanda, and in Casey Wanda recognized a hero of the Polish struggle in the war. They understood each other's experiences and past lives without explanation or confusion. What better way to settle into a new world than with someone who shared one's roots and understood one's past, someone who spoke the same language, whose culture, food, and religion were familiar? Both of them must have felt fortunate to have found the kind of partner they might have met and married in Poland, had the war never interrupted their lives, to help them adapt to life in a new country.

Photographs from this period of their lives show the couple among their friends, on picnics or other outings, laughing and enjoying themselves like any other group of Canadians on an adventure. Other photos show Wanda and her friends walking in the park, standing in front of their house, enjoying the idle pursuits of the young. Or celebrating: one of Wanda's friends is in her wedding dress, the others in gowns as her attendants. In one photo, Wanda and Niusia are standing outdoors in the winter. Snow is on the roof behind them, but they are wearing party dresses, and their arms are bare. They cling to each other for warmth, their faces happy. They show no sign of the ordeals they had been through.

When Mavis Gallant interviewed the young Polish women in Quebec, she found it troubling that no one had tried to make the women feel they had a "stake in the future of Canada." It's possible young women like Wanda didn't need to start out with a big vision of their future lives. What they were looking for, and what they eventually found, was simply an undisturbed place to work and make a home and a life, no different from any other Canadian.

Wanda and Casey married on a snowy day in November 1951, and one year later their first child, Jerzy, was born. Later, when he started school, Jerzy became George. For the first seven years of his life, until the birth of his brother, Chris, George lived the life of an only child. The family settled into life in a neighbourhood of other Polish immigrants. It was the kind of neighbourhood that unsympathetic politicians might have called an immigrant ghetto, as if the choice of neighbourhood posed a social problem and represented a rejection of Canada and a futile attempt to maintain a connection to their country of birth. Wanda and Casey, like many other immigrants, found housing they could afford and were happy to live among

Wanda and Casey on their wedding day

(Courtesy George Surdykowski)

others who understood them and their history. Their reception in a neighbourhood of established Canadians might not have been as welcoming.

It is true that their social world was like a bubble of Polish culture in the middle of a different country. They socialized exclusively with other Polish expatriates; George's childhood friends, at first, were the children of his parents' friends. If there were other children on his street to play with, he didn't notice them. He spoke only Polish, and there was no television in the house to suggest the existence of a different world outside the walls of his home. Wanda, more than Casey, became active in the Polish Legion, organizing events, cooking meals for celebrations, and meeting with other Polish women. If she had ever had any aspirations to become more educated or make an independent life, she buried them. She stayed home to look after her children and devoted herself to caring for them and her home.

When Wanda later told me that she preferred cleaning to cooking, it may have been that the act of cleaning had a deeper meaning for her. Wanda lived for many months in vermin-infested barracks, with few possessions or comforts, every part of her environment a denial of her humanity. In Canada, the simple act of keeping things clean and orderly was a daily affirmation that she would never descend to the depths she had once been forced to inhabit. For many years, long after most households had abandoned them, she still used an ancient wringer washer. After the clothes had agitated in the soapy water, she would pass them through the rollers, change the water for rinsing, and then repeat the wringing process all over again. She hung her laundry to dry on the line, winter or summer. She never owned a dishwasher, but her countertops were perpetually clean and uncluttered. George remembers her plying him with a sugar sandwich so he would sit quietly while she washed the floors.

Wanda kept another link to the past alive in regular visits to the Boston area where her mother, Helena, and her brother Joe were living. They and Wanda's sister Kasia had immigrated to the United States in 1949. Every second summer of George's childhood, he and his family drove from Kitchener to Lynn, a small city about ten miles north of

Boston, to visit with his *babcia*, Helena, and his uncle Joe. Once or twice, the family travelled to Long Island, where Kasia had settled with her husband, Henryk, instead. Nine hundred kilometres and a border separated Wanda from her family, and although her mother hoped the family would be reunited in the United States, Wanda was happy to remain in Canada, where she had already begun building a life. At least they were close enough for regular visits.

It might also be that life in the United States did not seem all that appealing to Wanda. At first, Joe could find work only as a labourer in the rag trade, sorting waste materials. Later, he took a job in a factory where he remained for the rest of his working life. Joe and Helena lived in a small two-bedroom apartment on the second floor of an old brick walk-up apartment building. The neighbourhood was rough. George watched fights break out in the alley below as local gangs jostled for territory. Strangers hung out in the apartment building's hallways and stairwells, and he knew to give them a wide berth. He was warned not to go outside alone. Used to his freedom outdoors at home in Kitchener, he was suddenly hostage to the plans of his parents. The visits were lifeblood for Wanda but interminable for a small boy with nothing to do and no playmates to keep him busy.

During their visits, the family crammed into the tiny space. George slept on the living room floor while the adults talked into the night. He longed to go to a ball game at Fenway, to see the Red Sox play his beloved Yankees, but such treats were out of reach. Sometimes, his father would take him to a park nearby and hit balls for him to catch, or the group would go to the ocean at Revere Beach, but he had little else to interest him.

The trips became more tolerable when Niusia drove her Lincoln (always her car of choice) over from Hartford, Connecticut. Niusia found the long afternoons of adult gossip as oppressive as George did. "Let's get out of here," she'd say, and they would set off in the big car looking for adventure. In her long pants and short hair, she was a Katharine Hepburn figure, a pal with a taste for mischief. They would end up at the bowling alley, where they would bowl game after game of tenpin. Then they might drive around, sometimes stopping for ice cream or french fries, before returning to the apartment in Lynn and more hours of boredom.

Engraved on George's memory, chafing at him over the years, is the time his father angrily cancelled plans he'd made to take George to Fenway for an evening game, a one-time treat that was never rescheduled.

The day started badly. Niusia and his father, and maybe others, had argued, and Niusia had stormed out of the apartment. George had escaped outside to the stoop, where he sat alone, moping. When Niusia came out, she spotted him and gestured at him to come along with her. Desperate to get out, George hopped over the railing and went with her, not telling anyone what he was doing. They stayed away longer than usual, for five or six hours.

George concedes that some discipline might have been in order. After all, most parents would be upset if their young child disappeared without a trace for hours, particularly in a neighbourhood they knew wasn't safe. But he remembers that at the time he thought Casey seemed relieved to have a reason to cancel their plans, and he brazenly told his father that he knew he never wanted to take him to the game anyway. In the tangled skein of cause and effect it is impossible to know whether this incident was a symptom of the rupture between father and son, a cause, or both, but George and Casey never had an easy relationship after that.

Once George started his first job in a shoe store at age thirteen, he simply refused to go to Boston. As a compromise, he stayed with a friend of Wanda's that first summer; in later years, he insisted on his independence and stayed home alone, fending for himself from the age of fourteen.

Joe got married in 1970. Maria had come from Poland to the United States on a three-month visa; they met at a Polish community dance while she was visiting an aunt in Boston. They decided to be married quickly before her visa expired. In one photo, taken in September, Wanda, Kasia, and Joe pose with Maria in her simple pink wedding suit. Wanda is smartly dressed in a short white dress; Kasia has adopted a more glamorous look. In a green chiffon dress, her platinum-blond hair piled in a high bouffant, curls resting on her shoulder, she outshines the rest of the group. George remembers that his aunt spoke in what sounded to his ears like a Brooklyn accent, so unlike his parents or Joe. Of the siblings, Kasia was also the most Americanized, naming her daughter Diane instead of a more conventionally Polish name. Kasia appears in no other photos of family visits after Joe's wedding. At some point, a dispute ended the relationship between the sisters, another loosening of family ties among the Gizmunts, for reasons George never learned.

Wanda's brother Ryszard made the trip to the United States for the occasion. In an earlier photo taken that August, Joe, Wanda, and Ryszard are seated in folding aluminum lawn chairs in front of what appears to be Joe's house. They are all well dressed, the two men in short-sleeved shirts and long pants, Wanda in a stylish navy dress and sandals. Ryszard seems impossibly youthful next to his siblings, especially Joe, who wears the years of work and struggle on his face and in his hands, one of them missing the two fingers that were severed in a work accident. They smile happily, seemingly at ease with each other in spite of the decades of separation. Ryszard's visit was well timed; a few months after Joe and Maria were married, Helena died. Joe and Maria started their family—two boys, just like Wanda's family—and bought a home in Peabody where they had a garden, and Maria cared for their sons while Joe worked.

As time went on, Wanda and Casey's world expanded. While they never lost their connection to the Polish community, they found a new home away from the old Polish neighbourhood, closer to Casey's work. Their lives came to resemble those of other Canadians. They prospered, just like everyone did in the post-war boom. They stayed in touch with and sent parcels to family members left behind—Casey's brothers and sisters, Wanda's brother Ryszard and her aunt and uncle—and recognized that they had a much more comfortable life than they would have had if they had returned to Poland. They absorbed English Canadian culture through radio, television, and books, and through the lives of their sons. Casey came home after work and read the newspaper, cover to cover. He became a hockey fan and was active in his union. Their sons attended public schools, played sports, joined clubs, and went to university. At some point, Wanda and Casey came to identify themselves as Polish Canadians and became citizens. Life assumed a familiar, peaceful, and regular rhythm, in which it would almost be possible to forget that the war had ever happened.

In Homer's epic poem *The Odyssey*, Odysseus is absent from his home for twenty years: ten voyaging to Troy and waging battle against the Trojans, and another ten making his way back, through a series of adventures and challenges, until he arrives, alone, at Ithaca. Not for him the unending glory of death in battle, like the hero Achilles. When Odysseus encounters Achilles's ghost in the Land of the Dead, Odysseus assures him he made the right choice, exchanging the possibility of a long life for glory. But Achilles rebukes Odysseus; he says he'd "rather serve another as a land-bound serf...than be the lord of all the withered dead."[9]

What about the hero who survives? What happens when the journey ends and the battles have been fought?

Casey returned to Poland only once, making a single unsatisfying visit in the 1970s. He packed a suitcase full of coffee, stockings, and other small luxuries that were unavailable in Poland. He must have given these things to the siblings he never talked about. Wanda and George drove to the airport to pick up Casey from his return flight. It was a stormy day, driving was difficult, and Casey's flight was delayed. On the way back to Kitchener, Wanda and Casey talked about the trip, speaking in Polish. Concentrating on driving in poor conditions, George remembers only his father's obvious disappointment in the trip and his claim that he would never return. His Ithaca had disappeared. Perhaps Casey understood that, like the hero of C.P. Cavafy's poem, his Ithaca had nothing left to give him, and the riches of life would have to come from elsewhere.[10]

Certainly all he endured during the war was heroic, from exile in Siberia to his life as a grunt in the Italian campaign, no less so because it was never celebrated. But his fate was the one Achilles's ghost says he would have chosen: a modern serf engaged in the drudgery of building tires in a factory, for the rest of his life. His job was probably not much different than the work he might have done in Poland after the war, but it gave him and his family a better life than he could have managed there. He may have ended up with everything he wanted. George believes that his father was very happy, secure, free, and able to prosper as much as any other Canadian in the years after the war.

The Odyssey is more than the story of a heroic journey; it also asks how a son may know his father, as Telemachus goes in search of the father he never knew. The answer is that a father, who knows his son from birth, will always know his son better. Our parents are, of necessity, a mystery to us, even when they share the intimate experiences of their past. I often ask George to tell me about things he did with his father. He remembers wandering with Casey through the woods near Kitchener, foraging for mushrooms, a favourite pastime of Poles and likely a fond childhood memory of Casey's. Mostly, he remembers fishing trips, leaving in the darkness of the morning before dawn and driving for what seemed to be hours to find Casey's favourite places to fish. He knows Casey must have shown him how to bait a hook and where to find fish and what kind are the best for eating. I ask, "Didn't you talk to him while you fished?" George says, "That's not how you do it. You have to spread out and stay quiet."

George didn't know, until after Casey died, that his father used to go to watch him play football in high school. He would arrive after George had suited up and watch unnoticed from the stands, leaving before George finished changing. I can picture him, still and silent. He might have cheered when he saw an exciting play, showing an exuberance I never saw in him. I wonder how it felt for Casey, standing with the dust of the factory still on his clothes, to watch his son, free to follow the aimless pursuits of the young in simulated battle, spared from the real one.

CHAPTER 13
SILENCE, MEMORY

Like Casey, Wanda made a single trip back to Poland, apparently in the early 1970s. She went without Casey, maybe because of the cost or because her Chris was not old enough to be left on his own. Although Joe had no interest in returning, adamant that there would be nothing in Poland for him, Wanda must have felt she had some unfinished business. In photographs, Wanda appears older, somehow more serious, than she did in the photographs with Joe and Ryszard the summer of Joe's wedding.

In one, Wanda stands in the middle of a square, sunglasses shielding her eyes. It must have been hot, but even so, she has tucked a silk scarf into the neck of her sleeveless top. Men carrying pieces of luggage pass nearby, possibly coming or going from a train station. In the distance, Communist-era concrete apartment towers loom over the barren streets. No trees or shrubs or other vegetation soften the dismal view. Wanda gazes into the distance, frowning and uncertain. She may have felt overwhelmed by the urban hustle, so different from the more human scale of life in Kitchener. Just as likely, amid the sterility of the Soviet-era architecture, she was unsettled at finding herself in a Poland she did not recognize.

Nothing in the photos indicates where they were taken. George knows Wanda would have spoken about her trip to his father and her friends, but he remembers no conversation with her about it. By then, he was a university student, absorbed in his own busy life: a summer job at an iron works, workouts at the gym, playing football with a summer league. The life of his parents took place offstage. Poland was even less interesting to him. In his own European odyssey in 1974, he never made his way to his parents' homeland. It was grey and backward and boring, when the rest of Europe was in lively technicolour.

When I first thought about Wanda's life as an exile, it was mainly to understand how she recovered from the events of the war: the death of her uncle, the loss of her brother, the Russian occupation, her time in the labour camp in Germany, and her adjustment to a new life in a strange country. Missing from this script, and from the photos she left behind, was any sense of her life before the war.

The brutal events of the war at least came to an end. Wanda's other trauma was intangible and unending. When she was taken from her home in Opaĺ, she left behind both past and future: the remnants of her childhood, and the life she expected to live as a woman. Did she nurture memories of her life before the war, before she lost her father? What dreams did she abandon when she left Europe for an unknown future? Did her vanished past haunt her?

Every exile understands this loss, and many find it impossible to speak of. But in their silence, they may still cherish dreams of the past, both painful and beautiful, untainted by the events that threw them out of the world they knew. All languages have a word for this. The Portuguese have the beautiful *saudade*, an exquisite suffering. In English, it is *nostalgia*, from the Greek *nostos* (return home) and *algos* (pain). For the exile, nostalgia is not merely an abstract wistfulness for a simpler time, but a profound sense of loss. Svetlana Boym, the Russian-born American intellectual, called it "a longing for a home that no longer exists or has never existed…a mourning for the impossibility of mythical return, for the loss of an enchanted world with clear borders and values."[1] For the Welsh, the word is *hiraeth*—to have a longing for a home that isn't the place it should have or could have been; to have a sense of incompleteness about home.[2]

In Polish, the word is *tęsknota*. Boym compares it to the Russian *toska*, giving "a similar sense of confining and overwhelming yearning with a touch of moody artistry unknown to the Russians, enamored by the gigantic and the absolute."[3] In her memoir *Lost in Translation*, Eva Hoffman describes *tęsknota* as a "magical preservative," crystallizing "like amber" around images of the life that was lost—the house, the garden, the country. Hoffman, born after the war, left Kraków for Canada with her parents when she was thirteen years old. Walking around Vancouver, her new home, Hoffman felt herself "pregnant with the images of Poland, pregnant and sick."[4]

How much more complicated are those yearnings when cataclysmic events tear one from one's home? It is not hard for me to understand Wanda's silence about her war experience. Forgetting, or at least avoiding remembering, could have been the most direct path to survival and gathering the strength needed to create a new life. But what of her life as a small girl? Thinking again of my mother's happy childhood reminiscences, I ask George whether Wanda ever shared anything about her life before the war. Did she tell stories about Christmas celebrations, of special gifts she received, of family life, or even the yard she played in? No, he said; mainly, she spoke in general terms about Polish customs. "In Poland, we have the main Christmas meal on Christmas Eve, for Wigilia," or, "For Wigilia, we set a place for those who have died or cannot be there," she would have said.

Boym speculates that nostalgia might be taboo for many exiles who left their homes under difficult political circumstances; the deeper the loss, the more difficult it can be to express it publicly. But if nostalgia is a romance with one's fantasy of another time, it does not fare well when confronted with reality. The ideal lover remains ideal only when viewed from a distance. On her return to Poland, Wanda came face to face with the home she thought she left behind, but no matter what part of the country she saw, the Poland of Wanda's travels could never be the Poland of her childhood. The photo of Wanda standing near a collection of apartment towers might have captured the moment of dissonance between her idealized past and the rather disappointing present. It might have been the moment Wanda realized that she was once a Pole, but now she was some other thing. A Canadian, yes, but not like those born in Canada. She was in some intermediate state, an exile's version of the Buddhist's bardo, suspended between death and rebirth.

George recalls only one thing his mother said about her trip on her return: she would never go back to Poland.

In 2017, I went to a conference where a panel of writers talked about their journey of immigration to Canada. One, a woman whose family was displaced by the civil war in the former Yugoslavia, spoke of her feelings of loss, and her tendency to romanticize her homeland. She eventually realized that her place of origin had a dark element to it, and her idealized version never existed. She came to think of herself as Odysseus, travelling between two Ithacas. Because anyone could become displaced, she believed that it was important to think about how best to adapt to that reality.

I was most struck, though, by another panellist's story. Coincidentally, she was born in Kitchener, at least forty years after George. Her first language was English; she later learned to speak her parents' native language but felt that she could never be fluent in their mother tongue. She spoke of her evolving concept of home, beginning with the idea that home was her parents' birthplace in a sub-Saharan African country. She had a longing to return there, as if that were where she'd started. When she did, though, she discovered that "even in my place I was the other." She lost her grasp on the concept of a geographic home and decided that home for her would be where she was with the people she loved.

Listening to the young speaker, I wondered how many other children of immigrants felt displaced in the country of their birth. There are many differences between her and George, not the least of which are their different generations and George's European heritage. But there may also be similarities that could explain how children of immigrants, no matter where their parents came from, can develop an uncertain relationship with their birthplace. Not unusually for immigrants to Canada, George's parents created a home that felt very much like their early homes in Poland. They spoke Polish, ate foods common in Poland, and wore clothing that, in its dated formality, appeared more Eastern European than North American. Their church, Sacred Heart, had a Polish-speaking priest and was the focus of the Polish community. Their social life took place at the Polish Legion or in the homes of their Polish friends.

These connections to the past—crystallized in amber, in the words of Eva Hoffman—can represent either the denial of a present reality or the comfort of tradition and transitional objects as the immigrant takes uncertain steps from one world into another. If adaptation occurs, it doesn't happen magically overnight, and sometimes, it is the children who force the next steps into the new world.

Most people can point to events that represent turning points or are in some way transformative. For George, one such event was his first day of kindergarten. Apart from an appendicitis attack when he was a toddler, George has no memory of his childhood before that day. It's almost as if the time he spent speaking only Polish was the equivalent of the preverbal stage, when we have no capacity to develop narrative memories of events. Because his family lived outside the Sacred Heart school catchment zone, where the children of other Polish immigrants would have gone, he went to the local school, St. Theresa's, instead. With no other Polish children to mediate or translate, George found himself in a classroom where he could not understand a word that was spoken.

Why didn't his mother do something to prepare him for this obvious challenge? She had to know what awaited him. But the more I think of it, the more I wonder whether George's recollection is entirely factual. It seems unlikely to me that, having lived in Kitchener for eight years by the time George entered school, Wanda spoke no English. She would have had to navigate the city, including the majority of stores where English was the only language of transaction. Even if they had no television, what about the radio? Or a newspaper? His father, who worked at the tire factory, would have had contact with English speakers, and his mother, clearly an intelligent woman, would surely have made an effort to teach herself some words of English. By the time I met her, she spoke English fluently, albeit with a Polish accent.

And, as someone who obviously valued education, wouldn't she have spent time teaching him numbers and letters and reading books to him? Some of this must have been in English.

George would be the first to concede the frailty of memory. He's spent his professional life as an arbitrator, listening to witnesses, and he knows the sometimes tenuous connection between one's memory of facts and the truth. But whatever the facts were, George's memory of his reaction to his first day of school is the truth. He remembers the terror he felt at being powerless and isolated from the other children, and he associates that with his foreignness. Even if he had a few words of English, he would have been acutely aware of how different he was from his classmates. His mother was not, could not, be there to protect him. In that moment, he understood that whatever world his parents lived in, he was now in a different one.

Not only was school a place to learn the usual lessons of reading and arithmetic, but it was also the place where he would absorb the habits and customs of a culture foreign to him. It was no different than if he were the immigrant, except in his case, he only had to walk down the street to arrive in a new country. The question for George was: would he move between the two worlds, or stake his place in only one?

George quickly learned to speak English. At some point, he adopted the anglicized version of his name. Maybe it was agreed he would be George when his mother registered him for school, the administrators suggesting that the name Jerzy would be too awkward for his Canadian schoolmates to pronounce. He made friends at school and in his neighbourhood, and he began living in this new country of children — the streets and the undeveloped fields that surrounded them. Although his parents sent him to Polish school on Saturday mornings, he refused to go after one year of lessons. He was discovering the power of the child of immigrants: he was his parents' interpreter of the outside world and the filter of information coming in. He threw away notes from school that he didn't want his parents to see. The arrival of his brother, when he was seven, made it even easier for him to escape attention. He assumed the freedom of a much older child, an independence undreamt of by today's youth.

As Wanda and Casey learned to speak English, it became the language George insisted on using when he spoke with them—and with his brother, who never became as fluent in Polish as George. In the words of linguist Julie Sedivy, this sacrifice of language is a "perennial immigrant equation" in which the family is betrayed for acceptance by society. The chasm between parents and child only grew as George realized that it was more than language that separated his family from those of his schoolmates. In comparison to the parents of his friends, their habits seemed foreign, and therefore backward and undesirable. Like most children, he wanted to fit in with his peers. He tolerated the minor insults about his Polish background—the football coach who called him "alphabet," the schoolyard taunts—overcoming them with his wits and, when needed, his fists. He hated the clothing his mother chose for him, so different from the others in the subtle ways that young people can detect. When he was thirteen and got his first job, he began buying his own clothes. His independence was complete.

For Wanda, this early separation from her son must have been another, unanticipated, loss. On the rare occasions when she spoke to him about his Polish heritage, George insisted that he was not Polish but Canadian. He identified with his own birthplace, not hers. The rejection she felt in his resolute avoidance of the very thing that defined her must have muted whatever satisfaction she took from George's ability to fend for himself.

During her visit to Poland, it's unlikely Wanda ventured into Belarus —still a Soviet republic in the 1970s—to seek out her hometown of Opaĺ. Her mistrust of the Soviets would have kept her from putting herself back into their orbit, and besides, twenty years before the Soviet Union's collapse, Belarus was still closed off. I don't know if she even could have obtained a visa to enter the country. Occasionally, I suggest to George that we travel there ourselves, to explore the area his mother came from. It doesn't surprise me when he objects. "What would we see there?" he asks. For him, the region holds no mystery.

Today, Belarus is a recovering post-Soviet republic under the control of a Soviet-style authoritarian dictatorship, going through a citizens' revolt against a fraudulent election that has, so far, only resulted in arrests and further oppression. Although a few hundred thousand Poles remain in Belarus, the country retains few remnants of the Polish culture that once existed inside its borders.[5] The world Wanda inhabited there no longer exists.

The Soviet and German occupations, with their deportations, intensive warfare, partisan activity, and mass atrocities, exacted a devastating toll on the people of Belarus. In his book *Bloodlands*, Timothy Snyder offers a chilling accounting of the losses. Nine million people lived in Soviet Belarus in 1941; 1.6 million non-combatants were killed by the Nazis, including 700,000 prisoners of war, 500,000 Jews, and 320,000 who were described as partisans. Two million people were moved from their homes or deported as forced labour. Another one million fled the Germans. When the Soviets returned, they deported a quarter million more people to Poland, and thousands more to the gulag (adding to the roughly quarter million they had deported there before the Nazi invasion). By the end of the war, Snyder says, half the population had been killed or moved, something that "cannot be said of any other European country."[6]

The country lay in ruins. Cities had been bombed and rural villages extensively damaged or entirely destroyed, burned in the Nazi hunt for Jews and partisans. In the first years after the war, the country was the scene of mass migrations. Hundreds of thousands of soldiers, partisans, forced labourers, and refugees moved through the republic. The formerly ethnically diverse region was transformed into a primarily Belarusian country. The homes of murdered Jews or deported Poles were now occupied by new owners, sanctioned by the state.

The existence of those who once lived in Belarus was scarcely acknowledged when Wanda returned to Poland in the early seventies. Many of the burned villages were never reconstructed and had disappeared from the map. The mass graves of the murdered Jews were covered over, left to nature's devices. The site at Bronna Góra

(Bronnaya Gara), about fifty kilometres from Opaĺ, is infamous among Holocaust researchers. The Nazis established this extermination site in May and June 1942. They conscripted hundreds of local residents to dig eight pits, sixty metres long by six metres wide, using shovels and explosives. Over the next six months, trains arrived frequently, bringing the Jews who were killed on arrival. By the end of the war, fifty thousand Jews were murdered and buried at Bronna Góra.[7]

These graves, and the mass graves of Jews throughout the country, remained unmarked for decades. After they liberated the area in 1944, the Soviets established a special commission to investigate the killing site. They excavated the bodies and interviewed witnesses for evidence at the Nuremberg trials. But the site was left to nature. The mass graves were not fenced in, and no memorial was erected. Indeed, no Soviet memorial specifically mentioned Jews as the victims of genocide. It wasn't until Jewish activists forced the issue, at the time of the fall of the Soviet Union, that the site was commemorated. Since then, through the determination of Jewish memorial societies and humanitarian organizations, a number of graves have been discovered and investigated and memorials dedicated in honour of the Jews of Belarus killed in the Holocaust.[8]

In *After Such Knowledge*, Eva Hoffman suggests that for all the losses non-Jewish Poles suffered in the Second World War, and the cult of memory that exists in Poland, the war is remembered "as tragedy rather than trauma." She wonders if tragic suffering is somehow more resolvable. The distinction, for her, is the agency of the victim. In tragic struggle, there may be "moral agony," but the victim's sense of identity and dignity remains intact.[9]

The trauma of the Holocaust was not Wanda's trauma, except as a witness. But it would be wrong to discount the oppressive and threatening experiences that affected her directly. In 1941, when much of the killing took place around her, Wanda would have been only fourteen years old. She had already suffered the loss of her father and an uncle, and the removal of her youngest brother from her immediate family. There had to have been many times during the war when her sense of identity and dignity were under attack, and her survival uncertain. I doubt she would have felt a sense of agency until she arrived in Canada, and even then, with constraints. I understand why Hoffman poses her questions, but I wonder whether the distinction she makes is more relevant at the level of culture or nationhood, where larger narratives are created. For Wanda, I feel certain there was both tragedy and trauma in all the losses, suffering, and deportation she experienced. How likely is it that she found comfort in the memories of her early life in a part of Poland that ceased to exist?

I no longer wonder why Wanda never spoke of the war to George; a parent's instinct is to shelter her children from disturbing information. In the ordinariness of life, such conversations would have seemed needless, even gratuitous. Just as likely, her experiences left her unable to articulate the full horror of years of suffering in the space of a few conversations. It must have been equally so for Casey, whose own journey had been no less arduous.

Sparing George and Chris from this knowledge was a gift, but the cost to Wanda must have been high. Unaware of the details of her past, George could not understand a central truth of his mother's life, or empathize with her struggle. This was a loss to him as much as to her. But in her silence, she communicated none of the hatred or prejudice that pervaded the world she grew up in. The grievances of the past can live in the hearts of children of immigrants, guaranteeing that somewhere in the world, someone is planning to exact revenge. Or immigrants can transfer their longing for a past life to their child, who, like the young woman who spoke at the conference I attended, may yearn for the land of her parents as a true, but unattainable, home. Without this inheritance, George was free to approach the world unencumbered.

Wanda likely had no reason to return to the scene of so much destruction and cruelty, to pull off the scab that had grown over the wound. If she couldn't talk about it, how could she revisit it? She undoubtedly knew it would look nothing like the place of her childhood, and as a Pole, she would not have been particularly welcome. If she had any memories of her time before the war, they would have to live on in her imagination, which was a better place for them. Boym says that reflective nostalgia "lingers on ruins, the patina of time and history, in the dreams of another place and another time." I want to believe that some fragments of her history made Wanda happy, some memories of a time when she was just a little girl with two loving parents.

Belarus was no place for her to find them.

At about the same time Wanda made her pilgrimage to Poland, Wolfgang Hamberger, Fulda's mayor, began to establish contact with the Jews who had fled the city before or during the war. Germany had begun the long, difficult process of reconciliation and atonement for its persecution of Jews, beginning a series of commemorations and Holocaust reunions that took place over the next two decades. One of the largest was in Fulda in 1987, when almost three hundred people from Israel, the United States, and twenty other countries converged on the city to remember the past and honour those who did not survive. Some were survivors, but many were their children or grandchildren, who encouraged their parents to confront a memory they had evaded for most of their lives. Some took part in walking tours, remembering the homes they once lived in, the stores they frequented, and the life they once had. They visited graves and spoke German for the first time in decades. Some even managed to reconnect with people they knew in their early years, a teacher or a friend. Although many dreaded their return, most felt satisfied to connect with their earlier selves and remember how they once lived, before the war. In spite of their trauma, they found meaning in revisiting the past.[10]

Historian Mary Fulbrook describes this period beginning in the late 1970s as the "era of the survivor," in contrast to the preceding "era of the witness," when the testimony of survivors as witnesses was important for the prosecution of war criminals and not for the meaning of their experiences in their own lives. She suggests that the era of the survivor was a discovery not of the persecuteds' voices but of an audience willing to listen. For example, every major French and

English publishing house rejected Elie Wiesel's *Night*, now considered a classic text on the horrors of Auschwitz and Buchenwald, when he wrote it in the late 1950s. Similarly, Primo Levi's *Ecce Homo* sold few copies when first published soon after the war; two decades passed before it reached a wide audience. In the last thirty years, the voices of Holocaust survivors have finally been heard in events like the one held in Fulda, in oral history and documentation projects, and in museums, books, and movies. Even in the face of all this evidence gathering, however, the most violent episode of the twentieth century is receding from view. Sadly, recent statistics suggest the number of students who lack knowledge of the Holocaust is increasing.

Although Wanda's experience of the war is categorically different from that of Holocaust survivors, it was profoundly traumatic. She was abused, stripped of her humanity, and forced to serve those who persecuted her, and she had to purchase her freedom with even more labour. Her experiences are little known. I assumed she never spoke of it first out of concern for her children and then because she preferred to put distance between her life in Canada and unpleasant thoughts of the past. But now, I wonder. Did she want to forget or was it simply that no one wanted to listen?

CHAPTER 14

THE RECKONING, PART II

After every war
someone has to tidy up.
. . . .
From time to time someone still must
dig up a rusted argument
from underneath a bush
and haul it off to the dump.

—Wisława Szymborska, *The End and the Beginning*[1]

The ad in the *New York Times* looked, at first, like any other advertisement for Mercedes-Benz. It wasn't until the third line that one realized it wasn't selling cars: "Mercedes-Benz. Design. Performance. Slave Labor." Fifty-five years after the war ended, the question of compensation for many of the victims of Nazi war crimes was still unresolved. In the early post-war period, the West German government had made a token effort to acknowledge responsibility toward the victims of the Holocaust. In November 1949, Chancellor Konrad Adenauer offered ten million deutschmarks (more than two million in Canadian dollars at the time) to Israel "as a first direct token that the injustice done to Jews all over the world has to be made good."[2] In the resulting negotiations with Israel (and the organization known as the Claims Conference), the West German government agreed to create a fund that, over the ensuing forty years, paid roughly one hundred billion DM to half a million Holocaust survivors.[3] The agreement excluded survivors who lived in communist countries and forced or slave labourers whose claims were considered within the realm of reparations under international law.[4] Millions of forced workers living behind the Iron Curtain and those, like Wanda, who had emigrated from Europe altogether received no compensation from Germany.

A variety of developments in Europe and the United States converged in the 1990s to bring this issue to the surface once again. Survivors and their descendants marked the fiftieth anniversary of various key events in the war: the Warsaw Ghetto Uprising, D-Day, and VE Day. In April 1993, the United States Holocaust Memorial Museum — the first official memorial to the Holocaust outside Israel — opened in Washington, DC. Historians, novelists, and filmmakers were retelling the story of the Holocaust in graphic detail for a public that may have known little of that part of history.

While the human cost of the war was well known, the magnitude of the financial impact on its victims was just coming under scrutiny. The Nazis had confiscated bank accounts, homes, and other valuable assets from Jews living in Germany and the conquered territories, much of it eventually passing through Swiss banks. As well, many of the victims of the Holocaust left behind dormant bank accounts and unclaimed insurance policies that remained unaccounted for.

In 1995, Edgar Bronfman and Isaac Singer, representing the World Jewish Congress, met with the Swiss Bankers Association to discuss the dormant bank accounts of Holocaust victims. Unhappy with the bankers' response, Bronfman and Singer turned to New York senator Alfonse D'Amato, chair of the Senate Banking Committee. For the next two years the committee investigated the conduct of the Swiss banks during the war. Lawyers, researchers, and Jewish organizations combed through newly available records to uncover dormant bank accounts and insurance policies. As more information came to light, one archivist described the Holocaust as not just the greatest murder in history but the "greatest robbery."[5]

Mercedes-Benz

DESIGN.
PERFORMANCE.
SLAVE LABOR.

"I was 15 when Daimler-Benz selected me from a concentration camp to work in its factory. My father, mother, two brothers and sister had all already been murdered."

Irving Kempler

When Daimler-Benz purchased Chrysler in 1998 for $36 billion, the company could point to a long history of efficient craftsmanship. What the company does not want to talk about is its equally efficient exploitation of tens of thousands of forced and slave laborers during World War II. Leased from the Nazis, these concentration camp inmates and abductees have never been compensated by Daimler-Benz for their labor, suffering and inhuman treatment.

Daimler-Benz owned or supervised factories throughout occupied Europe, including motor vehicle and tank facilities for the Nazi army, with many of the plants relying on slave labor for at least half their labor force, sometimes more. German companies were not required to use these people. They chose to use them. And to obtain workers from concentration camps, companies had to initiate formal bids. Many companies declined. But Daimler-Benz aggressively sought and received as much "disposable" forced and slave labor as possible. Daimler-Benz supervisors, in league with members of the SS, committed ongoing atrocities against these people, including imprisonment, torture and murder. Many were put to work digging out tunnels for underground facilities designed to protect Daimler-Benz equipment from Allied bombs. The death rate at Daimler-Benz was staggering.

Today, survivors of slave or forced labor at such companies as Daimler-Benz, BMW, Ford and Bayer await compensation for their work and suffering. Meanwhile, Nazi overseers received, and continue to receive, their salaries and pensions. Even some convicted war criminals collect their payments in prison.

No meaningful proposal to compensate these victims has yet been put forward. Time is running out. The survivors are dying. On October 6, negotiations between German companies and representatives of their victims will take place in Washington, D.C. Germany and those companies that used slave labor have a moral and legal obligation to pay these victims for their work, suffering and inhuman treatment. Surely, DaimlerChrysler, with $143 billion in assets, can afford to pay its debt to those it so brutally exploited.

From the makers of Mercedes-Benz, that's the level of performance we expect.

JUSTICE. COMPENSATION. NOW.

New York Times advertisement, October 1999

(REUTERS/Alamy Stock Photo)

The Clinton administration appointed Stuart Eizenstat as its special representative to broker a resolution to the dispute on behalf of the US government. As the pressure mounted, the Swiss bankers agreed to an independent audit of their accounts. But the arrival of lawyers who filed lawsuits in New York hijacked a diplomatic solution. Eizenstat considered the class-action lawyers a "witches' brew of egos and mutual jealousies" that threatened to push the negotiations beyond his diplomatic control. But the awkward union of law, politics, and diplomacy eventually resulted in a settlement that provided Jewish groups with $1.25 billion for lost assets of Holocaust victims and their heirs. It also created a template for resolution of the complex issue of compensation for slave and forced labourers.

On March 4, 1998, the first class action to deal with German forced labourers was filed in New Jersey against the Ford Motor Company and its German subsidiary, Ford-Werke, for their use of slave and forced labour to make trucks for the German army.[6] Eventually, US lawyers filed fifty cases in federal and state courts against more than a dozen German companies doing business in the United States, including Bayer, Volkswagen, Siemens, and BASF.[7] Although class actions are a growing segment of litigation in Canada, they have long been a prominent feature of the American legal system, and evolving jurisprudence in the US courts meant that foreigners could be held liable for violations of international law, even if the offences or crimes were committed outside the United States and against non-Americans.[8]

The timing for a resolution of these claims would never be better. In the increasingly complex global trade environment, German corporations were vulnerable to government and consumer pressures in the United States. Daimler-Benz had announced a pending merger with Chrysler, VW was about to introduce the new Beetle in the United States, and German companies generally were competing for new markets. German industry looked for ways to resolve the claims and end the negative publicity.

None of these cases went to trial. All were vulnerable to dismissal on the basis of expired limitation periods, and some others would have been rejected because the plaintiffs had worked for firms that no longer existed, or for the German government (including those, like Wanda, who worked for the railway), or for firms with no presence in the United States. Finally, many of the plaintiffs were excluded because post-war treaties with Germany's allies — Italy, Hungary, Romania, Bulgaria, and Austria — cut off the claims by nationals of those countries.[9] But in cases with important social dimensions, even where a successful outcome is doubtful, the filing of a lawsuit is an invitation to a conversation. The German companies were prepared to talk.

In August, representatives of twelve major German companies met to discuss their strategy. They had several conflicting object-ives. Even if they succeeded in defeating the lawsuits, they would lose in the court of public opinion in an important market. They needed to remove impediments to business, preferably without admitting liability for the sins of the past. But, as members of the post-war gen-eration, they also felt a moral obligation to treat the victims of the Nazis respectfully and reach an honourable settlement of their claims.

The Germans proposed to accept their historical responsibility to Holocaust survivors and others who had suffered under the Nazis in exchange for the settlement of pending and future class actions. Stuart Eizenstat again stepped into the negotiations. His objective was to ensure that any settlement would reach all those affected by the Nazis' forced-labour programs, and he expanded the stakeholder group to include representatives of the governments of Germany, the United States, Central and Eastern European nations whose forced labourers had never been paid, Israel, the Claims Conference (repre-senting all Jews regardless of country of origin), German industries, and class-action attorneys.[10]

Not surprisingly, the negotiations were messy, complex, and heated. As they dragged on, with disputes over the amount of the com-pensation fund and the classes of persons entitled to make claims, the claimant groups pressured the German government and industry. There were frequent skirmishes outside the negotiating boardrooms, with provocative tactics and statements on all sides. On February 17,

1999, the *New York Times* reported that the German chancellor, Gerhard Schröder, announced the establishment of a "Remembrance, Responsibility and Future" fund of up to $1.7 billion to compensate the victims of the Nazis; another purpose, frankly admitted, was to "counter law suits, particularly class action suits, and to remove the basis of the campaign being led against German industry and our country."[11] The advertisement that ran in the *New York Times* later that year was just a warning shot to the Germans from the litigants. More would follow if necessary.

Soon after, the parties came to an agreement in principle, leaving the details of the compensation scheme for further negotiation. A signing ceremony in Berlin on December 17, 1999, confirmed the settlement. In the news conference that followed, Chancellor Schröder expressed the hope that the agreement would bring an end to a "bloody century [when] Germany inflicted suffering on the world and perpetrated the Holocaust, a scar that cannot be healed." The same day, the German president, Johannes Rau, offered a public apology in which he "begged forgiveness" on behalf of the German people for the mistreatment of slave and forced labourers.[12]

The settlement became law in Germany with the proclamation of the Foundation Law on August 12, 2000. The law established a foundation to make financial compensation to those affected by Nazi injustice, to be processed through partner organizations. A fund of approximately $5.2 billion—one half from German industry, the other half from the German government—was created to fund claims by forced labourers as well as other Nazi-era property claims against Germany. From the fund, more than eight billion deutschmarks was allocated to payments to the Claims Conference, the five Eastern European nations, and claimants living in the rest of the world. Another seven hundred million was set aside for the Remembrance, Responsibility and Future fund to promote social justice and understanding and commemorate the victims of Nazi injustice.

The preamble to the Foundation Law acknowledged that the Nazis had "inflicted severe injustice on slave laborers and forced laborers through deportation, exploitation, and…human rights violations"; that the German enterprises also "bear a historic responsibility and must accept it"; and that "the Law comes too late for those who lost their lives or…have died in the meantime." It also declared the Bundestag's intention "to keep alive the memory of the injustice inflicted on the victims for the coming generations as well."[3]

George first heard about the compensation fund through a chance conversation with a lawyer who appeared before him in a labour arbitration. The lawyer, whose mother had coincidentally also been a forced labourer in Germany, asked George if he was aware of the fund. He was not, and so she faxed the application forms to him. The legislation set a tight timeline: applications had to be made by December 31, 2001, to qualify.

George called Wanda to tell her about her right to make a claim for compensation. She was unenthusiastic. "What's the point?" she said. "It was so long ago." George prodded her. She was entitled to make a claim, he said. After all this time, the harm done to her was acknowledged, and she should get what little compensation was available. To him, a busy arbitrator accustomed to hearing labour grievances, it was simple: fill out the form, send it in, wait for the decision. It seems insensitive, in retrospect, that we didn't consider that it might not have been simple to Wanda, digging up a memory that she preferred to leave undisturbed. We assumed she would be glad to know that someone was finally taking responsibility for what was done to her during the war. After a while, she relented; she would look at the forms with him. It never occurred to us that she was doing this just to please her son.

A few months later, in July 2001, George sat with Wanda in her kitchen to go over the questions on the application. By then, Wanda was seventy-four years old, her time in the labour camp almost sixty years in the past. I imagine her searching through the cookie tin for her old documents and possibly lingering over some of the

photographs that later absorbed my attention. I wonder now whether
the idea of talking about this time with George made her anxious. She
would have had to prepare herself to go into the detail needed to make
a claim. She would have been forced into a conversation with George
that she had avoided for a lifetime. She might have asked herself
whether it was worth the trouble.

I doubt the questions themselves surprised her. In the way of
bureaucracies everywhere, the foundation classified Nazi victims
based on the category of misery endured. Were they in a death camp,
a concentration camp, a labour camp? Were they injured or diseased?
Did they lose family members? In the form, Wanda recorded that she
was sent to Fulda in August 1943 to work in a factory making parts
for warplanes. This was different from the information Joe later
gave us, that they worked making parts for trains. Maybe George
misunderstood her, or perhaps she herself didn't know what the parts
were for and made her own assumptions. She could not remember the
name of the company.

The form asked for a description of what happened during the
period of her forced labour, including the conditions in which she was
held. For the first and last time, she told George what had happened to
her in Germany. He wrote it down for her:

> We lived in a barracks behind barbed wire. Every morning
> the guards took us to the work. We worked from 6 a.m.
> to 6 p.m., I think. There were armed guards in the factory
> watching us while we worked. In the morning before
> work they gave us one slice of bread and black coffee.
> For lunch we had kohlrabi soup and a slice of bread. For
> dinner we had a slice of bread and black coffee. There was
> one Italian, two Russian, and four Polish barracks. There
> were 21 of us in a 25-foot by 12-foot room in three-high
> bunks. We were not ever allowed to go outside for any
> reason except to go to work. There were armed guards
> outside the barracks. We worked seven days a week. The
> guards would beat at us [sic] for no reason. The barracks

were filthy and full of lice and bedbugs. When the Allies were bombing the area we were not allowed to leave the barracks to go to a bunker.

Wanda gave as little detail as possible. She didn't tell George about the day she was taken and deported to Germany. They didn't have a conversation about life during the Russian and German occupations or during her time in the camp. She didn't talk about being hungry or afraid or how she felt about losing her home. She didn't offer any of the details we later heard from Joe. The form didn't require this information, and she didn't volunteer it.

The International Organization for Migration was responsible for administering the applications of non-Jewish victims living outside the Czech Republic, Poland, and the republics of the former Soviet Union. In May 2002, it notified Wanda that her claim contained all the necessary information required for processing. Sometime later, the foundation awarded Wanda a sum in the neighbourhood of $1,600 for her forced labour as "voluntary humanitarian indemnification."

Sixteen hundred dollars. In our twenty-first-century rights-oriented world, we imagine that for every wrong there is a remedy; that offenders should be punished, and the innocent should be compensated for their losses and suffering. We believe that if the victim cannot be made whole, the remedy should be proportional to the wrong. Even in a robust justice system like Canada's, this belief is often more theoretical than real. But for Wanda, the idea was not even theoretical. It was ludicrous. Was the paltry cheque an insult to her injury, rubbing salt in a wound that had almost healed?

The foundation avoided using the term *compensation*, acknowledging that the payment was not intended to represent actual compensation for the harm suffered but was a symbolic material gesture and public recognition of the tragedy of her victimization. The symbolism of the result was not always reflected in the turbulent negotiations that led to the agreement, though. Stuart Eizenstat's description of the negotiation process offers an unflattering portrait of many of the players and of their motives. I was disturbed to read about one German representative's resistance to the compensation of non-Jewish forced labourers. Bodo Hombach wanted to keep the focus on the "singular notion of the Holocaust," where the Germans had a "particular historical obligation." He regarded the plight of the forced labourers as a "wage differential" problem that was a consequence of war, distinct from slave labourers who were worked to death. At one point, he unwisely informed Eizenstat that "the German mindset is ready to address the singular atrocities of the Holocaust, but forced labor is as old as time—for example, the building of the Pyramids." From Eizenstat's account, it seems obvious that many of the parties were clinging to longstanding views and grievances that stood in the way of resolution.[14]

They seemed united, though, in their disdain for the lawyers and their extreme tactics and excessive demands. I found myself conflicted about the role of the lawyers in this case. I wasn't disturbed by their tactics; for a lawyer, it is often better to be feared than liked. I can admire the fearlessness lawyers can demonstrate when pursuing their clients' interests, as long as they comply with their ethical duties to their clients and the courts. And without the lawyers, would any of this have occurred? But they were so handsomely compensated, while the people whose interests they represented came away with so little. Although a few of the key lawyers in the Swiss negotiations took no fees at all, fifty-two law firms involved in the German cases divided up $54 million in legal fees, with the average fee being a little over $1 million, for services that amounted to research, filing claims, and meetings and negotiations.[15] It isn't wrong that they were paid, but that fact sits uneasily beside the $1,600 Wanda got for her deportation, her labour, the loss of her youth and her country. On this point Eizenstat was unapologetic, pointing out that the lawyers' fees were minuscule compared with the contingency fees in mass-injury cases, which can range from 15 to over 30 percent of the settlements. This seems like cold comfort to me, but George is surprised the fees weren't higher. He is never surprised by the extremes of human nature.

My uneasiness about Wanda's claim, and the program as a whole, isn't really about legal fees. It's about the power money is thought to have as a symbol of justice or remorse for those who went through experiences like Wanda's, or worse. If the true loss can never be compensated, what is the purpose of the financial award? One of the claimants observed, poetically, that the money was "just to wipe tears."[16] Elie Wiesel, in his introduction to Eizenstat's book about the negotiations, wrote that the true damage of the war had to do with something other than financial losses. It was in the childhood that was lost, the small but meaningful possessions that disappeared, and the innocence that was stolen. Money cannot compensate for intangible but precious possessions. The claims were not really about money; in his words, they were about the "ethical value and weight of memory." The duty to remember includes not just the great or momentous but also the small possessions of the poor. "In other words," he writes, "the poor victims were robbed of their poverty."

Another observer, Abraham Foxman, the director of the Anti-Defamation League, was also concerned that the act of "monetizing" the Holocaust demeaned its victims, but he finally concluded that it was important to have accountability, not only for those affected but as a message to future generations.

Eizenstat acknowledged these concerns, and as the man who dedicated several years of his life to completing the negotiations, he undoubtedly spent much time wondering at the significance of his mission. In the end, he concluded that the legacy of his work was "simply the emergence of the truth" about the dimensions of the injustice visited on the innocent, which had never been redressed.

The truth that emerged from the forced-labour negotiations was already known to those who had experienced it, and to some extent it had been explored in the Nuremberg trials and in numerous books and other writings since then. No new facts emerged in the negotiations themselves. Unlike a court proceeding, which is open and transparent, negotiations take place in private settings. No witnesses were called, because the discussions were about money, responsibility, and the structure of a settlement. As for Wanda, I doubt that she considered that she was engaged in an exercise of exposing the truth. Her sparse statement could not — and was not intended to — convey her true losses: the life she was born to live, her identity as a Pole, and the culture she could not fully share with her children, a gap that could never be bridged.

Perhaps no agreement could bear the burden of such a mission, and nobody could have known this better than Wanda and the others who shared her losses. Still, the apologies by the German chancellor and president and the admission contained in the legislation that created the foundation were important acknowledgements of the injustice forced labourers had suffered. And, although the amounts paid to individual claimants were not high, the aggregate amount of the settlement was substantial enough to represent a true gesture of remorse and reconciliation. New sources of information were developed and made publicly available on the foundation's website and in the German national archives. Some of the funds were used for an international biographical documentation project, in which nearly six hundred people were interviewed about their forced-labour experiences. Of these, thirty were living in the United States (none were in Canada). The resulting book, *Hitler's Slaves: Life Stories of Forced Labourers in Nazi-Occupied Europe*, tempers dry academic research with the words of those who agreed to tell their stories, some of them for the first time. Oral histories were videotaped, educational materials were developed, a travelling exhibit produced by the Buchenwald and Mittelbau-Dora Memorials Foundation was compiled into a book about forced labour, and websites were created. All of this can educate future generations.

But mostly, the truth exists in the application forms of the 165 million claimants who received payments under the fund. It will be remembered by the hundreds of people who read the forms and searched through archival records to process the claims of the labourers. These humble documents contain the weight of the evidence about the Nazi forced-labour program as its victims experienced it. But the forms aren't searchable; someone who knows what they are looking for has to request them. Maybe someone has created an extract or database of the information from the applications—this would have been a burdensome addition to the already massive task of administering the fund—but if it exists, I didn't manage to find it. The forms and the words of the abused will remain buried in the German national archives until someone like me goes searching for information about a loved one or, more likely, until the whole episode recedes from view completely.

In a small park near Roncesvalles Avenue, once the heart of Toronto's Polish community, stands a monument to the dead of Katyń. Cast in bronze and erected in 1980, the large rectangular sculpture is cracked in the middle, the two jagged facing edges leaving an empty space between them until they meet at the bottom. Poland's broken heart, its fractured country, are movingly represented in the artwork. The monument is inscribed with the words, "In remembrance of fifteen thousand Polish prisoners of war who vanished in 1940 from the camps in USSR at Kozelsk, Ostashkov, Starobelsk. Of these over four thousand were later discovered in mass graves at Katyń, near Smolensk, murdered by the Soviet state security police."

The brutal massacre of the Polish soldiers has come to symbolize the historical antagonism of the Poles toward the Russians for crimes against them and is particularly resonant for the Polish diaspora, who were among those affected by the loss of part of Poland to the Soviet Union and the deportations in the early part of the war. Before the fall of communism in 1989, there were no monuments to Katyń in Poland itself, where the taboo against discussion of Soviet crimes against the Poles prevented such commemorations. The Poles knew the truth, though, and on All Souls' Day they erected wooden crosses in cemeteries, in defiance of the lie they were forced to live with. It was up to Poles in exile to make their own remembrances, exacting the only justice available for the crimes against Poland. Similar monuments to the dead at Katyń can be found where other Polish exiles settled around the world.

At Nuremberg, the Soviets had accused the Nazis of responsibility for the deaths of the Polish soldiers in the Katyń forest, citing evidence from their own commission into the deaths to prove it was the Nazis, and not the Soviets, who were guilty of the crime. The Nuremberg judges offered no vindication to the Soviets on this allegation, making no reference in their decision to the murder of the Polish soldiers. The Soviet claim that the crime was committed by the Nazis was ignored, as if it were never made. The lie persisted until 1990, when Soviet president Mikhail Gorbachev admitted guilt but implied that NKVD chief Lavrentiy Beria had acted on his own, without state authority, in directing the killing. But in 1992, his successor, Boris Yeltsin, went to Warsaw and handed the Polish president, Lech Wałęsa, the proof of what everyone knew was true. The March 5, 1940, order that led to the Polish deaths, signed by Stalin, said in part:

> In the NKVD camps for war prisoners and in prisons…
> is currently detained a large number of ex-officers of
> the Polish army, ex-members of the Polish police and
> intelligence services, members of Polish nationalist and
> counter-revolutionary parties, members of organisations
> exposed as counter-revolutionary and insurrectionist,
> fugitives and others. All are persistent enemies of Soviet
> power, and full of hatred for the Soviet outlook….To be
> treated in the special mode with the application in their
> case of the ultimate measure of punishment—shooting.

When Yeltsin went to Warsaw, he promised to punish the surviving murderers and pay reparations; neither of these was done. In 1994, the Polish and Russian governments signed an agreement for the mutual preservation of burial sites of victims of wars and repressions; two years later, the Russian government began construction of a memorial at the site of the mass grave at Katyń. Although the Polish government designated the site a Polish military cemetery, the Russians dedicated the memorial to "those Soviet and Polish citizens who fell victim of totalitarian repressions." Thus, the Polish soldiers were described not as prisoners of war and victims of Soviet war crimes but as victims of Stalin's repression. After all, the Soviet Union has consistently maintained that it was not at war with Poland in September 1939, let alone when the massacres were carried out in 1940.

Casey died before any of these events occurred, but it wouldn't have surprised him to know that this rapprochement was short-lived. In the last decade, both Polish and Russian governments have pursued nationalist policies, and the Katyń memorial is one of many that have become the scenes for contested historical narratives. Next to the burial site, the Russian government built a large monument dedicated to the victims of the Great Terror of 1937-38, including official recognition of about eight thousand Russian victims of Stalinism from the Smolensk region. A sign at the memorial entrance reads, "Here rest over 8,000 Soviet and over 4,000 Polish citizens," but only a small number of the eight thousand Soviet victims actually "rest" in Katyń; the others are buried elsewhere in the Smolensk region. The importance of this monument is the impression it creates: that twice as many Soviets as Poles were killed at Katyń, and that the site is to commemorate the suffering of all of them.

In 2017, Russia's first national memorial commemorating victims of Soviet repression, The Wall of Grief, was erected beside Moscow's central ring road. The massive, curved, bronze sculpture made up of dozens of faceless human figures is intended to represent the millions deported, imprisoned, and executed under Joseph Stalin, including Casey and all the other *sybiracy*. The memorial makes no reference to the circumstances of the deported. There was not and never will be any compensation offered to those whom these repressions affected. Although the Polish government recently established a compensation fund and created the Siberian Exile Cross in 2003, neither of these can be awarded posthumously except to those who were still alive in 2003.

Modern Russia has never embraced the language and gestures of reconciliation and transitional justice. The progress of the heady days of glasnost has been replaced by a return to suppression of information and human rights, and a centuries-old vision of a Slavic world under Russia. Memorial, the organization working to preserve the memories of the repressed (including the murdered Polish officers and the *sybiracy*) was declared a "foreign agent" and later shut down completely following a prosecution in the Russian Supreme Court in late 2021. A state prosecutor argued that the organization had "blackened the Soviet Union's wartime legacy," asking, "Why do we, the offspring of victors, have to repent and be embarrassed, instead of being proud of our glorious past?"[17] Masha Gessen has written that Russia was sensitive to the depiction of the USSR as a terrorist country, preferring the more benign term "political repression," making "the deaths and arrests of millions sound like something akin to a natural disaster or perhaps a pandemic—a tragedy beyond human control."[18]

Not long after these events, the Russian army invaded Ukraine under the guise of a "special military operation" for "restoring the peace" and aiding civilians, in a deafening echo of its 1939 occupation of the some of the same territory. Russia dropped bombs on Ukrainian cities, killing, maiming, or deporting civilians, creating refugees, and destroying land in a country that had the temerity to imagine a future without Russian oppression.

In the face of such an outrage, the injuries and insults of the past must fade into the background. For Casey and the other *sybiracy*, as for the millions of other victims, there will never be any justice from the Soviets, the Russians, or anyone representing them. With the Russian invasion of Ukraine still raging, it is too early to say whether there will ever be justice for today's victims.

When the foundation's cheque arrived, Wanda called George to tell him. "What should I do with the money?" she asked. George was confused by the question, because Wanda certainly knew how to deposit money in the bank. Without thinking further of it, he told her to cash the cheque.

Only too late did he wonder whether her question was more philosophical than literal. If the payment was a symbolic gesture, then was she really asking whether she should make some symbolic use of it? She was comfortable enough. Although Casey's pension had expired, she had some savings, a small government pension, and very modest expenses. I can imagine that the idea of using the money for daily living expenses would have seemed incongruous or somehow unworthy. Surely she had not returned to her troubled memories just for some additional spending money.

Perhaps Wanda already understood this when she asked George what would be the point in pursuing the application. She didn't need the money. She didn't crave justice, and anyway, what would that consist of? For many, the payment, even in the form of a token sum, would have been vindication for what was taken from them. Others believe that the public apology and admission of wrong, even if from a later generation, are important steps in bringing closure to historical injustice. Truth and reconciliation systems across the globe are dedicated to this form of healing.

I wish we had taken the time to ask Wanda what justice meant for her. She wouldn't have heard the public apology, although I have no doubt there were words of apology in the letter she received from the foundation. Her skeptical nature and her powerlessness during the war may have made her suspicious of the motives of the people behind the negotiations and settlement. It might even have pained her to think that her participation in the compensation process implied her forgiveness. The simple words, the terse description in her application form, tell me she had a wall around her memories. She hadn't forgotten, and I doubt she felt very forgiving.

It's a popular sentiment in today's world that forgiveness can bring peace to the wronged and talking about trauma can lead to healing. I don't think Wanda would have agreed with either of these ideas. Left on her own to recover from the war's upheaval, she had unique strategies to reconcile herself to a new and unexpected life. Some luck was involved. When her future was most uncertain, Canada offered her a home. Despite the price she paid for her immigration, she was fortunate to find herself among a group of women who shared her history, for whom no explanation was necessary. Together, they created new lives out of some very unpromising material, claiming their liberty in a new country where they could live undisturbed.

In Kitchener, in the modest home that she and her husband owned with no fear of being dispossessed, Wanda was free to live as she chose, finally immune to the big ideas of powerful men. It's not hard to see the compensation scheme as just another of those big ideas. It may have been a mistake to persuade her to participate in the process, a cheapening of the peace she had worked so hard to achieve on her own.

Now, when I think of the conversations we never had about Wanda's past life, I no longer regret the questions I failed to ask. Silence was Wanda's answer to the past and her protection in the present. Silence was her right. Who is to say that the burial of her memories, the simple life in a safe space, wasn't justice for her?

Acknowledgements

In my transition from lawyer to writer, I've been fortunate to have had many guides who supported and challenged me while writing this book. In the early going, Susan Scott saw the potential of Wanda's story in an essay, encouraged me to think of transforming the story into a book, and pointed me in the right direction. The faculty and fellow students at the University of King's College in Halifax, and in particular Dean Jobb and mentors Jane Silcott and Harry Thurston, had a profound influence on the development of the manuscript, and on my writing life more generally. Thank you, all of you, for sharing your knowledge and treating my ideas and writing with such care and respect.

I am so grateful to have a wonderful group of friends who have shared the joys and frustrations of writing with me in the last few years. Special thanks go to Rebecca Blissett, Alison Dowsett, Robin Duke, Karen Stiller, and Susan Lightstone; Alison Colvin went the extra distance, travelling to Quebec with me to explore Saint-Georges; and my writing group — Margaret Lynch, Catherine Fitton, Catherine Fogarty, and Katherine McCall — have helped to keep me on track. Jeremiah Bertram read an early version of the manuscript and offered great insight and wisdom about the book, and about life. To them, and many other friends and family members who have helped and supported me (and learned to be careful about asking how the book was coming), I appreciate all of you.

With few archival or written records and no surviving friends to consult about Wanda and Casey, I turned to Wanda's brother, Joe Gizmunt, for information about the family's life in Poland. Joe and his wife, Maria, and their sons, Robert and Chris, were extremely kind and generous with their time, and tolerant of my questions about a past they probably did not think about that much. Sadly, Joe died before this book was completed, but I want to express my (and George's) deep gratitude for him to his family.

I gained immeasurable respect for the work of historians and archivists while researching this book and benefitted from the input of several historians, both academic and amateur. Franziska Exeler was very generous in sharing her time and research about Belarus with me, even making her own search of maps to try to locate Casey's home. The Kresy-Siberia Foundation has a substantial online presence to provide resources, translation, maps, research aids, and so much more for me and thousands of others to research the little-known part of history of the exiled Poles from the *kresy*. I am also thankful to Łukasz Wodzyński for help with translations, as well as his literary and cultural insights about Poland. A former colleague, Voy Stelmaszynski, shared his own father's story with me and provided additional translation of an important article.

I've been privileged to work with the people at Goose Lane Editions, who have taken great care in the transformation of manuscript to book. I'm grateful to Matthew Halliday for his insightful comments and support in the early going, and to editors Jill Ainsley and Jess Shulman for their sensitive, detailed, and very thorough editorial work. Susanne Alexander's team, and especially Alan Sheppard and Julie Scriver, have eased the book's journey into its final form with great skill and good humour. I've been in good hands for this entire process.

I owe my greatest debt and deepest gratitude to George, who has supported me in every idea and project I've proposed during our decades-long relationship, no matter how ambitious or dubious (or both), usually at great cost to him as well. He tolerated my probing questions about his past without complaint, facilitated and organized research trips to Boston, Poland, and Germany, and tactfully offered his thoughts on earlier versions of the book. Dziękuję za wszystko co robisz.

Notes

INTRODUCTION: QUESTIONS

1. At various times in its history, modern Belarus was known as Byelorussia, Soviet Byelorussia, or Belorussia. Rather than require the reader to adapt to these different iterations in different time periods, I have taken a pragmatic approach, at all times referring to the territory as Belarus, Soviet Belarus, or the Belarusian Soviet Socialist Republic. When the country is referred to in quotations, I have preserved the spelling in the original.
2. Throughout the text, the spelling of Opol/Opaĺ will generally reflect the version in use at the time.

1: BORDERLANDS

1. Patrice M. Dabrowski, *Poland: The First Thousand Years* (Dekalb: Northern Illinois University Press, 2014), 130.
2. Timothy Snyder, *The Reconstruction of Nations: Poland, Ukraine, Lithuania, Belarus, 1569-1999* (New Haven: Yale University Press, 2003), 158–63, Kindle.
3. Czesław Miłosz and Catherine S. Leach, *Native Realm: A Search for Self-Definition* (New York: Farrar, Straus and Giroux, 2002), 129–30.
4. Jacob Shell, "Pripyat Marsh Culture (a half century before Chernobyl) — 1934 Photographs by American geographic explorer Louise A. Boyd," *Visual Work + Short Essays* (blog), accessed March 21, 2022, https://jacobshell.carbonmade.com/projects/7164197.
5. Louise Arner Boyd and Stanisław Gorzuchowski, *Polish Countrysides* (New York: American Geographical Society, 1937), 45–83.
6. Franziska Exeler, "Reckoning with Occupation: Soviet Power, Local Communities, and the Ghosts of Wartime Behavior in Post-1944 Belorussia" (PhD diss., Princeton University, 2013), 59.
7. Norman Davies, *God's Playground: A History of Poland*, Vol. 2, *1795 to the Present* (New York: Columbia University Press, 1982), 393.
8. Dabrowski, *Poland*, 384–90.
9. Adam Zamoyski, *Poland: A History* (London: William Collins, 2015), 296.
10. Dabrowski, *Poland*, 389.
11. Kiryl Kascian, "Belarus's Day of National Unity: A Controversial Public Holiday with a Flawed Logic," *New Eastern Europe*, November 2, 2021.

12. Zamoyski, *Poland: A History*, 297–311.
13. Matthew Kelly, *Finding Poland: From Tavistock to Hruzdowa and Back Again* (London: Jonathan Cape, 2010), 49.
14. Born in 1911 in Šeteniai in today's Lithuania, Miłosz is one of many Polish literary figures to have been born in the *kresy*, a list which includes Adam Mickiewicz, born in Zaosie (Belarus); Adam Zagajewski, born in Lwów (Lviv, Ukraine); and even Joseph Conrad (Józef Korzeniowski), born in Berdyczów (Berdychiv, Ukraine). Not unusually for the region, Miłosz's heritage was a mix of Polish, Lithuanian, German, and possibly even Serbian origin.
15. Kathryn Clare Ciancia, "Poland's Wild East: Imagined Landscapes and Everyday Life in the Volhynian Borderlands, 1918-1939" (PhD diss., Stanford University, 2011), 6.
16. Halik Kochanski, *The Eagle Unbowed: Poland and the Poles in the Second World War* (London: Penguin, 2013), 82–84.
17. Dabrowski, *Poland*, 406.
18. Exeler, "Reckoning with Occupation," 49–50.
19. Kelly, *Finding Poland*, 73.
20. Kelly, *Finding Poland*, 80.
21. Jan Tomasz Gross, *Revolution from Abroad: The Soviet Conquest of Poland's Western Ukraine and Western Belorussia* (Princeton, NJ: Princeton University Press, 2002), 35.
22. Exeler, "Reckoning with Occupation," 82–83; and Kelly, *Finding Poland*, 85.
23. Exeler, "Reckoning with Occupation."
24. Ryszard Kapuściński, *Imperium* (New York: Vintage, 1995), chap. 2, Kindle.

2: THE GULAG

1. "Victims of Political Terror in the USSR," Memorial International, accessed March 17, 2022, https://lists.memo.ru/index.htm.
2. Masha Gessen, "The Russian Memory Project that Became an Enemy of the State," *New Yorker*, January 6, 2022.
3. N.S. Lebedeva, "The Deportation of the Polish Population to the USSR, 1939–41," *Journal of Communist Studies and Transition Politics* 16, no. 1–2 (2000): 28.
4. Julija Šukys, *Siberian Exile: Blood, War, and a Granddaughter's Reckoning* (Lincoln NE: University of Nebraska Press, 2017), 87.
5. Lynne Viola, *The Unknown Gulag: The Lost World of Stalin's Special Settlements* (New York: Oxford University Press, 2007), 3–4, 32, 78, 132, 168.
6. Adam "Kaczor" Kaczyński, "Along the River Juły," *Kurier Galcyjski* 14, no. 162 (July 31-August 16, 2012).
7. Stefan W. Waydenfeld, *Ice Road: An Epic Journey from the Stalinist Labor Camps to Freedom* (Los Angeles: Aquila Polonica, 2011), chap. 6, Kindle.
8. Julius Margolin, Stefani Hoffman, Timothy Snyder, and Katherine R. Jolluck, *Journey into the Land of the Zeks and Back: A Memoir of the Gulag* (Oxford: Oxford University Press, 2020), chap. 6, Kindle.
9. Gustaw Herling, *A World Apart* (London: Heinemann, 1951), chap. 10, Kobo.
10. Waydenfeld, *Ice Road*.
11. Herling, *A World Apart*, chap. 11.
12. Margolin et al., *Land of the Zeks*, chap. 13.
13. Edward H. Herzbaum, *Lost between Worlds: A World War II Journey of Survival* (Leicester: Matador, 2010), 51–54.

3: WAR AND AMNESTY

1. Franziska Exeler, *Ghosts of War: Nazi Occupation and Its Aftermath in Soviet Belarus* (Ithaca, NY: Cornell University Press, 2022), chap. 2.
2. Henning Pieper, *Fegelein's Horsemen and Genocidal Warfare* (London: Palgrave Macmillan, 2015), 92.
3. A.L. Polick, "The Destruction of Motol," JewishGen (website), trans. Shimon Yojok and ed. Dov Yarden (Jerusalem: Former Residents of Motol in Israel, 1956), https://www.jewishgen.org/yizkor/motol/motol.html#title, accessed January 26, 2021.
4. Matthew Kelly, *Finding Poland: From Tavistock to Hruzdowa and Back Again* (London: Jonathan Cape, 2010), 132. The italics in the quotation are my addition.
5. Kelly, *Finding Poland*, 132–35.
6. Anne Applebaum, *Gulag: A History* (New York: Doubleday, 2003), chap. 21, Kindle.
7. Józef Czapski, *Inhuman Land: Searching for the Truth in Soviet Russia*, trans. Antonia Lloyd-Jones (New York: NYRB, 2018), 35.
8. Roman Olczyk, "Memories of Siberia," Poland in Exile (website), http://www.polandinexile.com/olczyk.html.
9. Kenneth K. Koskodan, *No Greater Ally: The Untold Story of Poland's Forces in World War II* (Oxford: Osprey, 2009), 117.
10. Norman Davies, *Trail of Hope: The Anders Army, an Odyssey across Three Continents* (Oxford: Osprey, 2015), 95; and Halik Kochanski, *The Eagle Unbowed: Poland and the Poles in the Second World War* (London: Penguin, 2013), 180.
11. Applebaum, *Gulag*, chap. 21.
12. Czapski, *Inhuman Land*, 361.
13. Exeler, *Ghosts of War*, chap. 2.
14. Richard J. Evans, *The Third Reich at War* (New York: Penguin, 2009), 195.
15. Exeler, *Ghosts of War*, 94.
16. Evans, *Third Reich*, 76.
17. Alexander von Plato, Almut Leh, and Christoph Thonfeld, *Hitler's Slaves: Life Stories of Forced Labourers in Nazi-Occupied Europe* (New York: Berghahn Books, 2010), 72, 88.
18. Ann Tusa and John Tusa, *The Nuremberg Trial* (London: Macmillan, 1984), chap. 15, Kindle.
19. Tusa and Tusa, *Nuremberg Trial*, Biographies of the Defendants.

4: OSTARBEITER IN GERMANY

1. Taras Kurylo, "'The Biggest Calamity That Overshadowed All Other Calamities': Recruitment of Ukrainian 'Eastern Workers' for the War Economy of the Third Reich, 1941–1944" (PhD diss., University of Alberta, 2009), 88.
2. Kurylo, "'The Biggest Calamity,'" 27–28. *Ostarbeiter* refers to non-German Soviet citizens, including residents of Soviet Ukraine (except Galicia), Soviet Belarus, and the territories of interwar Poland in western Belarus and Volhynia.
3. Kurylo, "'The Biggest Calamity,'" 28.
4. Ulrich Herbert, *Hitler's Foreign Workers: Enforced Foreign Labor in Germany under the Third Reich* (Cambridge: Cambridge University Press, 1997), 189-90.

5. International Military Tribunal Prosecution, "Fritz Sauckel letter to Alfred Rosenberg and report concerning plans for the mobilization of labor," April 24, 1942. Harvard Law School Library, *Nuremberg Trials Project*.

6. IMT Prosecution, Fritz Sauckel, "Instructions Regarding the Conscription and Treatment of Foreign Workers," May 7, 1942. Harvard Law School Library, *Nuremberg Trials Project*.

7. Friedrich Didier, *Europe Works for Germany: Sauckel Mobilizes the Labor Reserves* (Munich: Zentralverlag der NSDAP, 1943), https://research.calvin.edu/german -propaganda-archive/sauckel.htm, accessed July 18, 2022.

8. Herbert, *Hitler's Foreign Workers*, 169–70.

9. IMT Prosecution, "Letter from Alfred Rosenberg to Fritz Sauckel concerning abuses in the transfer of Eastern workers to Germany," December 21, 1942. Harvard Law School Library, *Nuremberg Trials Project*.

10. IMT Prosecution, "Memoranda concerning the conduct of Councillor Fritz Mueller in the conscription of workers," October 29, 1943. Harvard Law School Library, *Nuremberg Trials Project*.

11. A sculptor and painter, Mataré was expelled from his position as professor at the Dusseldorf Art Academy when the Nazis took control of the cultural and artistic institutions in Germany to transform them into vehicles of Nazi ideology. He was among the artists swept up in the Entartete Kunst action, in which the Nazis denounced artists accused of creating "degenerate" art. One of his works, the monument "Dead Warrior" (erected in Kleve in 1934 in honour of the soldiers of Kleve who fell in the First World War), was removed by the Nazis, dismantled, and buried. It was created as a symbol of the tragedy of war, but the Nazis rejected it as a symbol of German humiliation. In 1977, the statue was excavated and reinstalled in Kleve. In the post-war period, Mataré completed several significant works, including the doors of the Church of Peace in Hiroshima.

12. "Fulda 1933-1939: Eine schwarze Stadt wird braun," *Fuldaer Zeitung*, July 20, 2016.

13. Judith Miller, *One, by One, by One: Facing the Holocaust* (New York: Simon & Schuster, 1990), "Germany." Kindle.

14. "Kristallnacht in the City of Fulda," Goldschmidt testimony, Yad Vashem Archives O.3/V.T/3246.

15. "Fulda 1945. End of WW2," https://youtu.be/qFiPtbvQRPw, accessed July 18, 2022.

16. Detailed records of bombing missions by the US Army Air Force are posted in a vast array of official and unofficial archival and historical sites. The descriptions of these missions over Fulda are mainly derived from records kept by the 8th Air Force Historical Society, at https://www.8thafhs.org/research/.

17. "The "Krätzbach Disaster," *Osthessen News*, December 27, 2004.

18. Ian Buruma, *Year Zero: A History of 1945* (New York: Penguin, 2013), 336.

19. International Labour Office, *The Exploitation of Foreign Labour by Germany*, Studies and Reports Series C (Employment and Unemployment), no. 25, 1945, 193.

20. Himmler quoted in Richard J. Evans, *The Third Reich at War* (New York: Penguin, 2009), 81.

21. E.M. Collingham, *The Taste of War: World War II and the Battle for Food* (New York: Penguin, 2012), 371–72.

22. IMT Prosecution, "Petition to the Government General of Poland concerning the treatment of Polish workers in Germany," May 17, 1944. Harvard Law School Library, *Nuremberg Trials Project*.

23. International Labour Office, *Exploitation of Foreign Labour*, 195.

24. IMT Prosecution, "Letter to Adolf Hitler concerning the use of foreign labor and prisoners of war in Germany," June 3, 1943. Harvard Law School Library, *Nuremberg Trials Project*; "Letter to Adolf Hitler concerning the use of workers from Eastern Europe, Belgium, and France in Germany," April 14, 1943. Harvard Law School Library, *Nuremberg Trials Project*.

25. Alexander von Plato, Almut Leh, and Christoph Thonfeld, *Hitler's Slaves: Life Stories of Forced Labourers in Nazi-Occupied Europe* (New York: Berghahn Books, 2010), 3–4.

26. Mark Spoerer, "Forced Labour in the Third Reich," Norbert Wollheim Memorial (J.W. Goethe-Universitat/Fritz Bauer Institut. Frankfurt am Main, 2010), 24, http://www.wollheim-memorial.de/files/1065/original/pdf_Mark _Spoerer_Forced_Labor_in_the_Third_Reich.pdf, accessed March 21, 2022.

27. Richard J. Evans, reply to John Diebold, "Sabotaging Hitler's Bombs," *New York Review of Books*, February 14, 2008.

5: DISPLACED

1. William I. Hitchcock, *The Bitter Road to Freedom: A New History of the Liberation of Europe* (New York: Free Press, 2008), 187–88. See also Tony Judt, *Postwar: A History of Europe since 1945* (New York: Penguin, 2005), 17. Judt's estimate of the number of homeless Germans was as many as twenty million. It's common to find that estimates of numbers of dead, homeless, or displaced vary significantly from one source to another, but in all cases the numbers are horrifying.

2. Greg Bradsher, "Operation Clarion: February 22-23, 1945," *The Text Message*, National Archives and Records Administration, February 24, 2015.

3. Richard J. Evans, *The Third Reich at War* (New York: Penguin, 2009), 679.

4. "Fulda 1939-1945: Massenmord und Bombenterror," *Fuldaer Zeitung*, August 17, 2016.

5. Sophie Hodorowicz Knab, *Wearing the Letter "P": Polish Women as Forced Laborers in Nazi Germany, 1939–1945* (New York: Hippocrene Books, 2016), 231.

6. Hitchcock, *Bitter Road to Freedom*, 292.

7. Volkhard Knigge, Rikola-Gunnar Lüttgenau, Jens-Christian Wagner, and Jens Binner, *Forced Labor: The Germans, the Forced Laborers, and the War*, Companion Volume to the Exhibition (Weimar: Buchenwald and Mittelbau-Dora Memorials Foundation, 2010), 140.

8. Knigge et al., *Forced Labor*, 141.

9. Timothy Snyder, *Bloodlands: Europe between Hitler and Stalin* (New York: Basic Books, 2010), 317–18.

10. Vincent Slatt, "Nowhere to Go: Displaced Persons in Post–VE Day Germany," *Historian* 64, no. 2 (2002), 279; Hitchcock, *Bitter Road to Freedom*, 250.

11. Knab, *Wearing the Letter "P"*, 235.

12. Jessica Reinisch, "Old Wine in New Bottles? UNRRA and the Mid-Century World of Refugees," in *Refugees in Europe, 1919–1959: A Forty Years' Crisis?* ed. Matthew Frank and Jessica Reinisch (London: Bloomsbury, 2017), 149.

13. Dan Plesch, "Aftermath: Institutional Responses to Displaced Persons and Refugees after 1945," in *Refugee Policies from 1933 until Today: Challenges and*

Responsibilities, ed. Steven T. Katz and Juliane Wetzel, International Holocaust Remembrance Alliance Series, vol. 4 (Berlin: Metropol, 2018), 130–31.

14. Reinisch, "Old Wine," 157.

15. Hitchcock, *Bitter Road to Freedom*, 255.

16. Juliane Wetzel, "On the Move: Postwar German Territory as a Transit Area for Survivors, Displaced Persons, Refugees and Expellees," in *Refugee Policies from 1933 until Today*, 149.

17. Slatt, "Nowhere to Go," 286.

18. Ben Shephard, *The Long Road Home: The Aftermath of the Second World War* (London: Vintage Books, 2011), 84.

19. Shephard, *Long Road Home*, 84.

20. Hilary St. George Saunders, *The Left Handshake: The Boy Scout Movement during the War, 1939–1945* (London: Collins St. James's Place, 1949).

21. Slatt, "Nowhere to Go," 284.

6: ENEMIES AND ALLIES

1. Halik Kochanski, *The Eagle Unbowed: Poland and the Poles in the Second World War* (London: Penguin, 2013), 337.

2. Kochanski, *Eagle Unbowed*, 200.

3. Eric Karpeles, *Almost Nothing: The 20th-Century Art and Life of Józef Czapski* (New York: NYRB, 2018), 204.

4. Karpeles, *Almost Nothing*, 201.

5. Kochanski, *Eagle Unbowed*, 342.

6. Norman Davies, *Trail of Hope: The Anders Army, an Odyssey across Three Continents* (Oxford: Osprey, 2015), 255.

7. Józef Czapski, *Inhuman Land: Searching for the Truth in Soviet Russia*, trans. Antonia Lloyd-Jones (New York: NYRB, 2018), 366.

8. Kochanski, *Eagle Unbowed*, 480.

9. Czapski, *Inhuman Land*, 369–71.

10. Karpeles, *Almost Nothing*, 233.

11. Kochanski, *Eagle Unbowed*, 507.

12. Shephard, *Long Road Home*, 93.

7: THE WILD PLACE

1. Kathryn Hulme, *The Wild Place* (Boston: Little, Brown, 1953), 14.

2. Hulme, *Wild Place*, 67.

3. Hulme, *Wild Place*, 108–12.

4. United Nations Archives (UNA), Fonds AG-018—United Nations Relief and Rehabilitation Administration (UNRRA) (1943–1946), Item S-1260-0000-0024-00001—Germany—DP Operations—Supporting Documents Illustrating Problems of a DP Camp—Wildflecken, Helen Zilka, Relief Service Division letter, August 14, 1946.

5. Hulme, *Wild Place*, 114.

6. UNA, Fonds AG-018—United Nations Relief and Rehabilitation Administration (UNRRA) (1943-1946), Item S-1260-0000-0023-00001—Germany Mission—Station List of UNRRA Teams in Germany, William J. Holman memo, October 16, 1946.

7. Shephard, *Long Road Home*, 147–59.

8. Vincent Slatt, "Nowhere to Go: Displaced Persons in Post–VE Day Germany," *Historian* 64, no. 2 (2002), 285.

9. Dana Adams Schmidt, "DP's in Camp Riot Mob 'Soviet' Aides," *New York Times*, February 7, 1947.

10. Hulme, *Wild Place*, 156.

8: THE RECKONING, PART I

1. Ernie Pyle, *Brave Men* (New York: H. Holt, 1944), chap. 10; Sian MacKay, *Von Ripper's Odyssey* (n.p.: Thistle Publishing, 2016), chap. 7–9, Kindle.

2. Edgar Snow, "They're Getting Their Alibis Ready," *Saturday Evening Post*, July 28, 1945.

3. Ian Buruma, *Year Zero: A History of 1945* (New York: Penguin, 2013), chap. 3, Kindle.

4. Greg Dawson, *Judgment before Nuremberg* (New York: Pegasus, 2012), chap. 23, Kindle.

5. Jeremy Hicks, "'Soul Destroyers': Soviet Reporting of Nazi Genocide and Its Perpetrators at the Krasnodar and Kharkov Trials," *History* 98, no. 4 (2013), 539–40.

6. Mary Fulbrook, *Reckonings: Legacies of Nazi Persecution and the Quest for Justice* (New York: Oxford University Press, 2018), chap. 8, Kindle.

7. Ann Tusa and John Tusa, *The Nuremberg Trial* (London: Macmillan, 1984), chap. 2, Kindle.

8. Tusa and Tusa, *Nuremberg Trial*, chap. 2.

9. Francine Hirsch, *Soviet Judgment at Nuremberg: A New History of the International Military Tribunal after World War II* (Oxford: Oxford University Press, 2020), 30–31.

10. Hirsch, *Soviet Judgment at Nuremberg*, 32.

11. Bradley F. Smith, *The Road to Nuremberg* (New York: Basic Books, 1981), 47.

12. Oona A. Hathaway and Scott Shapiro, *The Internationalists: How a Radical Plan to Outlaw War Remade the World* (New York: Simon & Schuster, 2017), 254–55.

13. Francine Hirsch, "The Soviets at Nuremberg: International Law, Propaganda, and the Making of the Postwar Order," *The American Historical Review* 113, no. 3 (2008): 701–30.

14. Rebecca West, *A Train of Powder* (n.p. Open Road Media, 2010), chap. 1 ("Greenhouse with Cyclamens 1 (1946)"), Kindle.

15. "Nuremberg Trial Proceedings, Volume 2" in William C. Fray and Lisa A. Spar, *The Avalon Project at the Yale Law School: Documents in Law, History and Diplomacy* (New Haven, CT: Avalon Project, 1996), 98–102.

16. West, *A Train of Powder*.

17. Nuremberg Trial Archives, "The International Court of Justice: Custodian of the Archives of the International Military Tribunal at Nuremberg," 2nd ed., 2018, 29.

18. IMT (International Military Tribunal) Prosecution, "Alfred Rosenberg letter to Fritz Sauckel concerning abuses in the transfer of Eastern workers to Germany," December 21, 1942. Harvard Law School Library, *Nuremberg Trials Project*.

19. IMT Prosecution, "Extracts from the minutes of the 54th meeting of the Central Planning Board concerning the conscription of workers," March 1, 1944. Harvard Law School Library, *Nuremberg Trials Project*.

20. Steffen Rassloff, "Fritz Sauckel: Hitler's 'Model Gauleiter'" (Thuringia, Leaflets on regional studies 36), Erfurt 2004. https://tinyurl.com/2zsy4nk5, accessed on March 23, 2022.

21. IMT Prosecution, "Extract from the Judgment of the International Military Tribunal, concerning the use of forced labor," September 30, 1946. Harvard Law School Library, *Nuremberg Trials Project*.

22. Douglas M. Kelley, *22 Cells in Nuremberg: A Psychiatrist Examines the Nazi Criminals* (New York: Greenberg, 1947), 195–97.

23. Charles E. Wyzanski, "Nuremberg: A Fair Trial? A Dangerous Precedent," *Atlantic*, April 1946.

24. E.B. White, "Comment," *New Yorker*, October 20, 1945.

25. In *The Internationalists*, the authors argue that the creation of the United Nations, the Paris Pact of 1928, and the unfolding of the Nuremberg trials represented the dawn of a New World Order, which today appears under threat by nationalist governments across the world.

26. Fulbrook, *Reckonings*, chap. 8.

9: WINDS OF CHANGE

1. Blair Fraser, "They Won't Go Home," *Maclean's*, November 1, 1946.

2. Kathryn Hulme, *The Wild Place* (Boston: Little, Brown, 1953), 115.

3. H.R. Hare, "Report of Activities of Canadian Polish Movement Unit," Library and Archives Canada (LAC), Department of Employment and Immigration Fonds, RG76-I-A-1, vol. 648, microfilm reel C-10588, file A85451, file part 1, "Admission of 4000 former Polish Soldiers for Agricultural Work," 1946.

4. Martin Thornton, *The Domestic and International Dimensions of the Resettlement of Polish Ex-Servicemen in Canada, 1943–1948* (Lewiston, NY: Edwin Mellen Press, 2000), 148–49, 206.

5. Thornton, *Resettlement of Polish Ex-Servicemen*, 114.

6. Thornton, *Resettlement of Polish Ex-Servicemen*, 149.

7. Thornton, *Resettlement of Polish Ex-Servicemen*, 168–76.

8. "Bring Workers into Canada to Replace Nazis," *Ottawa Citizen*, May 30, 1946.

9. Parliament of Canada, *House of Commons Debates*, 20th Parl., 2nd Sess., vol. 5, August 28, 1946, 5,515.

10. Isabelle Lussier, *Dionne Spinning Mills Co.: Histoire d'une Famille Industrieuse de Saint-Georges de Beauce* (Québec: Éditions GID, 2005), 251.

11. Austin F. Cross, "Parliamentary Personalities," *Canadian Business*, September 1947.

12. Gail Cuthbert Brandt, *Through the Mill: Girls and Women in the Quebec Cotton Textile Industry, 1881–1951* (Montréal: Baraka Books, 2018), 260–61.

13. H. Hickey, "Order to Import Polish Girls for MP's Mills Recommended by Glen after Others Balked," *Globe and Mail*, May 27, 1947.

14. "100 Immigrées," Notes of S. St.-Égide, Supérieure. Dionne fonds, Société Historique Sartigan.

10: ONE HUNDRED GIRLS AND A SCANDAL

1. Kathryn Hulme, *The Wild Place* (Boston: Little, Brown, 1953), 131–36.

2. Jessamine Fenner, "Flight to Freedom," *Survey Midmonthly* 84 (January 1948): 7–31.

3. Fenner, "Flight to Freedom."

4. "Forty Polish Girls Land in Maine on Way to Canada," *Lewiston Daily Sun*, May 30, 1947.

5. "100 Immigrées," Notes of S. St.-Égide, Supérieure, Dionne fonds, Société Historique Sartigan.

6. *House of Commons Debates*, 20th Parl., 3rd Sess., vol. 3, April 21, 1947, 2,279.

7. *House of Commons Debates*, 20th Parl., 3rd Sess., vol. 3, April 23, 1947, 2,331 and April 24, 1947, 2,406.

8. *House of Commons Debates*, 20th Parl., 3rd Sess., vol. 3, May 1, 1947, 2,644–46.

9. "Canadian Firms File 24 Requests for 5,400 DP's," *Globe and Mail*, July 11, 1947.

10. Valerie Knowles, *Strangers at Our Gates: Canadian Immigration and Immigration Policy, 1540-2015*, 4th ed. (Toronto: Dundurn, 2016), 164–67.

11. Will Lang, "100 Girls and a Dionne," *Life*, June 2, 1947.

12. Allan Dreyfuss, "100 Polish Girls Chosen For MP's Quebec Mills," *Globe and Mail*, May 22, 1947.

13. Editorial, "Contract Citizenship by Political Favor," *Montreal Gazette*, May 26, 1947.

14. Editorial, "'Policy' at Bankrupt Level," *Globe and Mail*, May 26, 1947; H. Hickey, "Order to Import Polish Girls for MP's Mills Recommended by Glen after Others Balked," *Globe and Mail*, May 27, 1947.

15. Joan Sangster, "The Polish 'Dionnes': Gender, Ethnicity, and Immigrant Workers in Post–Second World War Canada," *Canadian Historical Review* 88, no. 3 (2007), 469–500.

16. *House of Commons Debates*, 20th Parl., 3rd Sess., vol. 4, June 2, 1947, 3,668–706.

17. Sangster, "Polish 'Dionnes,'" 486.

18. *House of Commons Debates*, 20th Parl., 3rd Sess., vol. 5, June 13, 1947, at 4,117–121.

19. Editorial, "The Verdict Is Unaltered," *Globe and Mail*, June 16, 1947.

20. Editorial, "How Not to Import People," *Maclean's*, July 15, 1947.

21. Serge Courville, Pierre C. Poulin, and Barry Rodrigue, eds., *Histoire de Beauce-Etchemin-Amiante, Québec* (Institut québécois de recherche sur la culture, 2003), 667.

22. Patryk Polec, "Hurrah Revolutionaries and Polish Patriots: The Polish Communist Movement in Canada, 1918–1950" (PhD diss., University of Ottawa, 2012), 245–46; Joseph Ledit, "Letter-Writers, Visitors Pester Polish Girls," *Amherst Daily News*, September 12, 1947.

23. J. Langlois, "No Time for Boys: St. Georges DP Girls Work, Study," *Globe and Mail*, August 2, 1947.

24. Fenner, "Flight to Freedom."

25. Library and Archives Canada (LAC), Wiktor Podoski Fonds, item 102575, R2467-0-7-E, MG30-E230, 1920–1975.

26. Richard J. Needham, "One Man's Opinion," *Calgary Herald*, September 23, 1947.

27. Library and Archives Canada (LAC), Department of External Affairs Fonds, RG25-A-3-b, Volume number: 3952, File number: 9626-40, File part: 1, "Admission into Canada of Textile Workers Recruited by Mr. Ludger Dionne, M.P. in Europe," 1947/04/01-1948/11/09.

28. LAC, Department of External Affairs Fonds, RG25-A-3-b, "Admission into Canada of Textile Workers Recruited by Mr. Ludger Dionne, M.P. in Europe."

11: FREE BUT NOT FREE

1. "Union Says, 'Welcome, Girls' Rushes to Organize Them," *Toronto Daily Star*, May 31, 1947.
2. "Brisez les chaines de l'esclavage: L'Union des ouvriers de textile," Dionne fonds, Société Historique Sartigan (author translation).
3. Serge Courville, Pierre C. Poulin, and Barry Rodrigue, eds., *Histoire de Beauce-Etchemin-Amiante, Québec* (Institut québécois de recherche sur la culture, 2003), 659.
4. Courville et al., *Histoire de Beauce*.
5. "Spinning Mill Boss Blasts Unions for Threatening Protest," *Montreal Herald*, June 2, 1947.
6. "Dionne Says Polish Girls Cannot Return to Europe," *Toronto Daily Star*, June 2, 1947.
7. Joan Sangster, "The Polish 'Dionnes': Gender, Ethnicity, and Immigrant Workers in Post–Second World War Canada," *Canadian Historical Review* 88, no. 3 (2007), 469–500.
8. Isabelle Lussier, *Dionne Spinning Mills Co.: Histoire d'une Famille Industrieuse de Saint-Georges de Beauce* (Québec: Éditions GID, 2005), 206–21.
9. "100 Immigrées," Notes of S. St.-Égide, Supérieure, Dionne fonds, Société Historique Sartigan.
10. Mavis Gallant, "DP Test Case—A Failure," *The Standard Magazine*, Montréal, August 28, 1948, 3, 16–17, 22.
11. "Toronto Nearer Heaven than Mills in Quebec," *Globe and Mail*, October 7, 1947.
12. Lussier, *Dionne Spinning Mills*, 231–2.
13. Gallant, "DP Test Case," 22.
14. Lussier, *Dionne Spinning Mills*, 298.
15. Lussier, *Dionne Spinning Mills*, 344–348.
16. Lussier, *Dionne Spinning Mills*, 232–3.

12: JOURNEY'S END

1. Henry Prysky, "Polish War Veterans Arrive on Aquitania; Head for Farm Work," *Halifax Herald*, May 27, 1947; "328 Polish Men Arrive," *Halifax Herald*, June 30, 1947.
2. Vic Satzewich, "Unfree Labour and Canadian Capitalism: The Incorporation of Polish War Veterans," *Studies in Political Economy*, no. 28 (1989): 101.
3. Satzewich, "Unfree Labour," 104.
4. Valerie Knowles, *Strangers at Our Gates: Canadian Immigration and Immigration Policy, 1540–2015*, 4th ed. (Toronto: Dundurn, 2016), 165–67.
5. Julie Gilmour, "'The Kind of People Canada Wants': Canada and the Displaced Persons, 1943-1953" (PhD diss., University of Toronto, 2009), 27.
6. H.R. Hardy, "Plan Make [sic] Poles Good Canadians," *The Edmonton Journal*, November 13, 1946.
7. Aleksandar Hemon, "Mapping Home," *New Yorker*, December 5, 2011.
8. Adam Zagajewski, *Two Cities: On Exile, History, and the Imagination* (Athens, GA: University of Georgia Press, 2002).
9. Translation from Daniel Mendelsohn, *An Odyssey: A Father, a Son, and an Epic* (New York: Alfred A. Knopf, 2017), chap. "Apologoi." Kindle.

10. C.P. Cavafy, "Ithaka," in Constantine Cavafy, Edmund Keeley, Geōrgios P. Savvidēs, and Philip Sherrard, *C.P. Cavafy, Collected Poems* (Princeton, NJ: Princeton University Press, 1975).

13: SILENCE, MEMORY

1. Svetlana Boym, *The Future of Nostalgia* (New York: Basic Books, 2008), chap. 5, Kindle.
2. Pamela Petros, "Dreaming in Welsh," *Paris Review Daily*, September 18, 2012.
3. Boym, *Future of Nostalgia*, chap. 1.
4. Eva Hoffman, *Lost in Translation: A Life in a New Language* (New York: Penguin, 1990), 115.
5. Andrej Kotljarchuk, "World War II Memory Politics: Jewish, Polish and Roma Minorities of Belarus," *Journal of Belarusian Studies* 1 (2013): 24.
6. Timothy Snyder, *Bloodlands: Europe between Hitler and Stalin* (New York: Basic Books, 2010), 225–52 and 251 in particular. Other writers have offered different estimates of the number of Jews and others killed by the Einsatzgruppen (e.g., Headland, who writes that irregular reporting makes it difficult to reach accurate estimates. Reports indicate a minimum of 1,152,731 were killed, 134,000 by Einsatzgruppen B, who operated mainly in Belarus: Ronald Headland, *Messages of Murder: A Study of the Reports of the Einsatzgruppen of the Security Police and the Security Service, 1941–1943* [Rutherford, NJ: Fairleigh Dickinson, 1992], 105.)
7. Yahad In Unum, "In Evidence, The Map of Holocaust by Bullets," Bronnaya Gora, https://yahadmap.org/#village/bronnaya-gora-brona-gora-brest-belarus.375, accessed July 20, 2022.
8. Information Portal to European Sites of Remembrance, "Memorial to the Victims of the Extermination Site at Bronnaya Gora." https://www.memorialmuseums.org/eng/denkmaeler/view/1569/Memorial-to-the-victims-of-the-extermination-site-Bronnaya-Gora, accessed July 20, 2022.
9. Eva Hoffman, *After Such Knowledge: Memory, History, and the Legacy of the Holocaust* (New York: Public Affairs, 2004), 41.
10. Judith Miller, *One, by One, by One: Facing the Holocaust* (New York: Simon and Schuster, 1990), "Germany," Kindle.

14: THE RECKONING, PART II

1. "The End and the Beginning," in *Map: Collected and Last Poems* by Wislawa Szymborska, trans. Clare Cavanagh and Stanisław Barańczak (New York: Ecco, 2016), 286-87. Used by permission of Ecco, an imprint of Harper Collins. All rights reserved.
2. Patricia Chappine, "Delayed Justice: Forced and Slave Labor Restitution After the Holocaust," *Journal of Ecumenical Studies* 46, no. 4 (2011): 616.
3. Ann L. Phillips, "The Politics of Reconciliation Revisited: Germany and East-Central Europe," *World Affairs* 163, no. 4 (2001): 176; Stuart E. Eizenstat, *Imperfect Justice: Looted Assets, Slave Labor, and the Unfinished Business of World War II* (New York: Public Affairs, 2004).
4. Chappine, "Delayed Justice," 617.
5. Thomas Huber, "Holocaust Compensation Payments and the Global Search for Justice for Victims of Nazi Persecution," *Australian Journal of Politics & History* 48, no. 1 (2002): 97.

6. Chappine, "Delayed Justice," 617.

7. Eizenstat, *Imperfect Justice*, chap. 10.

8. Anne-Marie Slaughter and David Bosco, "Plaintiff's Diplomacy," *Foreign Affairs* 79, no. 5 (2000): 102–16.

9. D. Vagts and P. Murray, "Litigating the Nazi Labor Claims: The Path Not Taken," *Harvard International Law Journal* 43, no. 2 (2002): 510–11.

10. These events are discussed generally in each of Chappine, Phillips, and Huber.

11. Roger Cohen, "German Companies Adopt Fund for Slave Laborers under Nazis," *The New York Times*, February 17, 1999, 1.

12. Eizenstat, *Imperfect Justice*, chap. 13.

13. Günter Saathoff, Uta Gerlant, Friederike Mieth, and Norbert Wühler, eds., *The German Compensation Program for Forced Labor: Practice and Experiences* (Berlin: Remembrance, Responsibility and Future Foundation, 2017), Annex 1.

14. Eizenstat, *Imperfect Justice*, chap. 11.

15. Eizenstat, *Imperfect Justice*, Conclusion.

16. Alexander von Plato, Almut Leh, and Christoph Thonfeld, *Hitler's Slaves: Life Stories of Forced Labourers in Nazi-Occupied Europe* (New York: Berghahn Books, 2010), 80.

17. Felix Light, "Russian Court Orders Closure of Renowned Rights Group Memorial," *Moscow Times*, December 28, 2021, https://www.themoscowtimes.com/2021/12/28/russian-court-orders-closure-of-renowned-rights-group-memorial-a75674, accessed March 22, 2022.

18. Masha Gessen, "The Russian Memory Project That Became an Enemy of the State," *New Yorker*, January 6, 2022.

Selected Sources

Wanda and Casey's story is about two of the "little people," or "little great people," as the Belarusian writer Svetlana Alexievich describes them in her Nobel speech, "because suffering expands people." An oral historian, Alexievich believes that in telling "their own, little histories, big history is told along the way."

Casey and Wanda's life stories were embedded in a larger story of war, displacement, forced labour, and exile, but with few archival records to consult, and no survivors to tell their story in their own words, their "little history" emerged mainly by piecing together the fragments of "big history" that they lived through. The literature on the civilian experience of the Second World War has evolved, particularly in the last twenty years. Archives in Russia have opened up; archivists there and in Europe have digitized records to make them accessible to researchers; museums and memorial organizations have gathered oral histories and other testimonies from survivors; and historians have interpreted this newly available information. Without all of their work, this book would not have been possible.

What follows is a selection of sources that may be of interest to readers who would like to learn more about aspects of Wanda's and Casey's stories. More detailed and comprehensive references appear in the endnotes. Special mention should go to several archival sources that were important to my research. The Arolsen Archives (formerly the International Tracing Service) hold the records of the millions who were deported to forced-labour or concentration camps in Nazi Germany. Memorial, the Russian organization dedicated to recovering the memory of the millions who were oppressed by Soviet state terror, and Poland's Institute of National Remembrance have collected and recorded the details of the Polish victims of Soviet repression in their databases. The proceedings of the Nuremberg trials are available in digital format through two projects: the foundational documents, judgment, and trial transcripts can be found in the Avalon Project at Yale University (https://avalon.law.yale.edu/subject_menus/imt.asp); and many of the trial exhibits and related documents are offered in digital format by the Nuremberg Trials Project of Harvard University's Law Library (https://nuremberg.law.harvard.edu).

POLAND, BELARUS, UKRAINE, AND THE KRESY

Bartov, Omer. *Anatomy of a Genocide: The Life and Death of a Town Called Buczacz.* New York: Simon & Schuster, 2018.

Boyd, Louise Arner, and Stanisław Gorzuchowski. *Polish Countrysides.* New York: American Geographical Society, 1937.

Brown, Kate. *A Biography of No Place: From Ethnic Borderland to Soviet Heartland.* Cambridge, MA: Harvard University Press, 2004.

Dabrowski, Patrice M. *Poland: The First Thousand Years.* Dekalb: Northern Illinois University Press, 2014.

Exeler, Franziska. *Ghosts of War: Nazi Occupation and Its Aftermath in Soviet Belarus.* Ithaca, NY: Cornell University Press, 2022.

Gross, Jan Tomasz. *Revolution from Abroad: The Soviet Conquest of Poland's Western Ukraine and Western Belorussia.* Princeton, NJ: Princeton University Press, 2002.

Kelly, Matthew. *Finding Poland: From Tavistock to Hruzdowa and Back Again.* London: Jonathan Cape, 2010.

Reid, Anna. *Borderland: A Journey through the History of Ukraine.* London: Weidenfeld & Nicolson, 1997.

Snyder, Timothy. *Bloodlands: Europe between Hitler and Stalin.* New York: Basic Books, 2010.

———. *The Reconstruction of Nations: Poland, Ukraine, Lithuania, Belarus, 1569-1999.* New Haven: Yale University Press, 2003.

Sword, Keith, ed. *The Soviet Takeover of the Polish Eastern Provinces, 1939-41.* London: Macmillan Press, 1999.

Zamoyski, Adam. *Poland: A History.* London: William Collins, 2015.

SOVIET DEPORTATIONS AND THE ANDERS ARMY

Applebaum, Anne. *Gulag: A History.* New York: Doubleday, 2003.

Berkovits, Annette Libeskind. *In the Unlikeliest of Places: How Nachman Libeskind Survived the Nazis, Gulags, and Soviet Communism.* With a foreword by Daniel Libeskind. Waterloo, ON: Wilfrid Laurier University Press, 2014.

Czapski, Józef. *Inhuman Land: Searching for the Truth in Soviet Russia.* Translated by Antonia Lloyd-Jones and with an introduction by Timothy Snyder. New York Review Books Classics. New York: NYRB, 2018.

Davies, Norman. *Trail of Hope: The Anders Army, an Odyssey Across Three Continents.* Oxford: Osprey, 2015.

Dekel, Mikhal. *Tehran Children: A Holocaust Refugee Odyssey.* New York: W.W. Norton, 2019.

Herling, Gustaw. *A World Apart.* London: Heinemann, 1951.

Herzbaum, Edward H. *Lost between Worlds: A World War II Journey of Survival.* Leicester: Matador, 2010.

Karpeles, Eric. *Almost Nothing: The 20th-Century Art and Life of Józef Czapski.* New York: NYRB, 2018.

Margolin, Julius, Stefani Hoffman, Timothy Snyder, and Katherine R. Jolluck. *Journey into the Land of the Zeks and Back: A Memoir of the Gulag*. Oxford: Oxford University Press, 2020.

Viola, Lynne. *The Unknown Gulag: The Lost World of Stalin's Special Settlements*. New York: Oxford University Press, 2007.

Waydenfeld, Stefan W. *Ice Road: An Epic Journey from the Stalinist Labor Camps to Freedom*. Los Angeles: Aquila Polonica, 2011.

NAZI OCCUPATION OF POLAND AND FORCED LABOUR IN GERMANY
Desbois, Patrick. *The Holocaust by Bullets: A Priest's Journey to Uncover the Truth behind the Murder of 1.5 Million Jews*. New York: Palgrave Macmillan, 2008.

Evans, Richard J. *The Third Reich at War*. 1st American ed. New York: Penguin, 2009.

Herbert, Ulrich. *Hitler's Foreign Workers: Enforced Foreign Labor in Germany under the Third Reich*. Cambridge: Cambridge University Press, 1997.

Homze, Edward L. *Foreign Labor in Nazi Germany*. Princeton Legacy Library. Princeton, NJ: Princeton University Press, 1967.

Knab, Sophie Hodorowicz. *Wearing the Letter "P": Polish Women as Forced Laborers in Nazi Germany, 1939-1945*. New York: Hippocrene Books, 2016.

Knigge, Volkhard, Rikola-Gunnar Lüttgenau, Jens-Christian Wagner, and Jens Binner. *Forced Labor: The Germans, the Forced Laborers, and the War*, Companion Volume to the Exhibition. Weimar: Buchenwald and Mittelbau-Dora Memorials Foundation, 2010.

Kochanski, Halik. *The Eagle Unbowed: Poland and the Poles in the Second World War*. London: Penguin, 2013.

Plato, Alexander von, Almut Leh, and Christoph Thonfeld. *Hitler's Slaves: Life Stories of Forced Labourers in Nazi-Occupied Europe*. New York: Berghahn Books, 2010.

Richie, Alexandra. *Warsaw 1944: The Fateful Uprising*. London: William Collins, 2013.

POST-WAR DISPLACEMENT
Buruma, Ian. *Year Zero: A History of 1945*. New York: Penguin, 2013.

Gatrell, Peter. *The Unsettling of Europe: How Migration Shaped a Continent*. New York: Basic Books, 2019.

Hitchcock, William I. *The Bitter Road to Freedom: A New History of the Liberation of Europe*. New York: Free Press, 2008.

Hulme, Kathryn. *The Wild Place*. Boston: Little, Brown, 1953.

Judt, Tony. *Postwar: A History of Europe since 1945*. New York: Penguin, 2005.

Katz, Steven T., and Juliane Wetzel, eds. *Refugee Policies from 1933 until Today: Challenges and Responsibilities*. International Holocaust Remembrance Alliance Series, vol. 4. Berlin: Metropol, 2018.

Lowe, Keith. *Savage Continent: Europe in the Aftermath of World War II*. London: Viking, 2012.

Nasaw, David. *The Last Million: Europe's Displaced Persons from World War to Cold War*. New York: Penguin Press, 2020.

Shephard, Ben. *The Long Road Home: The Aftermath of the Second World War*. London: Vintage Books, 2011.

POST-WAR LABOUR AND IMMIGRATION IN CANADA
Abella, Irving M., and Harold Martin Troper. *None Is Too Many: Canada and the Jews of Europe 1933-1948*. Toronto: University of Toronto Press, 2012.

Cuthbert Brandt, Gail. *Through the Mill: Girls and Women in the Quebec Cotton Textile Industry, 1881-1951*. Montréal: Baraka Books, 2018.

Knowles, Valerie. *Strangers at Our Gates: Canadian Immigration and Immigration Policy, 1540-2015*. 4th ed. Toronto: Dundurn Press, 2016.

Lussier, Isabelle. *Dionne Spinning Mills Co.: Histoire d'une Famille Industrieuse de Saint-Georges de Beauce*. Québec: Éditions GID, 2005.

Sangster, Joan. *Transforming Labour: Women and Work in Post-War Canada*. Studies in Gender and History. Toronto: University of Toronto Press, 2010.

Thornton, Martin. *The Domestic and International Dimensions of the Resettlement of Polish Ex-Servicemen in Canada, 1943-1948*. Canadian Studies, vol. 25. Lewiston, NY: Edwin Mellen Press, 2000.

NUREMBERG AND TRANSITIONAL JUSTICE
Conot, Robert E. *Justice at Nuremberg*. 1st ed. New York: Harper & Row, 1983.

Eizenstat, Stuart E. *Imperfect Justice: Looted Assets, Slave Labor, and the Unfinished Business of World War II*. New York: Public Affairs, 2004.

Fulbrook, Mary. *Reckonings: Legacies of Nazi Persecution and the Quest for Justice*. New York: Oxford University Press, 2018.

Gilbert, G.M. *Nuremberg Diary*. London: Eyre & Spottiswoode, 1948.

Goldensohn, Leon, and Robert Gellately. *The Nuremberg Interviews*. New York: Knopf, 2004.

Hirsch, Francine. *Soviet Judgment at Nuremberg: A New History of the International Military Tribunal after World War II*. Oxford: Oxford University Press, 2020.

Kelley, Douglas M. *22 Cells in Nuremberg: A Psychiatrist Examines the Nazi Criminals*. New York: Greenberg, 1947.

Sands, Philippe. *East West Street: On the Origins of "Genocide" and "Crimes Against Humanity."* New York: Knopf, 2016.

Tusa, Ann, and John Tusa. *The Nuremberg Trial*. London: Macmillan, 1984.

Marsha Faubert is a Toronto-based lawyer with a
lengthy history of public service in the administrative
justice system in Ontario. She has worked as a
litigator, an arbitrator, an adjudicator of appeals
in workplace injury and disease claims, and as
the director of a provincial tribunal.
Wanda's War is her first book.

Photo: Rebecca Blissett